THE
Great Tradition
OF THE
American Churches

THE
Great Tradition
OF THE
American Churches

by *WINTHROP S. HUDSON*

HARPER & BROTHERS
Publishers, New York

Library of Congress catalog card number: 53-6417

To Lois

CONTENTS

CONTENTS

FOREWORD

A carefully defined equilibrium of church and state has been the great tradition of American religious and political life. There are many who are concerned lest this equilibrium be disrupted by encroachments of the state. An equally great danger—not always so clearly recognized—is that the partnership so carefully devised may be upset and destroyed by the churches themselves.

When churches succumb to the pressures of secular life and fail to exhibit a distinctive quality of faith and life, the separation of church and state with its clearly distinguished spheres of responsibility loses its point. As churches give less and less evidence of the prior claim of God upon their corporate existence, the reason which made it necessary for them to assert their independence from the state progressively diminishes. Ultimately, the churches find themselves with little to say that is not already being said by the generality of the community. In this situation, with nothing to lose, the churches will be tempted to renounce the specific responsibilities assigned to them, and an insistent clamor will arise among people of good will to have the state participate in the support of religious goals which have become indistinguishable from personal and national self-interest.

It is important that this danger be made clear so that both the churches and the state may be rescued from the inevitable consequences of an ill-considered policy.

American experience over the past century and a half has abundantly demonstrated the frequently forgotten truth that churches tend to flourish and become strong and influential when they are subjected to the coercion of a purely voluntary status. This is the clear meaning of Kenneth Scott Latourette's designation of the nineteenth century as "the great century" in the history of Christianity.

American experience also has demonstrated the parallel truth that complete voluntarism alone—indispensable as it is —is not an automatic guarantee of the health and vitality of the churches. It is only when the coercion of voluntarism is translated into a compulsion to fulfill a distinctive and specific vocation in society that the churches are enabled to kindle the urgent enthusiasm and wholehearted commitment which constitute the bedrock of vigorous institutional life. Furthermore, it is only in terms of their distinctiveness—made possible by the separation of church and state—that the churches are able to participate creatively and constructively in the shaping of the society and its culture.

It is when this process is reversed that danger comes. With the fading of a sense of distinctive vocation, church life inevitably begins to languish. As the vigor and vitality of the churches decline, the pressure to call upon the state for help becomes almost irresistible—the more so because it is no longer possible to distinguish clearly between the gods of society and the God of the church. If the surrender of responsibility is successfully effected and the carefully devised equilibrium of church and state is destroyed, the consequence can only be a further emasculation of the churches and an increasing secularization of society.

This, then, is the argument of this book, and it involves certain uncomfortable conclusions concerning the necessity for a thoroughgoing reconstruction of contemporary church life.

While an analysis of the present plight of the churches cannot be made intelligible apart from the changing theological outlook of the past century and a half, an attempt has been made to keep the theological discussion to the barest minimum necessary to provide an understandable frame of reference. The intention is not to describe or define the theology that is needed if a quickening of spiritual life is to take place within the churches, but merely to suggest that the churches in a democratic society must stand for something definite and specific if they are to avoid surrendering to the dominant cultural tendencies of the time.

The necessity for the churches to exhibit a distinctive faith and life would suggest that there must be some normative content to their message. What that content is to be, however, can only be determined by the churches themselves through procedures of democratic discussion. Fortunately, these discussions have been taking place and what amounts to a theological revolution is rapidly being pushed to completion. No single theological system, to be sure, can ever fully represent the total claim of God upon the minds and hearts of men, a fact which constitutes the major justification for what otherwise might be described as the sin and scandal of denominationalism. Consequently, we can expect diversity to persist, and the striving within denominations to achieve disciplined communities of Christians who seek to bear witness in their corporate life to the demands of the Eternal God in the midst of changing circumstances should constitute no serious threat to that liberty of the spirit which must always be preserved if the divine initiative is to be safeguarded.

When biographical material has been utilized to illustrate the course of American church life during the century and a half between 1800 and 1950, the men selected have been chiefly preachers who occupied the pulpits of the churches. Theological professors have been left largely unmentioned in order to avoid the suspicion that the tendencies described represent merely academic opinion and not the major stream of life within the churches. Some distortion, in terms of the essential integrity of the diverse individuals who are discussed, is inevitable. Full-scale biographies are impossible within the scope of a few pages, and only those aspects of their thought and activity have been selected and emphasized which indicate their significance within the particular context of the interest of this book. Thus Dwight L. Moody, who can readily be "debunked" as a nonintellectual, gains in stature as a not unworthy representative of what had been the noble tradition of Jonathan Edwards, Lyman Beecher, and Charles G. Finney. Phillips Brooks, in contrast, suffers by identification with tendencies whose ultimate consequences would have horrified him.

The question may arise in the minds of some readers as to why a discussion of the significance of the Fundamentalist movement does not find a place within these pages. In brief, the reason is simply that Fundamentalism did not succeed in capturing and placing its stamp on a single major denomination and therefore it represents in terms of influence a minor current in American religious life. Consequently, the Fundamentalist movement yields little information concerning the dominant tendencies within the American churches. This omission, on the other hand, has meant that something less than justice has been done to the men who struggled valiantly at the turn of the century to save the churches from the utter irrationality of identifying the Christian faith with antiquated knowledge which was demonstrably false. Rejecting the attempt to solve the problems raised by new methods of scientific inquiry and historical study by isolating themselves from the modern world, the proponents of what was then called the New Theology retained for the churches the spirit of self-criticism and won from the churches the acknowledgment that they must not become irrelevant by refusing to face squarely and unblinkingly the plain facts of life. Above all, by an emphasis upon the necessity for a historical point of view, an instrument was provided whereby men might be freed from bondage to cultural forms and a way was prepared for a renewal of genuinely prophetic religion.

One further admission and apology must be made. I have

tried to write clearly so that I may be understood. While the measure of my performance does not equal the sincerity of my intentions, the attempt I fear has occasionally led to over-simplification and the casting of alternatives into too sharp relief. The nineteenth century, which was not without its superficialities and petty legalism, will appear overidealized, while the twentieth century, which possesses many redeeming qualities, will seem to be portrayed in much too somber a hue. My only excuse is that I have sought to make plain the contrast which does exist so that the present plight of the churches will be clearly apparent. Unfortunately, when a careful shading of qualification seemed called for, the felicitous phrase sometimes escaped me, and I am sure that the central argument has been stated at several places with undue bluntness. For this I can ask of the reader only the benefit of a charitable judgment, and trust that the basic contentions concerning the importance of preserving the voluntary nature and responsibility of the churches and of their need to be something more than indiscriminate companies of believers in anything and nothing will have been made sufficiently evident to win assent.

Grateful acknowledgment must be made to many who have contributed to this study in ways both known and unknown— to Sidney E. Mead whose biography of Nathaniel W. Taylor has contributed much of the material for Chaper IV, and from whom I have drawn many other insights; to James Hastings Nichols who, through various articles and books, has provided material and points of view which are only inadequately acknowledged in the annotations; to H. Richard Niebuhr for his perceptive account of the course of American religious thought in his book, *The Kingdom of God in America*; and to many others, including Eugene M. Austin, Henry Steele Commager, Whitney R. Cross, Ralph H. Gabriel, W. E. Garrison, C. H. Hopkins, Hugh Thompson Kerr, Jr., K. S. Latourette, H. F. May, J. T. McNeill, Wilhelm Pauck, H. Shelton Smith, Willard L. Sperry, W. W. Sweet, and E. T. Thompson. Above all, appreciation must be expressed to my students and to my colleagues on the faculty of the Colgate-Rochester Divinity School for their sympathetic interest and helpfulness at many points; to President Wilbour E. Saunders for his generous concern; to my wife for her long forbearance during those weeks of preoccupation when the book was being written and for her never-failing cheerfulness and encouragement; to Dudley Zuver of Harper & Brothers for his thoughtful interest and discerning suggestions; and to Conrad Henry Moehlman who early taught me never to fear fact nor to evade truth, no matter how unpleasant the conclusions might be.

WINTHROP S. HUDSON

Colgate-Rochester Divinity School
January 1, 1953

THE
Great Tradition
OF THE
American Churches

CHAPTER I

THE PROBLEM THE CHURCH IS
FACING: *The Re-examination of the*
Great Tradition

As the vigor and vitality of the churches decline, the pressure to call upon the state for help becomes almost irresistible—the more so because it is no longer possible to distinguish clearly between the gods of society and the God of the church.

A day of reckoning has come for the churches. Statesmen, scientists, educators—indeed, all men who can discern the signs of the times—are agreed that the basic problem confronting mankind today is a spiritual problem. They are likewise agreed that the spiritual capital available to us in our time of need has been largely depleted. For several decades the American people have been becoming increasingly illiterate religiously. We are largely ignorant of theology and have little or no awareness of belonging to any historic religious tradition. "There can have been few times in our era," writes Dean Willard L. Sperry, "when the continuity of the Christian tradition as a cultural fact has worn as thin as is the case today, or when the vital succession is as seriously impaired." More than thirty years ago, it was already apparent to a group of chaplains and Y.M.C.A. workers who had returned to America after serving with the troops overseas that the United States had become "a needy mission field" in which "the knowledge of the Christian religion, its beliefs and its moral ideals," was in "pathetic default."[1]

I

How to begin again the task of evangelizing a society that has lost its spiritual rootage is the crucial question confronting the churches. It is not an easy question to answer. Commenting upon the steady decrease in church school attendance and the sharp decline in religious training in the home, one prominent clergyman has acknowledged that he is confronted by an "unsolved dilemma." The churches are apparently increasingly ineffective, the homes have abdicated their responsibility, and the state is restrained from taking any action to recover the spiritual heritage upon which "our way of life depends." Unable to suggest a positive program for the churches which would seem to give real hope of rekindling the embers of spiritual life and yet unwilling to sacrifice the evident political values of the separation of church and state, he concluded that he must "frankly confess" that he did not have "the solution for this basic dilemma of religious freedom and democracy."[2]

This clergyman reflects a common mood. Many earnest Christians today are questioning the validity of that principle which hitherto has been celebrated by preachers and politicians alike as the chief glory of the American Republic. The voluntary principle in religion, finding constitutional expression in the provision for the separation of church and state, is now being subjected to a frank re-examination and reappraisal. It is not surprising that thoughtful people who are disturbed by the growth of a secular spirit should begin to consider whether or not the state should assume some definite responsibility for encouraging and aiding religion so that the advance of secularism may be arrested and the springs of spiritual life renewed. What is surprising in the contemporary discussions of the subject is that the separation of church and state can be described as a "threadbare phrase"[3] and defended, when it is defended, almost exclusively on secular grounds. Practical political considerations stemming from the diversity of religious belief and practice in our society, together with an insistence upon the necessity of safeguarding civil liberties if democracy is to survive, now constitute almost the sole apologetic for the maintenance of the free church system in American life. This strange silence is the justification for this book.

The voluntary principle in religion has been the great tradition of the American churches, and it ought not to be lightly repudiated without a thoroughgoing consideration of the consequences of such a repudiation and without a voice having been raised in its behalf on religious grounds. If it is true that the churches have a large stake in the outcome of the current discussions, careful attention should be given to the verdict of past experience. No pattern of social organization is ever unambiguously good in the sense that a perfect harmony of all possible values is secured, and therefore heed must always be taken lest a proximate good be sacrificed in the illusion that an unambiguous good might be achieved.

II

The value judgment implicit in Kenneth Scott Latourette's characterization of the nineteenth century as "the great century" in the history of Christianity should give us pause in any hasty reconsideration of the validity of the separation of church and state, for the greatness of the nineteenth century was in a very real sense the achievement of the free churches. Deprived of state support, the free churches had been compelled to assume responsibility for maintaining and perpetuating themselves on a voluntary basis. They had to be both relevant and effective, or perish. They had to make themselves both heard and felt. As a result of this "moral coercion," church life became strong and vigorous, being based upon personal conviction rather than nominal adherence, and a new surge of spiritual vitality produced a missionary outreach that brought the gospel to every new settlement established in the westward march of the American people, sent missionaries into every corner of the earth, and created colleges and hospitals and charitable foundations. Nor were the evils of society forgotten. Reform movements of every kind and description began to flourish. Slavery was abolished, temperance became respectable, wages and hours and conditions of labor began to be regulated, and legislation was adopted to improve the lot of the wards of society—the blind, the fatherless, the mentally deficient, the prisoner, the indigent. These reform movements, as Alice Tyler has pointed out in *Freedom's Ferment* and Arthur Schlesinger has confirmed in *The American As Reformer,* were "the product of evangelical religion." And evangelical religion, in turn, was the product of an acceptance by the churches of the responsibility for recruiting their membership on a purely voluntary basis.

Even more impressive than the vigorous life within the churches and the tremendous missionary and reform activities fathered by them was the positive impact of religion upon culture and society as a whole. The separation of church and state removed the temptation to think that something was accomplished by mere tinkering with the externals of institutional arrangements. No longer could men comfort themselves with the thought that they were living in a Christian society because the churches were formally recognized and hats were tipped when the clergy passed. Dependent solely upon the powers of persuasion, the churches were compelled to deal with the very springs of belief and conviction. The result was one of the most successful penetrations of culture by a religious faith that the world has ever known. The free church pattern, James Hastings Nichols has asserted, demonstrated its ability "to maintain a greater hold for Christian ethics on the common life than is the case of any other major tradition. . . . Puritan denominationalism and separation of church and state have resisted moral corrosion conspiciously better than the state-church system. . . . By means of this pattern the Puritan group of denominations have had a greater positive impact on Western civilization in the last three centuries than any other branch of Christianity."[4]

The most obvious inference to be drawn from our present low spiritual estate would seem to be that the churches are no longer fully measuring up to the specific responsibility imposed upon them by their voluntary status in society. It is precisely such an admission of failure that many of our religious leaders seem unwilling to make. Lacking incisive theological insight and yielding to the all too human temptation to "pass the buck," there has been on the part of many a persistent refusal to acknowledge that the churches have been either derelict in their duty or ineffective in their ministry, and there has been an equally persistent effort to pin the responsibility for our present spiritual plight upon the state. The absence of formal religious instruction in the public schools is the chief scapegoat. What the churches have failed to do, the public schools must now do. They must teach the great fundamental truths of religion and thus restore the moral and spiritual foundations of society. The state must not be either neutral or indifferent. It must definitely assume the obligation to encourage, promote, and support the interests of religion. In no other way, it is suggested, can the spiritual health of the nation be restored.

A moment's reflection should be sufficient to indicate how ill-equipped the state is to provide such spiritual leadership. In a democracy, the state and its schools can never do much more than reflect the spiritual climate of the community at large. Our mayors and our aldermen, our governors and our legislators, our superintendents of public instruction and our boards of education—chosen as they are by the total electorate—cannot be expected to be lay bishops who are markedly in advance of the voters they represent. To expect them to be peerless spiritual leaders of the people who will bring about a quickening of new spiritual life is to expect the impossible. Such a quickening of spiritual life must come from voluntary associations of the concerned and committed within the larger community. Nor shall we develop the needed spiritual resources by relying upon the notion that religion is simply a body of information to be mastered. It is that, to be sure, but it is far more than that. The objective of the Sunday School used to be defined as "the conversion of the scholar and the growth in grace of the young convert."[5] Such an objective is quite impossible within the framework of the public schools, and yet such a revolution in our ultimate values and goals is precisely the thing we so desperately need. Furthermore, from the religious point of view, the redeemed life must also be a shared life within the sustaining fellowship of the church, but the public schools are public and not church schools. Consequently, they are not organized in such a way as readily to relate a "young convert" to the churches. Finally, our problem is not so much the younger generation as it is the older generation. We live in an adult world, and it is the adults who call the tune—write our textbooks, teach our children, elect our officials, determine our policies, establish our customs. The unhappy truth is that whatever idealism and spiritual sensitivity we may be able to instill in the youth of any particular generation will soon vanish unless some change is made in the adult world. Whatever we might wish it to be, the actual fact is that the vast majority of our youth upon reaching maturity must conform to the patterns of adult life. The school children are not our problem; it is their parents. And of all the institutions in society, the churches, not the schools, are best equipped to make a frontal assault upon the adult world.[6]

From the perspective of a trained historian, Henry Steele Commager in his book, *The American Mind,* suggests that the responsibility for our present spiritual plight does rest squarely upon the churches. "Never before," he asserts, have the churches "been materially more powerful or spiritually less effective." The clergy play "only a timid role." "The great moral crises of two world wars failed to elicit any authoritative religious leadership or even to inspire any spiritual interpretation, and not the clergy but the scientists instructed the American people in the moral consequences of the use of the atomic bomb." The root of the failure Commager locates in the "steady secularization" of the churches themselves.

Religion became increasingly a social activity rather than a spiritual experience. William Dean Howells, the most acute observer of the social habits of plain people, noted the ravages of secularization, even in Puritan New England. "Religion there," he wrote of Equity, New Hampshire, "has largely ceased to be a fact of spiritual experience, and the visible church flourished on condition of providing for the social needs of the community. It was practically held that the salvation of one's soul must not be made too depressing, or the young people would have nothing to do with it. Professors of the sternest creeds temporized with the sinners, and did what might be done to win them to heaven by helping them to have a good time here. The church embraced and included the world."[7]

The failure of the churches can almost be dated. It largely occurred during the fateful decade of the eighteen nineties, when Russell Conwell was identifying Christian virtue with alertness to economic opportunities and sin with its opposite; when Newell Dwight Hillis was preaching on timely topics and proclaiming contradictory gospels on successive Sundays; when Phillips Brooks was insisting that the church must be as broad as humanity; when other preachers were spending their time demonstrating how one could be both a skeptic and a believer, or beating the drums for an increasingly jingoistic nationalism, or retreating with Charles Sheldon into the realm of romantic sentimentality. In a certain sense, these are caricatures of men who were indeed more than mere prisoners of their time, but they are caricatures which reveal only too clearly the unhappy truth that the churches were losing the distinctive note of the Christian gospel and the distinctive quality of the Christian life.

If it is the churches that have failed, it is with the churches that we must begin in any attempt to reach both the churched and the unchurched pagans in our midst. We shall not begin by making demands upon the state. We must begin by looking to the churches and seeing what we are doing there. Harry Emerson Fosdick has said that we need a renewal of powerful, ethical, and spiritual religion, adding that if we get it, it will come "from the religious community, from renewal of life in the churches."

If we want better education, we must get better schools. If we want better children, we much get better homes. If we want better justice done, we must have better courts. If we want better civic conditions, we must have better government.[8]

Just so! And if we want our spiritual life improved, we must turn to the institutions of religion and charge them with that task. If we are to have a revival of real religious interest and concern in our time, we must begin by acknowledging that it is not the state but the churches that have failed to preserve in full measure our spiritual heritage. When the churches take courage and assume responsibility for the spiritual life of the community and begin once more to make a successful penetration of our culture, we shall not need to worry about a secular state or secular schools for they will reflect the general spiritual climate.

The problems confronting the churches, to be sure, are varied and acute, but they are not insoluble nor is there any need for counsels of despair. In many ways, the problems are no more difficult than the problems faced successfully by the churches in dealing with the lawless and turbulent frontier communities which marked the westward expansion of the American people throughout the eighteenth and nineteenth centuries. Indeed, in one respect, the present situation is more hopeful. Then a large segment of the rowdy and boisterous population on the frontier was openly contemptuous of religion, whereas today there are many indications of a widespread and almost wistful interest in religion. It is an interest that has not sprung from the churches nor has it as yet been channeled in any significant way into the churches, but it is there and it is real. On the other hand, there is little hope that the present opportunity will be grasped and a new awakening of spiritual life will take place, if the churches remain content to say only what everyone is saying and exhibit in the quality of their corporate life nothing that serves to distinguish their members from the generality of the community.

III

This book will seek to set forth, first of all, in clear and simple terms the basic theological convictions which led the American churches to adopt the voluntary principle as the basis of church life and to urge its incorporation into the fundamental law of the land. It is then proposed to examine the effect of the acceptance of the voluntary principle upon the churches themselves, to document the actual achievements of the voluntary churches in meeting the new problems with which they were confronted, and to evaluate their relative success in making a positive impact upon society as a whole. Finally, an effort will be made to identify the specific failures which have occurred so that intelligent consideration can then be given to the alternative courses of action which are being urged upon the churches. If an adequate strategy to meet the spiritual need of the day in which we live is to be devised, we must first of all understand how we got to where we are. The "lessons of the past" must be taken into account in the formulation of any positive program which will give real hope of bringing about a renewal of powerful, ethical, and spiritual religion in our time.

In our present perplexity, it should be helpful to go back initially to those years just before the eighteen nineties when the morale of the churches was high and when the voluntary principle in religion was one of the unquestioned postulates of the American people. Such a survey of the religious scene on the eve of the twentieth century should serve to give us perspective in a day when the situation of the churches has been radically altered, should provide us with some insight into the traditional understanding of the implications of the free church system, and should help us to understand why the voluntary principle was then regarded as the secret of the power and influence which religion so obviously had exerted in American life. It may also provide us with some clues as to the nature of our present difficulties when, in a later chapter, we return to the nineties and seek to identify the specific surrenders which then took place.

CHAPTER II

AN AXIOM OF ALL AMERICANS:
The Voluntary Principle in Religion

It is accepted as an axiom by all Americans that the civil power ought to be not only neutral and impartial as between different forms of faith, but ought to leave these matters entirely on one side, regarding them no more than it regards the artistic or literary pursuits of the citizens. There seem to be no two opinions on this subject in the United States. JAMES BRYCE[1]

No one is better equipped to give us a detached view and a balanced appraisal of American religious life on the eve of the eighteen nineties than James Bryce. As a discriminating observer of the American scene Lord Bryce is still unsurpassed, and *The American Commonwealth* remains the most penetrating analysis of American institutions and mores that has yet been written. When it was first published in 1888, it received almost universal acclaim, and for several decades no college man could count his education complete until he was sufficiently acquainted with Bryce to be able to quote him with assurance. Bryce's work was accepted as a normative account of American society, because Americans almost intuitively recognized within its pages an accurate and discerning portrait of themselves. Bryce had succeeded in verbalizing the common assumptions and the frequently unconscious practices which every American took for granted, and at the same time he was able to single out the tensions and contradictions which were beginning to be felt as the nation moved forward into an urbanized and industrialized society.

I

The Americans, Bryce reported, were a religious people.
"There are churches everywhere, and everywhere equally: in
the cities and in the country, in the North and in the South,
in the quiet nooks of New England, in the settlements which
have sprung up along railroads in the West." Not only were
churches numerous, they were well attended. "In cities of
moderate size, as well as in small towns and country places,
a stranger is told that possibly a half of the native population
go to church at least once every Sunday." Even "the ordinary
reading of the average family has a religious tinge," being supplied in large part by "religious or semi-religious weekly and
monthly magazines."[2]

The most striking feature of American religious life, to
Bryce as a European visitor to these shores, was the legal status of the churches. "Of all the differences between the Old
World and the New," he wrote, "this is perhaps the most
salient. . . . All religious bodies are absolutely equal before the
law and unrecognized by law, except as voluntary associations
of private citizens." The fact that, in describing the national
and state governments, he "never once had occasion to advert
to any ecclesiastical body or question" should not be regarded
as an oversight, Bryce assured his European readers, "because
with such matters government in the United States has absolutely nothing to do." Unlike its status in European lands, "the
legal position of a Christian church is in the United States
simply that of a voluntary association, or group of associations,
corporate or unincorporate, under the ordinary law. There is
no such thing as a special ecclesiastical law: all questions, not
only of property but of church discipline and jurisdiction, are,
if brought before the courts of the land, dealt with as questions
of contract." Every religious group, in turn, is left free to "organize itself in whatever way it pleases, lay down its own

rules of faith and discipline, create and administer its own system of judicature, raise and apply its funds at its uncontrolled discretion."[3]

Had Bryce known that within the compass of a single lifetime, this principle of complete separation of church and state would be seriously questioned by many American churchmen, he would have been utterly astounded. For Bryce thought the matter had been settled once and for all. What seemed most remarkable to him was that the separation had been "accomplished with no great effort and left very little rancour behind." Even the Congregational ministers of Connecticut and Massachusetts, who had predicted dire evils to result from disestablishment, afterward acknowledged that the change had turned out to be "a blessing to their own churches." Since that time, Bryce reported, "no voice has . . . been raised in favor of reverting—I will not say to a state establishment—but even to any state endowment or state regulation of ecclesiastical bodies." All Americans, he observed, were agreed at this point. "It is accepted as an axiom by all Americans that the civil power ought to be not only neutral and impartial as between different forms of faith, but ought to leave these matters entirely on one side, regarding them no more than it regards the artistic or literary pursuits of the citizens. There seem to be no two opinions on this subject in the United States."[4]

It is well to have Bryce remind us how widespread the agreement was at this point. A heritage of colonial days, derived from the new conception of the church worked out among the English Puritans and finding initial expression in Rhode Island and Pennsylvania, the principle of separation of church and state had commended itself to a majority of Americans by the end of the colonial period. Even the adherents of denominations with a state church tradition in the Old World had begun to accept the voluntary conception of the church and were soon to be among its most ardent defenders. Thus the guarantees of religious freedom in the Constitution of the new republic did not constitute such a marked departure from previous sentiment and practice as is sometimes suggested. Technically, it is true that "establishment and religious tests for office were not prohibited in the United States by the Constitution," and "were simply referred to local option."[5] The national government was restrained at this point, but the states were not. And an establishment of religion—with each taxpayer assigning his rates to the church of his choice—did linger on for a generation in three of the New England states. But long before the adoption of the Fourteenth Amendment in 1868 imposed the restrictions of the First Amendment upon state governments, the principle of separation had been incorporated in the constitutions of the individual states and was taken for granted by everyone. Roughly by 1830, the complete separation of church and state had become an unquestioned postulate of all Americans.

Occasionally it is suggested that the religious clauses of the Constitution imply nothing more than that no religious denomination can enjoy any special privileges and that all religious communities must be treated alike, and that, therefore, it follows that all churches may share in an equal and just distribution of government funds for the support of religion. Nothing could be further from the truth, and so to understand the American doctrine of separation of church and state is to miss its very genius. The heart of the matter resides in the fact that the churches are placed on a purely voluntary basis and given sole responsibility for the religious life of the nation. This was the general understanding throughout the nineteenth century, as Bryce sought to make clear.

The confusion at this point is primarily due to the terminology that was employed. Connecticut, for example, adopted a constitutional provision in 1818 which stated that henceforth "no preference shall be given by law to any Christian sect or mode of worship." But this was further defined to mean that "each and every society or denomination of Christians in this state shall have and enjoy the same and equal powers, rights and privileges; and shall have power and authority to support and maintain the ministers and teachers of their respective denominations, and to build and repair houses for public worship, *by a tax on the members of any such society only.*"[6] James Madison, looking back in 1822, declared that in order to put all churches "on a footing of equal and entire freedom," the various states had "rejected religious establishments altogether."[7] Thus was it understood by all. Daniel Dorchester, in his pioneering work *Christianity in the United States* (1888), speaks of it as "the purely voluntary principle in religion"; and Philip Schaff, America's most distinguished church historian, in the same year affirmed: "The necessary consequence of the separation of church and state is the voluntary principle of self-support and self-government." Heinrich A. Rommen, the Roman Catholic authority on constitutional law and political theory, adds his word of confirmation:

> The constitutional principle of separation implies the following. First, no religious group or Church enjoys any juridical or political privileges, none receives any direct or indirect financial support from the state. . . . Secondly, the Churches and the religious associations . . . are legally organized upon the basis of the civil law . . . like any other of the free associations of the citizens in the state. . . . The state gives full religious freedom, [and] retires from any positive or negative intervention into the religious life of its citizen.

Perhaps the best modern summary of the general understanding of the constitutional principle is provided by Charles A. Beard:

> The Constitution does not confer upon the Federal Government any power whatever to deal with religion in any form or manner. . . .
> Congress can make no law respecting an establishment of religion. This meant that Congress cannot adopt any form of religion as the

national religion. It cannot set up one church as the national church, establish its creed, lay taxes generally to support it, compel people to attend it, and punish them for non-attendance. Nor can Congress any more vote money for the support of all churches than it can establish one of them as a national church. That would be a form of establishment.

Schaff put the matter even more succinctly when he said that the Constitution "is neither hostile nor friendly to any religion; it is simply silent on the subject, as lying beyond the jurisdiction of the general government."*[8]

II

Many thoughtful people today are asking if the idea of a religiously neutral state is not a contributing factor to the depressed status of religious life and itself a manifestation of the secular spirit. Quite obviously, the neutral state is the antithesis of the medieval ideal of a coercive church-state society. But to suggest that it is secular, Bryce would say, is completely to misunderstand the American principle, which is rooted in a distinctly religious idea. Bryce was entirely clear at this point. "The refusal of the civil power to protect or endow any form of religion," he observed, "is commonly represented in Europe as equivalent to a declaration of contemptuous indifference on the part of the state to the spiritual interests of its people. A

* In view of the confusion which has been introduced into discussions of this subject, a few illustrations of the type of restriction incorporated in the early state constitutions should serve to indicate that Bryce and Schaff and Dorchester in 1888 were not reflecting a novel view which had developed only late in the nineteenth century.

The Constitution of Pennsylvania (1776) reads: "No man ought or of right can be compelled to attend any religious worship, or erect or support any place of worship, or maintain any ministry, contrary to, or against, his own free will and consent."

The Constitution of New Jersey (1776) states: "No person shall . . . ever be obliged to pay tithes, taxes, or any other rates, for the purpose of building or repairing any other church or churches, place or places of worship, or for the maintenance of any minister or ministry, contrary to what he believes to be right, or has deliberately or voluntarily engaged himself to perform."

state recognizing no church is called a godless state; the disestablishment of a church is described as an act of national
impiety. Nothing can be farther from the American view."⁹

The American view, Bryce points out, is rooted in "the conception of the church as a spiritual body existing for spiritual
purposes, and moving along spiritual paths," and consequently
it never occurred to "the average American that there is any
reason why state churches should exist."

> Compulsion of any kind is contrary to the nature of such a
> body. . . . It desires no state help. . . . It does not seek for exclusive
> privileges, conceiving that these would not only create bitterness
> between itself and other religious bodies, but might attract persons
> who did not really share its sentiments, while corrupting the sim-
> plicity of those who are already its members. Least of all can it
> submit to be controlled by the state, for the state, in such a world
> as the present, means persons many or most of whom are alien to its
> beliefs and cold to its emotions.

From this conception of the church, the conclusion naturally
follows that "the church as a spiritual entity will be happiest
and strongest when it is left absolutely to itself, not patronized
by the civil power, not restrained by law except when and in
so far as it may attempt to quit its proper sphere and
intermeddle in secular affairs." The state, for its part, being a
democracy, will necessarily reflect the spiritual and ethical principles of its citizens. "So far from thinking their commonwealth godless, the Americans conceive that the religious
character of a government consists in nothing but the religious
belief of individual citizens, and the conformity of their conduct
to that belief. They deem the general acceptance of Christianity to be one of the main sources of their national prosperity,
and their nation a special object of the Divine favour."¹⁰

This is the theory. What have been the consequences of its
application? As a European, Bryce could not avoid this question. "Considering that the absence of state interference in

matters of religion is one of the most striking differences between all the European countries on the one hand and the
United States on the other, the European reader may naturally
expect some further remarks on the practical results of this
divergence." European defenders of established churches, he
commented, always seek to terrify the advocates of disestablishment and disendowment with the certain prospect that "the
authority and influence of religion will wane if state recognition is withdrawn."[11] To what extent did American experience
justify or discredit such a fear? What were the actual results?

The most obvious consequence of the American experiment
in religious freedom, Bryce noted, was the general sense of
religious peace pervading the country. "Social jealousies connected with religion scarcely exist in America."

> There are no quarrels of churches and sects. . . . No established
> church looks down scornfully upon dissenters from the height of
> its titles and endowments, and talks of them as hindrances in the
> way of its work. No dissenters pursue an established church in a
> spirit of watchful jealousy, nor agitate for its overthrow.[12]

"Half the wars of Europe, half the internal troubles that have
vexed European states . . . have arisen from theological differences or from the rival claims of church and state. This
whole vast chapter of debate and strife has remained virtually
unopened in the United States." There is, to be sure, a rivalry
between denominations "to extend their bounds, to erect and
fill new churches, to raise great sums for church purposes," but
it is not an "unfriendly" rivalry and it does not "provoke bad
blood." Indeed, "one notes a kindlier feeling between all denominations, Roman Catholics included," than is true in Europe, because "the state stands neutral and all churches have
a free field." Not even the skeptic is "under a social ban," and
"discussions on the essentials of Christianity and of theism
are conducted with good temper." To the weary European,

concluded Bryce, this general sense of peace and harmony among the citizens is soothing indeed, and it "contributes not a little to sweeten the lives of ordinary people."[13]

American experience also demonstrated, Bryce observed, that religious freedom was of equal benefit to the churches themselves. A half century earlier, Alexis de Tocqueville had remarked with pleasant surprise that in the United States "the people fulfill with fervor all the outward duties of religion."[14] Bryce was no less impressed by this fact. The churches, he concluded, were stronger, attendance was larger, the percentage of the better educated actively interested in the church greater, and the clergy on the whole somewhat better paid than in any country of continental Europe. There can be no doubt, he affirmed, that "the voluntary system . . . makes men more liberal in giving for the support of religious ordinances among themselves and of missions elsewhere," and certainly no country has equaled the sums collected in the United States for all sorts of philanthropic purposes. As for the ministers, they "are among the first citizens and exercise an influence often wider and more powerful than that of any layman." Great Britain, with a strong free church tradition, alone of all the European countries could be compared to the United States in terms of the vitality and vigor of church life. "So far from suffering from the want of state support, religion seems in the United States to stand all the firmer because, standing alone, she is seen to stand by her own strength."[15]

A frequent indictment of a policy of unlimited religious freedom is that it results in a vast proliferation of distinct religious groups, and thus divides the resources of the churches, impairs their effectiveness, and weakens their influence. While it was true, Bryce acknowledged, that in America there was a wide variety of denominational bodies, he thought that the sectarianism of the American religious scene had been vastly overemphasized and its disadvantages overestimated.

In the first place, European travelers had greatly exaggerated the importance of strange sects and abnormal religious developments. "Such sects and developments there certainly are, but they play no greater part in the whole life of the nation than similar sects do in Germany and England, far less than the various dissenting communities do in Russia." Most of them are very small, attract little attention, and exist for a very brief time. "In a country seething with religious emotion and whose conditions seem to tempt to new departures and experiments of all kinds, the philosophic traveler may rather wonder that men have stood so generally upon the old paths."[16]

In the second place, religious freedom was not responsible for the multiplicity of religious bodies. "The churches of the United States," Bryce pointed out, "are the churches of the British Isles, modified by recent Roman Catholic, Lutheran, and Jewish immigration from the European continent." Actually, "no new religious forces have sprung up on American soil to give a new turn to her religious history." The Mormons constituted the only religious community of any considerable size which could be regarded as truly indigenous, and even the Mormons, Bryce had reason to believe, drew their recruits principally from abroad.[17]

In the third place, barriers among the major Protestant groups did not exist in any sectarian sense. "Exchanges of pulpit" were common, and "the comparative frequency with which persons pass from one denomination to another" was regarded as both normal and natural, and occasioned no ill-will. Between some of the denominations, Bryce noted, there has been a general agreement, "for the sake of efficiency and economy, not to plant two rival churches in a place where one will suffice," and among them all there has been a "readiness to work together for common charitable aims." Proposals for union between some of the leading Protestant denominations, he reported, were being "freely canvassed," and it seemed entirely likely that "before many years more than one such union will be carried through."[18]

Most significant of all, religious freedom had effectively prevented the rise of the anticlerical and antireligious sentiment so characteristic of European societies. Tocqueville, in his *Democracy in America,* had noted the strong impression this aspect of American life had made upon him.

On my arrival in the United States the religious aspect of the country was the first thing that struck my attention; and the longer I stayed there, the more I perceived the great political consequences resulting from this new state of things. In France I had almost always seen the spirit of religion and the spirit of freedom marching in opposite directions. But in America I found they were intimately united and that they reigned in common over the same country. My desire to discover the causes of this phenomenon increased from day to day. In order to satisfy it I questioned the members of all the different sects; I sought especially the society of the clergy, who are the depositaries of the different creeds and are especially interested in their duration. As a member of the Roman Catholic Church, I was more particularly brought into contact with several of its priests, with whom I became intimately acquainted. To each of these men I expressed my astonishment and explained my doubts. I found that they differed upon matters of detail alone, and that they all attributed the peaceful dominion of religion in their country mainly to the separation of church and state.[19]

Bryce was no less struck by this happy state of affairs. "No political party, no class in the community," he reported, "has any hostility either to Christianity or to any particular Christian body." Nowhere did Bryce find that "sharp opposition and antagonism of Christians and anti-Christians which lacerates the private as well as public life of France." Even among those who are not formal adherents, the churches were "thoroughly popular, in the best sense of the word." The fact that ecclesiastical considerations play no part in secular politics "gives the enemy less occasion to blaspheme than he is apt to have in Europe," and the person who becomes disaffected with his church does not become hostile to religion but simply joins some other denomination in which he feels more at home.[20]

So far as externals were concerned, it was quite apparent to Bryce that Christianity in the United States had maintained both its dignity and its authority, "planting its houses of worship all over the country and raising enormous revenues from its adherents." But a question of greater consequence was the extent to which it was able to influence conduct and direct the life of society as a whole. On this score, Bryce was equally positive concerning the beneficent effect of the separation of church and state. The Americans he found to be a truly religious people. "It is not merely that they respect religion and its ministers . . . , not merely that they are assiduous churchgoers and Sunday school teachers, but that they have an intelligent interest in the faith they profess, are pious without superstition, and zealous without bigotry." "Christianity," he continued, "influences conduct, not indeed half as much as in theory it ought, but probably more than it does in any other modern country, and far more than it did in the so-called ages of faith." Nor was it a mere personal piety cloaked in "the soft haze of self-complacent sentiment." Moral energy was as conspicuous as religious feeling. "The desire to expunge or cure the visible evils of the world is strong. Nowhere are so many philanthropic and reformatory agencies at work."[21]

Tocqueville also had commented on this aspect of American life. Although "religion in America takes no direct part in the government of society," he had written, "it must be regarded as the first of their political institutions."

There is no country in the world where the Christian religion retains a greater influence over the souls of men than in America; and there can be no greater proof of its utility and of its conformity to

human nature than that its influence is powerfully felt over the most
enlightened and free nation of the earth. . . .

In the United States religion exercises but little influence upon
the laws and upon the details of public opinion; but it directs the
customs of the community, and, by regulating domestic life, it
regulates the state.[22]

Two years later, Francis Grund, a Czech, was to assert, in
his book on *The Americans in their Moral, Social, and Political
Relations,* that "the religious habits of the Americans form not
only the basis of their private and public morals, but have become so thoroughly interwoven with their whole course of legislation that it would be impossible to change them without af-
fecting the very essence of their government." "Religion," in
fact, "presides over their councils, aids in the execution of the
laws, and adds to the dignity of the judges."[23]

III

Few things are more remarkable than the unanimity with
which Americans, in Bryce's day, ascribed the influence of
religion in their society to a firm adherence to the principle
of the voluntary church. No less remarkable is the fact that
what was then regarded an axiom by all Americans should have
been brought into serious question during the threescore years
that came after 1890. In a certain sense, however, it is not
strange that this should occur. For the headlong rush into a
new era precipitated critical problems for the churches and
religion, and religious leaders were forced to reconsider questions of fundamental strategy. Nor is it strange, as problems
became more acute, that some should come to regard the traditional separation of church and state as quite illogical.
Tocqueville had also recognized the apparent illogic involved.
"The philosophers of the eighteenth century," he wrote, "explained in a very simple manner the gradual decay of religious
faith. Religious zeal, said they, must necessarily fail the more

generally liberty is established and knowledge diffused. Unfortunately, the facts by no means accord with the theory."* It was because of this apparent paradox that Tocqueville began his investigations "to inquire how it happened that the real authority of religion was increased by a state of things which diminished its apparent force." "On every side in Europe," he had heard "voices complaining of the absence of religious faith and inquiring the means of restoring to religion some remnant of its former authority." And yet these very people, he discovered, hold that the idea of complete religious freedom was the thing most amiss in America. "I can only reply," he commented, "that those who hold this language have never been in America and that they have never seen a religious or a free nation. When they return from a visit to that country, we shall hear what they have to say."[24]

Is it not possible that the reason for the present low estate of religion in our national life and the seeming impotence of the churches may lie in another direction than is frequently supposed? Instead of placing the blame upon the fact that the state is restrained from taking any positive action to undergird the religious life of the nation, may not our present plight be due to the failure of the churches themselves effectively to nourish and quicken the spiritual life of their members? Spiritual life must always be renewed from generation to generation. Constantly expiring, it needs constantly to be replenished. Before we lightly dismiss the tradition which our father cherished and staunchly defended, ought we not to make sure that in doing so we are not seeking to avoid facing the fundamental issue by shifting the responsibility for the spiritual well-being of society from the churches, where it has traditionally rested in America, to the state, which has yet to prove itself capable

* Philip Schaff was to make a similar observation: "It is easy to make a plausible logical argument in favor of the proposition that the state cannot be neutral, that no-religion is irreligion, and that non-Christian is anti-Christian. But facts disprove the logic." (*Church and State*, 42.)

of fostering a genuine renewal of spiritual life? The fact that European theologians, with a state-church background, are increasingly looking with favor upon the American pattern of a confessing, voluntary church should be sufficient to make us hesitate to prejudge the issue. At the very least, we ought honestly to examine the reasons which led the American churches to adopt the voluntary principle in the first place, and then we ought to follow Tocqueville's advice really to study the principle at work among a free people before we ask people to listen to what we have to say.

CHAPTER III

FAITH AND FREEDOM: The Roots of a Great Tradition

It is better that the commonwealth be fashioned to the setting forth of God's house, which is his church, than to accommodate the church to the civil state. JOHN COTTON[1]

Unlike the churches in most other lands where the separation of church and state has taken place, the larger portion of the American churches did not have independence from the state thrust upon them; they claimed independence for themselves. No did they claim it simply as minority groups on the basis of expediency; they claimed it for good theological reasons. In recent years, this fact has been obscured, neglected, and forgotten. A distinctly religious principle in America, separation of church and state is now defended primarily on secular grounds, a phenomenon which reflects the confusion in present theological thinking.

No intelligent person, to be sure, would pretend that economic and sociological factors had nothing to do with the achievement of religious freedom in the United States. In an unpopulated frontier area, the economic pressure to attract settlers, on any basis, to clear the forests, till the soil, and pay quitrents is very great. And in the American colonies, this pressure did result in a religiously heterogeneous population, which in turn tended to make religious freedom a practical necessity. On the other hand, French and Spanish experience in dealing with an American frontier demonstrated that economic pressure could be restrained in the interest of maintain-

ing a uniform religious establishment, if the colonial authorities believed in the importance of such an establishment.[2] In
the English colonies, most notably in Roger Williams' sanc-
tuary of Rhode Island and in the Quaker domain of the Jer-
seys, Pennsylvania, and Delaware, the authorities did not so
believe. In the other colonies, the influence of this type of
thinking was also present and was soon to be reinforced by
the policy of a government at home which, for religious reasons, had ceased to believe in either the virtue or the value of
a uniform religious establishment. Consequently, the economic
pressure to recruit colonists on any basis was not resisted, the
development of religious diversity through immigration was
looked upon with equanimity, and the giving of a purely voluntary status to the churches was ultimately welcomed as con-
sonant with sound theology and good churchmanship.

I

Ernst Troeltsch, the great German sociologist and historian,
has pointed out that the American tradition of religious freedom is the distinctive contribution of left-wing Puritanism to
American life. Left-wing Puritanism came to power during the
English Civil Wars, and during the two decades between 1640
and 1660 the Protestant Reformation—with its insistence upon
the necessity for an explicit faith, its confidence in the power
of God's Word, and its profound skepticism of the claims of
men and institutions to infallibility—was carried to its logical
conclusion. With the emergence of the Independent party
(which included Congregationalists, Baptists, and other "sectaries") to a position of dominance, the great attack of the
English Revolution was directed against the concept of a state
church. A state church, the Independents maintained, tended
to foster a false reliance upon an institution and a deceptive
confidence in the sufficiency of a purely formal relationship to
it. Furthermore, such a relationship either subordinated the

church to the interests of the state or it created a monopoly of religion in the hands of divines, who inevitably would be confronted by the all too human temptation to abuse their monopoly, become self-seekers, and pervert the gospel. Samuel Richardson spoke the common mind when he contended that a monopoly in religion is as bad as a monopoly in the cloth trade, for to have a monopoly in religion is to have the divine will measured out at the whim and caprice of fallible men who are apt to trim and tailor it to fit their own self-interest. It is only by free trade in religion that truth can be tested and abuses prevented.

Contradictory as it may seem, the aim of the Puritan revolution was the creation of a Christian society. With regard to forms of worship and confessions of faith, the state was to be officially neutral. These things were to be left to the free determination of the independent congregations. But there was no surrender of a concern for society as a whole. Puritanism, by definition, meant "a determined and varied effort to erect the holy community,"[3] and from this ideal the Independents did not depart. The apparent conflict between their zeal for liberty and their concern for reform was resolved for them by their firm trust in the efficacy of discussion and the power of persuasion. To achieve and preserve the Christian character of society, they relied on the power of a godly public opinion created by the preaching of the Word. Persuasion rather than coercion was the means upon which they depended to attain their end. The civil power could not be utilized to compel a man to "this or that judgment or opinion or faith," or to coerce him into "this or that practice in religion," the author of *The Ancient Bounds* asserted. A man could only "be persuaded, induced by exhortation, example, or such means, and that's all."[4] Quite typical of the Puritan point of view was Oliver Cromwell's response to a complaint by a group of divines concerning the damage being done by unlicensed preaching. He told them they had the remedy at hand, since they had equal freedom to preach. Nor did the Commonwealth Puritans regard this reliance upon the power of persuasion as a frail reed.

For more than a generation, the Puritan preachers had been largely cut off from state support and forced to resort to the extralegal expedient of becoming "lecturers." Their livelihood was thus dependent upon their ability to secure voluntary contributions. Consequently, if they wished to survive, they had had "to find means to stir imaginations, wring the hearts of sinners, win souls to the Lord, in other words make themselves heard and felt."[5] And so successful were they, with no resources other than that of persuasion at their disposal, that within two generations they had been able to transform the entire moral and spiritual climate of England. The measure of their success is amply evidenced by the tributes of their opponents. Thomas Fuller quaintly observed: "What won them most repute was their ministers' painful preaching in populous places"; while Selden commented wryly: "The lecturers are friars and they stole the people's hearts away from the clergy and also took away their money."

The Christian society, as conceived by the Puritans of the Commonwealth period, presupposed a representative form of government. Otherwise the power of a godly public opinion would be impeded. This is the fundamental reason, we must assume, why Cromwell exhibited such a consistent reluctance to assume arbitrary power. This is unquestionably the explanation of Sir Harry Vane's remaining such an unreconstructed republican, and it is the key to the development of the Leveler movement among the sectaries. A simple democracy, of course, would not do, for the majority itself might conceivably become tyrannical. The freedom of the Word had to be preserved, and therefore the "rights of man," in terms of freedom of speech, of assembly, and of the press, as well as of freedom from arbitrary arrest, had to be guaranteed. The result was the overthrow of a system of absolutism in the state as well as in the church.

"The Cromwellian Commonwealth, which was avowedly intended to be a Christian state," says Troeltsch, "for a short time realized this ideal." Its downfall was due to the fact that the English people had not as yet mastered the techniques of democratic government. Nevertheless, Troeltsch continues, "short as was the time during which this grandiose edifice lasted, its influence on the history of the world was extraordinarily great." As a legacy to the future, it left four great ideas: the separation of church and state, toleration of different church societies alongside one another, the principle of voluntarism in the formation of these churches, and liberty of opinion in all matters of world view and religion.[6] These ideas the Restoration government could neither wholly eradicate nor suppress, and a partial adjustment to them had to be made in the revolutionary settlement of 1688 and 1689.

It was this type of thinking which became dominant in the American colonies, and in the colonies Puritanism had a freer hand. The selective process of migration increased the numerical importance of the left-wing groups, and both distance from the mother country and geographical space within and beyond the colonies made it difficult to implement the coercive policies of the Stuart reaction. Indeed, by seeking to extend the domain of Anglicanism in the new territories beyond the sea, local attempts to maintain a uniform establishment of Congregationalism in New England were weakened. Thus, the heritage of the Cromwellian period lived on. By the time of the American Revolution, partially as a result of the Great Awakening, "free church" ideas had penetrated all the major denominations, and practically all of them had come to accept the four great principles which were the legacy of the Puritan revolution in England. Only New England lagged behind, but even there the "Standing Order" was on the defensive within Congregational-

ism and was soon to surrender and adopt the point of view
that had become characteristic of the Congregationalists of
old England. Since the holy commonwealth of the English
Puritans had presupposed a representative form of government,
the era of the American Revolution and the American Constitution cannot be regarded as quite so revolutionary or creative
as is sometimes supposed. As James Hastings Nichols has
pointed out in his *Democracy and the Churches,* the pattern
which was then imposed on American life had been forged more
than a century earlier by the leaders of the Puritan revolt.
James Bryce saw this quite clearly when he wrote:

> There is a hearty Puritanism in the view of human nature which
> pervades the instrument of 1787. . . . It is the work of men who
> believed in original sin, and were resolved to leave open for trans-
> gressors no door which they could possibly shut. Compare this spirit
> with the enthusiastic optimism of the Frenchman of 1789. It is not
> merely a difference of race and temperaments; it is a difference of
> fundamental ideas.

André Siegfried, a French observer of the contemporary American scene, echoes Bryce's conclusion, saying: "If we wish to
understand the real sources of American inspiration, we must
go back to the English Puritanism of the seventeenth century."[7]

We can fully appreciate the force of these observations only
when we recall the religious coloration of the American colonies.
The colonies were solidly Protestant in terms of religious affiliation. As late as 1776, there were only fifty-six small Roman
Catholic congregations in all the colonies, constituting a tiny
minority of scarcely more than 1 per cent of all the churches
and perhaps an even smaller percentage of the total church
membership. On the other hand, fully 91 per cent of all the
churches belonged within the Puritan-Calvinist-Reformed
tradition.[8] While it is true that the majority group within New
England Congregationalism moved to the right during the
colonial period, left-wing Puritan sentiment—finding major

institutional expression among the Quakers* and the Baptists —was the dynamic religious force in colonial society, and it exerted an increasing influence within all the Protestant churches. The Congregationalists themselves were far from immune to this influence, and were frequently embarrassed by their movement to the right at a time when their fellow Independents in England were shifting rapidly to the left. Repeated left-wing rebellions arose within the churches of the Standing Order, and many, who did not secede as did Hooker and who were not driven out as was Williams, were tainted with left-wing views.

The difference between right-wing, center, and left-wing Puritan views probably should not be overmagnified. They shared common presuppositions and the sole heresy of the left-wing was its greater consistency in following out the logic of assumptions shared by all. It was because the left-wing so obviously had "the root of the matter" in them, as Cotton Mather put it, that the leaders of New England Congregationalism were frequently goaded to intemperate expressions. Since the "good theological reasons" which led to the adoption of the voluntary principle in religion were reasons drawn from the common treasury of Reformation faith, it is not at all surprising that such formerly right-wing groups as the Presbyterians, Anglicans, Lutherans, Reformed, and even the New England Congregationalists, driven by the logic of their own fundamental affirmations, should ultimately accept the left-wing point of view. The pressure to do so was especially great in a new and fluid society where ancient custom imposed no obstacle to logical and consistent ecclesiastical construction and where practical objections to the left-wing contentions were difficult to sustain. Indeed, these contentions had been set forth initially by the New England Congregationalists themselves.

* It should be remembered that the Quakers were one of the five major denominations at the close of the colonial period, and were widely dispersed throughout all the colonies.

II

The fundamental Puritan contention was that the commonwealth should be shaped to fit the design of the church rather than the reverse. They sought a holy commonwealth, but they were ecclesiastical architects first and political architects second. The ecclesiastical structure preceded and determined the pattern of the political structure. "It is better that the commonwealth be fashioned to the setting forth of God's house, which is his church, than to accommodate the church to the civil state."[9] So wrote John Cotton to Lord Say and Sele, and every Puritan would have agreed. Important as were political issues to the Puritans, they yielded always to the prior consideration of church organization. Their first concern was how the invisible church might be made visible, and their second concern was how the visible church might maintain itself as a reasonably pure approximation of the church invisible. The political order must be shaped to serve these two ends. This is a difficult point for us to grasp. Far removed from the days of constitution making, we are accustomed to think of the status of the church as determined by the political order, the more so because we no longer think of politics in theological terms.

Separation of church and state was not derived from any abstract philosophical ideas as to human freedom and equality. It was derived in the first instance from the two theological doctrines of the sovereignty of God and of human bondage to sin. From these two fundamental notions, the Puritans drew as a necessary corollary the conviction that all unchecked human power will lead inevitably to rebellion against God. On the basis of this analysis of the divine economy in the world, they arrived at three convictions concerning the visible church which were defended by all parties, although with varying emphasis. Any visible church, they affirmed, must be independent in its government, voluntary in its membership, and limited in power.

The first corollary of the basic theological presuppositions of the Puritans was the independence of the church. Stated positively, it was the affirmation of the dependence of the church upon God alone. "The converse of dependence upon God is independence of everything less than God."[10] This was not a particularly novel idea in the seventeenth century, although it did run counter to both the theory and practice of political Anglicanism. Gregory VII had asserted and defended the independence of the church in the eleventh century, and John Calvin had been equally jealous of the right of the church, always with reference to the will of God set forth in Scripture, to determine its own constitution, define the conditions of communion, and discipline its members. If God is sovereign and God in Christ is the sole head of the church, the Puritan would assert, then Christ as revealed in Scripture is the sole law to which the church must yield obedience. Roger Williams spoke the common mind when he said that to subject the church to control and direction by the state would be "to pull God and Christ and Spirit out of heaven, and subject them unto natural, sinful, inconstant men, and so consequently to Satan himself, by whom all peoples naturally are guided."[11] On this point there was no disagreement. "Even the established churches of Massachusetts Bay and Connecticut were never state churches which yielded any rights to the state in the appointment of officers, the administration of discipline, or the setting up of the form of church government."[12] From the very beginning, there was never any question as to the necessity for such independence.

The second principle to which the Puritans were committed was that the church must be voluntary in membership. In its most consistent form—exemplified by the Congregationalists, Baptists, and Quakers—the church, so conceived, was consti-

tuted by the voluntary adherence of those whom God had
"called out" of the world and gathered by a covenant, express
or implied, into a fellowship of believers. Thus Robert Baillie,
the Scottish divine, found the distinguishing mark of Congregationalism in "an explicit covenant, wherein all and every one
of the members by a voluntary association . . . do bind themselves under a solemn oath to walk in the ways of the Gospel."[13]
If the divine initiative were to be safeguarded, the church could
be constituted in no other way. Only by the outwardly un-
coerced act of free men in Christ could the church be brought
into being, and only thus could it be perpetuated. The church,
therefore, included only those who were able to give evident
proofs of grace and who were ready to assume exacting religious obligations in a covenant. Conversely, the authority of
the church, as a voluntary association of those in whom faith
had been awakened, extended only to those who had acknowledged its authority, and only for so long as they continued to
acquiesce in its exercise. "Churches," declared Richard Mather,
"have no power over such as have not engaged themselves by
covenant, and committed power unto them by professing to be
subject to all the ordinances of Christ amongst them." Or as the
author of *The Saints' Apology* put it: "Which jurisdiction no
man can lawfully be subjected unto but by his own agreement."[14]

The essential concurrence of the Presbyterians with this
point of view can easily be seen. They also drew a sharp distinction between the visible and the invisible church, with the
latter being the true church and the former only an approximation of it. The visible church was a body whose ultimate authority under God was exercised by the generality of the members
in a carefully devised representative system of government.
The unregenerate were excluded from membership and the
sacraments were not regarded as " 'general' means of grace,
open to any and all indiscriminately." The Presbyterians, to

be sure, were less willing than their fellow believers to the left to limit church membership only to those who could fulfill the most rigorous requirements, and consequently their churches were more capable of taking on the character of community churches.

Among Presbyterians the conviction was strongly held that in the final analysis the elect of God were known to him alone. . . . In admitting a person to the local congregation, the Presbyterians felt obligated to claim no more than that, in a charitable judgment, they had reason, based upon an examination of his faith and life by the minister and the elders who represented the people, to hope that God had numbered him within the great Church Universal.[15]

But, even if it was capable of embracing a larger portion of the community, the church for the American Presbyterians, no less than for the other Puritan groups, rested finally upon the voluntary adherence of the individual. Not only was this true, but throughout the colonial period the tendency among Presbyterians was to move in the direction of a more narrowly defined, gathered conception of the church. This was the meaning of their increasing insistence upon the necessity of a converted membership.

The fundamental theological convictions of the Puritans led them to insist, in the third place, that the visible church must be limited in power. Indeed, all human power must be limited. For they knew the human mind to be darkened, human affections corrupted, and human power forever subject to the temptation to exalt itself in rebellion against God. With Robert Barclay, the great Quaker theologian, they would all acknowledge that "all Adam's posterity, or mankind . . . is fallen, degenerated and dead . . . , and is subject unto the power, nature, and seed of the Serpent."[16] With Isaac Pennington, they would all confess that "man is captive, his understanding captive, his will captive, all his affections and nature in captivity."[17] Short of the harmonization of all powers in God's final act of redemption, the only possible procedure in dealing with the universal tendency of human power to absolutize itself was to surround it with limitations. Human nature being what it is, all unchecked power could lead only to a defiance of God and a contemptuous indifference to the common good.

> Let all the world learn to give mortal man no greater power than they are content they shall use, for use it they will. . . . It is necessary . . . that all power that is on earth be limited, church-power or other. . . . It is counted a matter of danger to the state to limit prerogatives, but it is a further danger not to have them limited.[18]

The words are John Cotton's, but the conviction they express was the common possession of all—Quakers and Presbyterians alike—who had gone to school to John Calvin.

As Cotton implied, the limitation of power is necessary in every area of life, in the church as well as in the state. Especially is this true of the church, for "the great usurpation of the kingdom which belonged only to God had taken place, they all believed, in the church."[19] Ecclesiastical absolutism was the anti-Christ itself, more to be feared than anything else. To give any civil power or authority to the church, Cotton insisted, would be to make "the church a monster." Magistrates who surrender any of their authority to the church, so that if the church condemns anyone, they must do so too, create a "monstrous deformity." It is necessary, therefore, "for Magistrates to keep their power in their own hands, and not to take things *Ipso facto* from the Church." The magistrates, warned Cotton, may neither "give their power to us, nor may we take it from them."[20]

> The careful distinction between the powers of church and state which the New Englanders sought to enforce was inspired no less by the desire to limit the church than by the wish to limit the civic power. In all this they were following Calvin and other reformers who had protested against the exercise of dominion by the church in the same breath with which they had declared its independence.[21]

Thus, from the very beginning, American Protestants were as opposed to church domination of the state as they were to state domination of the church, and they were opposed to it on the basis of good churchmanship informed by sound theology. Neither a state church nor a church-state would do.*

Logically, the principles of independence, voluntary membership, and limitation of church power would seem to lead inevitably to a complete separation of church and state, and the force of this logic was not missed by the left-wing Puritans. The Presbyterians, however, still clung to the ideal of a church recognized by law and enjoying the protection and support of the state. While the church must maintain its independence from the state and must preserve its voluntary character to safeguard the divine initiative and above all must not usurp the civil power, nevertheless, the state as a separate order of society had its own obligation to God. The state could be expected, on its own account, to honor God and yield obedience to him by providing the church with financial support and by denying the right of false worship to exist. The New England Congregationalists also adopted this position. Feeling the pull of tradition, fearing the consequences of complete separation, and possessing a sense of divine mission to create a new Zion in the American wilderness, they hesitated to accept the full logic of their presuppositions and, like the Presbyterians, appealed to the independent obligation of the state to God in support of their position.

Among the Presbyterians the notion of a uniform religious

---

*It is interesting to note that the congregational type of church organization, with its insistence upon the autonomy of the local church, was due in part to this principle of limitation. A concern for the restriction of church power quite as much as a belief in the rights of the local church led to the advocacy of only an "associational connectionalism." Ursurpation of the divine sovereignty by national, provincial, or episcopal institutions was what their experience had led them to fear; they had yet to learn that a local church could be quite as wayward and that perhaps some more positive check than "brotherly counsel" might be necessary. This problem will be considered in the final chapter.

establishment had no possibility of being applied in America, and under the pressure of a minority status it was difficult to maintain even as an ideal. The Congregationalists, on the other hand, constituted in the beginning a religiously homogeneous community and were able to translate their dream of a godly society into what was, to all intents and purposes, a confessional state. They were, however, in a particularly vulnerable position when it came to defending the course they had adopted. Their conception of the church left them with no ready answers to the arguments advanced by their more consistent brethren to the left, and a defense of a confessional state in terms of the obligation of the state to God could be made only by ignoring a theological conviction which was the common heritage of Protestantism in colonial America.

III

It was in terms of the doctrine of revelation that the notion that the state was obligated to honor God by providing the church with financial support and by denying the right of false worship to exist became untenable. How was the state to identify the true faith and the true church? In the Protestant understanding of the divine economy, no mortal man and no human institution was infallible, and any attempt to absolutize the fallible could only be interpreted as idolatry. The self-disclosure of God in Scripture, Calvin had insisted, could not be regarded as self-explanatory. The understanding of divine truth was dependent upon the gift of the Holy Spirit. This introduced both an element of humility and of tentativeness into Protestant formulations of faith.* "We doubt not what we practice," declared Thomas Hooker, "but it's beyond all

---

*In the century following the Reformation, in the heat of controversy, Protestants tended to retreat into an authoritative creedalism. To the extent that they removed their creedal formulations from discussion and regarded them as final statements of divine truth, they had abandoned Protestantism. The Puritan movement recovered the earlier Reformation perspective at this point.

doubt that all men are liars and we are in the number of those poor feeble men; either we do or may err, though we do not know it; what we have learned we do profess, and yet profess still to live that we may learn." This, of course, was no mere relativism or subjectivism. The possibility that the human apprehension of the divine self-disclosure might be imperfect must be affirmed, but the objective reality of the revelation of God in Christ was not questioned, and it served as a constant corrective in all attempts to formulate definite creedal statements. As the Scots Confession puts it:

> If any man will note in this our confession any article or sentence repugnant to God's Holy Word, . . . it would please him of his gentleness and for Christian charity's sake to admonish us of the same in writing; and we upon our honor and fidelity, by God's grace, do promise unto him satisfaction from the mouth of God, that is, from his Holy Scriptures, or else reformation of that which he shall prove to be amiss.

A similar point of view was echoed in the Particular Baptist Confession of 1646: "We confess that we know but in part, and that we are ignorant of many things which we desire and seek to know; and if any shall do us that friendly part to show us from the word of God that we see not, we shall have cause to be thankful to God and them.[22]

The generality of the Puritans, moreover, were conscious of living in a new dispensation in which they confidently expected new truth to be vouchsafed to them. They were vividly aware of the presence of the Holy Spirit, whose work it was not simply to confirm the old but to reveal the new, and they waited expectantly upon its leading for guidance. "I am verily persuaded," said John Robinson to the departing Pilgrims: "the Lord hath more truth yet to break forth out of his Holy Word. . . . I beseech you remember it is an article of your church covenant that you be ready to receive whatever truth shall be made known to you from the written word of God. . . .

It is not possible that the Christian world should come so lately out of such thick Antichristian darkness and that perfection of knowledge should break forth at once." And John Smyth explained his own practice in these words: "I have in all my writings hitherto received instruction of others, and professed my readiness to be taught by others, and therefore have I so oftentimes been accused of inconstancy. Well, let them think of me as they please. I profess I have changed, and shall be ready still to change for the better."[23]

The only way in which new disclosures of divine truth could be made and confirmed was through unfettered discussion.

We have a proverb that they that will find must as well seek where a thing is not, as where it is. Let us look upon the truth as God's and not ours, and let us look upon ourselves in all our discourses as hunting after it; every one . . . acknowledging that God must lead every man. . . . And this liberty of free disquisition is as great a means to keep the truth as to find it. The running water keeps pure and clear, when the standing pool corrupts. . . . The true temper and proper employment of a Christian is always to be working like the sea, and purging ignorance out of his understanding, and exchanging notions and apprehensions imperfect for more perfect, and forgetting things behind to press forward.[24]

Such a free and unconstrained recognition of truth—the exchange of the imperfect for the more perfect—through discussion, could be realized only if the Spirit remained unbound. And the Spirit was no respecter of persons. Even the humblest layman might be its instrument. Light might break forth "from the meanest of the brethren." Truth might be perceived by any man. Every man, therefore, must be free to be convinced and in turn to convince.

This type of thinking was at the farthest pole removed from the type of thinking implicit in the idea of a confessional state. The distinction is, perhaps, nowhere stated more clearly than by Nichols:

The confessional state . . . rested on the dogmatic theory of truth —that revelation is found in a closed objective body of propositions with stated institutionalized interpreters. Left-wing Puritanism, and the free churches that are their heirs, disbelieve that absolute truth can be exhaustively stated in any dogmatic formulation.

From this latter perspective, the spiritual sphere must ever remain open. Not only the church but the individual must be free to follow the leading of the Spirit. The motivation, however, was less to assert the rights either of the church or the individual than it was to protect the liberty of the Spirit and to permit the fulfillment of the consequent religious duties. The ultimate consequence of this line of thought is denominationalism—involving, on the one hand, freedom to organize ecclesiastical communities and, on the other hand, equal opportunity for individuals and churches to submit their claims in the forum of public discussion. Roger Williams states both the premises and the conclusion in explicit terms, and notes that among those that have divided themselves "into many several professions, . . . they that go furthest profess they must yet come nearer to the ways of the Son of God." The relation of theological assumptions to political principles, at this point, is clearly evident in the vivid words of Philip Schaff: "To talk about any particular denomination as the Church . . . has no meaning, and betrays ignorance or conceit. . . . The American laws know no such institution as 'the Church' but only separate and independent organizations."[25]

Quite obviously, the concern of the left-wing Puritans for liberty was a concern for the freedom of the Christian, and it poses the problem as to whether a similar freedom should be extended to the non-Christian. The answer was to be that it should be so extended. Unable to claim for itself the prerogative of any final determination of God's will and unable to rely upon the pretensions of any authoritarian church, the state was ill-equipped to judge as to who was to be numbered among the regenerate and what groups might properly be considered Christian. If the church could not do this in any final sense, how much less could the generality of the citizens—the obviously unregenerate as well as the regenerate. It is true that the church, as a voluntary body, could determine conditions of membership and communion, for it could do so without restricting either the liberty of the Christian or the liberty of the Spirit. The Christian was free to withdraw, and no orthodox Puritan ever thought of limiting the operation of the Spirit to any particular church. The state, on the other hand, was an inclusive body to which men must perforce belong, and by any action of which in the spiritual realm both they and the Spirit must inevitably be coerced. If the civil magistrate, says Williams, is to be made "the suppressor of schismatics and heretics, the protector and defender of the church, etc., what is this in true plain English but to make him the judge of the true and false church, judge of what is truth and what error, who is schismatical, who heretical?"[26] But practical considerations were equally compelling. Cromwell, Milton, and Williams all recognized the impossibility of guaranteeing the liberty of the regenerate without guaranteeing the liberty of all. The Christian liberty of the believer, they insisted, must be grounded on the natural liberty of all. Freedom was not just the birthright of the Christian; it was one of the natural rights of man. To hold otherwise would be to compromise the initiative and sovereignty of God.

A. S. P. Woodhouse, in his introduction to the Army Debates, suggests that the extension of liberty to all men was also made possible by the adoption of the principle of segregation, whereby a strict line was drawn between the realm of grace and the realm of nature. The realm of grace was restricted to the church, whereas the state should be guided in its action only by moral laws accessible to the reason and conscience of even unregenerate men. Such a distinction was made by some of the extreme left wing, but, with the possible exception of Williams, it was made by men who had become religiously indifferent. While such a distinction was not without influence, the principle of segregation was not necessary to account for the extension of freedom to all men. Actually, almost without exception, the Puritans held that the natural law could be clear only to the freed minds of the regenerate, and never in any full sense to the captive reason of the unregenerate. The significant contribution of left-wing Puritan thought at this point was not segregation but the restriction of the powers of the state. No real problem is presented by the contrast between Williams' conception of the church—rigorously restricted to visible saints, which can "be regarded only as an aristocracy of the elect"— and his conception of the state which is "pure democracy."[27] The point to be remembered is that a church is a wholly voluntary body, whereas the state is not.

Nor did the advocacy of separation, as distinguished from segregation, lead to a surrender of the Puritan's religious concern for society. It was a separation of church and state; not of the Christian and society. The Christian had the potent powers of discussion and persuasion at his disposal, and the church retained the two-edged sword of the Spirit, the Word of God. "Separatism in essence" never meant, as Woodhouse states, "separation from the world and its cares." It simply meant, in the first instance, separation from a corrupt church, and later the independence and freedom of all churches as voluntary societies. "It is action," said Richard Baxter, "that God is most served and honored by," and no Puritan would have dissented. The cry of reform was ever upon his lips, and the vision of a holy community always quickened his laggard steps.[28]

IV

The orthodox Protestants of the various American denominations, of course, did not stand alone in the struggle for the separation of church and state. The members of other minority groups stood staunchly by their side, even at a time when there was still dissent within the Protestant ranks. Especially notable was the leadership provided by the religiously emancipated intellectuals, the so-called "extra-church liberals," but while their role in the winning of religious freedom should never be minimized, it also should not be overstated. They had no mass following, and "the substantial popular support of the movement . . . was orthodox Puritan, whether Presbyterian, Baptist, Congregationalist, or Low Anglican."[29] H. Richard Niebuhr puts it even more vividly in describing the parallel struggle for democracy: "In America as in England the Christian enlightenment stood beside the rational enlightenment in the battle for democracy, and it furnished ten soldiers to the cause where the latter furnished one, for it dealt with the common men about whom the rationalists wrote books."[30] Above all, it is well to have Nichols remind us, in this connection, that

the eye of reason alone discovers very different things to be "natural" in a Roman Catholic monarchist society from what appears such in a society shaped by Puritanism. To this day the moral presuppositions of liberal democracy have never seemed "natural" to the self-consciously enlightened minds of Europeans shaped by Roman Catholic or Lutheran cultures. One may even suspect that the cultured rationalist generally restates in abstract terms the fundamental motifs he has heard from the despised and uncultured spokesmen for positive religious affirmations.[31]

In France, the *philosophes*, almost to a man, were led by an appeal to "natural reason" to defend the principle of an established, state-regulated church. It is not without significance, therefore, to recall that James Madison pursued his graduate studies under President Witherspoon, that Patrick Henry was indebted to Samuel Davies for his political ethics as well as his oratory, that Samuel Adams and John Hancock had been fed a steady diet of Election and Fast Day sermons, and that

Jefferson drew his ideas from the political Calvinism of Milton, Locke, and Sidney.

Far from being the product of indifference to religion, the separation of church and state was sought for sound and orthodox religious reasons. The subsequent development of the free church system was made necessary by convictions which were implicit in the thought of Puritanism from the beginning. The complete voluntarism of the Cromwellian era was a foretaste of what could be expected when the strength of the Puritan movement was transplanted to American soil.

CHAPTER IV

LYMAN BEECHER'S GREAT DISCOVERY: The Best Thing That Ever Happened in Connecticut

Voluntarism is so obvious a principle, as it is exhibited in American churches, that its significance is overlooked, but it is one of the revolutionary principles adopted by modern ecclesiastical organizations. H. K. ROWE[1]

If it is true, as Theodore Parker once said, that Lyman Beecher was "the father of more brains than any man in America," it is also true that he more than matched the stature of his illustrious sons and daughters. With the single exception of Charles G. Finney whose methods and views were closely to parallel his own, Lyman Beecher stood easily in the forefront of the outstanding religious leaders of the first half of the nineteenth century. "He had a singular gift for encountering major movements in his period—for crashing into them, glancing past them, or riding them as a skilled swimmer rides a wave."[2] Equipped with the uncanny sagacity of a practical politician, Beecher always knew what needed to be done and how to do it, and with his superabundance of energy he usually saw to it that it was done. Seldom daunted, one of the few mistakes in judgment he ever admitted was his defense of the Standing Order in Connecticut.

I

When the victory of the Fusion party, in the May election of 1818, made certain the withdrawal of state support for the churches in Connecticut, Lyman Beecher was utterly cast down. "I remember," said his son Charles, "seeing father, the day after the election, sitting on one of the old-fashioned, rush-bottomed kitchen chairs, his head drooping on his breast, and his arms hanging down. 'Father,' said I, 'what are you think-ing of?' He answered solemnly, 'THE CHURCH OF GOD.'" And Beecher himself confessed that "It was a time of great depres-sion and suffering. . . . It was as dark a day as ever I saw. The odium thrown upon the ministry was inconceivable. The injury done to the cause of Christ, as we then supposed, was irrepa-rable. For several days I suffered what no tongue can tell."[3]

For almost a decade, Beecher had led the fight and master-minded the campaign in defense of the establishment. To him, the establishment meant the preservation of true religion, good morals, and sound government. Without these three supports, he was convinced, society would rush headlong to disaster. Like Timothy Dwight, his good friend and great teacher, Beecher was unable "to conceive of true religion and good morals without the support of a sound government or, conversely, of a sound government without true religion." The three, in his mind, were indissolubly linked. Sound government could not endure without good morals, and good morals were dependent upon true religion. Disestablishment, therefore, could mean nothing less than the triumph of irreligion and immorality, and the destruction of society. "The great object" of those who were seeking to undermine the existing order, wrote Theodore Dwight, "is to destroy every trace of civilization in the world, and to force mankind back into a savage state."[4] It never occurred to Beecher that true religion, good morals, and sound government might survive disestablishment, and so he waged his war and battled valiantly to stave off the seeming forces of evil which had already won the day outside of New England.

After the churches had been disestablished, Beecher was obliged to confess that he had been mistaken. He found himself forced to acknowledge that what he had feared as the worst thing that could happen had turned out to be "the best thing that ever happened in the State of Connecticut." For, as he said, "it cut the churches loose from dependence on state support," and "threw them wholly on their own resources and God." Before the change, he declared, "our people thought they should be destroyed if the law should be taken away from under them. . . . But the effect, when it did come, was just the reverse of the expectation." Being "thrown on God and ourselves," there was "created that moral coercion which makes men work. Before we had been standing on what our fathers had done, but now we were obliged to develop all our energy." There were some who felt that ministers had "lost their influence," but "the fact is," asserted Beecher, "they have gained. By voluntary efforts, societies, missions, and revivals, they exert a deeper influence than ever they could by queues, and shoes buckles, and cocked hats, and gold-headed canes."[5]

II

Practical rather than theological considerations had led to Beecher's conversion from a defender of the establishment to an advocate of complete voluntarism in religion. He was interested in results, and it was his discovery that the voluntary principle, when applied to religious life, produced the results he desired that caused him to change his views. "The results he desired" is the key phrase, and Beecher's shift of position can be understood only when it is set over against the "actual condition of things" during the century and a half preceding his great discovery.

New England Congregationalism had fallen on evil days.[6] Beginning with the conception of the church as a body of convinced believers, Congregationalism soon found itself in the impossible situation of attempting to be both the church of the regenerate alone and the church of the community at large. To resolve this tension, they gradually shifted their position. First, the adoption of the "halfway covenant" admitted the unconverted children of church members to a rather anomalous status within the church. Then, the breach thus effected was widened by the doctrine of Stoddardism to the end that the full privileges of the church were extended to all who had not been convicted of "scandalous conduct or heresy." "These innovations in church order," reports Beecher, "though resisted by many and not introduced without considerable agitation, became at length almost universal throughout New England."[7] The results were drastic.

Religious experience, being no longer a test of church membership, disappeared from the pulpits as a theme of discourse. . . . Moralizing and speculation constituted the topic of pulpit ministrations. Church discipline, too, was relaxed, for unregenerate men would not call others to an account. Laxity of belief and morals prevailed, creeds and confession of faith were discarded, and candidates for the ministry often refused to answer inquiries in regard to both faith and experience.

The ultimate consequence was to include the entire community within the membership of the church. One aged minister, Leonard Bacon informs us, expressed his regret that he had not kept an accurate record of baptisms, but he was able to remedy the deficiency "by certifying, once for all, that to his best knowledge and belief, everybody then living in the parish was baptized."[8]

As the bars of the church were lowered, the influence of the church waned. It became to a large degree a secular institution, embracing and including the world. Accident of birth rather than conviction determined its membership, and with the decline of church discipline effective control over the life of its members was considerably weakened. Lamentations concerning the low ebb of moral and spiritual life were numerous enough, but conditions remained largely unchanged. Except for the brief interval of the Great Awakening, when an earnest attempt was made to return to the earlier pattern of a converted membership, New England Congregationalism could conceive of no other way to come to grips with the problem than an unyielding defense of its prerogatives as the established church. Elsewhere in the colonies, most of the American churches labored under the necessity of maintaining and perpetuating themselves as voluntary institutions and could not lightly dismiss the seeking and securing of conviction as the basis of church membership. But the Congregationalists of New England were under no such necessity. Consequently, the revivalism of the Awakening was not domesticated within the Standing Order, the Edwardeans or Consistent Calvinists of the back country lost themselves in theological speculation, and most of the constructive religious effort was left to the "sects" which had been either strengthened or created by the revival.

It was not until after the Revolution that New England Congregationalism began to rethink its position. Particularly distressing to earnest Christians was the growth of what was variously termed "free-thinking," "infidelity," and "atheism." For at least a generation, the natural religion of the English Deists had been gaining adherents among the emancipated intellectuals without causing any great stir, but now these rationalistic notions were beginning to be associated with the excesses of the French Revolution, and some people began to suspect the existence of a world-wide conspiracy to overthrow all government and all religion. Alarmed by the threat which seemed implicit in this French infidelity, a small coterie of Old Calvinists—heirs of the opponents of the earlier revivalism —began a vigorous counterattack—a counterattack which was ultimately to cause them to reconsider all the assumptions which had characterized their ecclesiastical views. Timothy Dwight, president of Yale, led the way, and out of his "efforts to rally Christian people to the defense of their religion," a "new revivalism was born."[9] At first, it was simply an effort, by means of a renewal of personal religious experience and conviction, to save society from the disastrous consequences of infidelity. Then, when disestablishment began to be agitated, Dwight and his cohorts, who were unable to "dissociate true religion from the state-established Congregational church,"[10] pushed the revival as a means to win support for the Standing Order.

III

The essence of the new revivalism, which was the major feature of the Old Calvinist counterattack, was a direct appeal to the minds of men to commit themselves to the fundamental truths of Christianity. Only thus, it seemed clear to them, could the advance of infidelity be arrested and the old order preserved. Without such a commitment among the people, firmly grounded in a personal religious experience, the battle—in a society where the majority vote prevailed—would most certainly be lost. In such a situation, where immediate and tangible results were demanded, the cold, formal discourses which had so largely replaced the personal preaching of the early Puritan clergy would no longer do. What was needed were sermons that would prick the conscience, convict men of sin, and lead them to Christ. On no other foundation could true religion and its necessary support—the state-established church—be secure.

This new revivalism was quite markedly different from the revivalism of the First Awakening under Jonathan Edwards. It was much more akin, in spirit and design, to the revivalism of popular churches in the West. "Edwards preached sincerely and vividly of what he had experienced and apparently was genuinely surprised when the revival began."[11] There was no deliberate design, no element of calculation. It was absolutely spontaneous. Discipline, to be sure, had been restored in the Northampton church, and Edwards' intense preaching of the doctrine of God's complete sovereignty and his oft-expressed longing for the conversion of those to whom he spoke, undoubtedly served to awaken the consciences of his hearers. But these were not premeditated "means." Edwards saw in it all only the hand of God. Dwight, on the other hand, deliberately set out to provoke a revival, and Beecher and Nathaniel W. Taylor perfected the techniques by which it might be fostered. To Edwards the revival was a by-product of the preaching of the Word; to the leaders of the Second Awakening it was something to be sought for very tangible ends.

Taylor was the theologian who worked out the appeal and provided the intellectual defense. Beecher was the organizer and the promoter, the strategist who devised the campaign and the commander who marshaled the forces, and he proceeded directly and effectively to go about the business of winning people to Christ. "Immediate repentance" and "immediate submission" were his watchwords.[12] "Where Dwight had moderately urged the use of 'means,' Beecher bluntly told the clergy that they were 'no longer to trust Providence, and expect God will vindicate his cause while we neglect the use of appropriate means.'" If the necessary exertions were made, Beecher had no doubt that truth would prevail, but it would not if the churches were asleep. "It is high time to awake," he insisted. "I foresaw what was coming," he said. "I saw the enemy digging at the foundations of the standing order," and "I went to work with deliberate calculation to defend it."[13] He not only rallied the ministers and pushed revivals; he launched a periodical, he encouraged the publication of tracts, and he organized voluntary societies for the reformation of morals and the promotion of missionary activity in "the waste places." And by doing so he systematized the pattern of activity which was to become characteristic of the American churches in their struggle for the souls of men and the creation of a godly society.

But to return to the revival phase of the campaign. Beecher's activity in stirring up his fellow ministers and organizing them for "systematic itineration" among the neighboring parishes in the interest of bringing "new life and revivals to one another's churches" need not detain us. Nor does our present concern require us to distinguish the "carefully controlled" revivals which developed under the capable leadership of Beecher from the more extravagant and enthusiastic awakenings of the colonial revivalists and of Beecher's western contemporaries. In terms of the specific function they were designed to serve and the ends they had in view, the two types of revivalism may be regarded as indistinguishable. In both instances the revival was a "means" and was definitely fostered.

What was of considerable importance in terms of the great light which dawned upon Beecher following disestablishment was his clear recognition that revivalism goes hand in hand with the idea of a purified church. It was only after the covenant had been renewed and two or three excommunications had demonstrated the determination of his church at Litchfield to "restore purity and preserve order" that a revival had begun there. In no other way could the necessity for a definite conversion experience be brought home to people long accustomed to claim, by right of birth, the name Christian and the privileges of church membership. "To form churches without reference to doctrinal opinion or experimental religion, and only by location within certain parish limits and by certain civil qualifications," Beecher was later to declare, "is the most pernicious infidelity that was ever broached. It breaks the spring of motion in the center of God's system of good will to men and stops the work of salvation." The qualifications for membership in a church of Christ, he insisted, must always be "personal holiness in the sight of God, and a credible profession of holiness before men." To hold otherwise is to "throw the church and the world together in one common field" and

to blot out "the doctrine of regeneration." Such a practical denial of the necessity of regeneration, it was evident to Beecher,
was quite as great an obstacle to the outbreak of a revival as
any theoretical denial might be.[14]

Beecher's campaign to combat the forces of infidelity and
save the establishment included more than revivals. He was
acutely aware of the good use to which the printed page could
be put in any appeal to the public. Books and periodicals could
reach a wider audience than any sermon, and Beecher did not
neglect them in his program of publication. But he was especially impressed with the value of pamphlet literature. Displaying a thorough understanding of modern advertising principles,
he set forth the advantages of tracts: they are "cheap and
easily multiplied; short and easily read; plain and easily understood; numerous and capable of being spread everywhere; and
as to answering them, of that there would be no end should it
be attempted." Matching his words with appropriate action, he
summoned his colleagues to meet at his home to initiate the
venture. "We must have a set of doctrinal tracts just right, and
to have such we must make them."[15]

Of greater long-term importance was the technique which
Beecher adopted and perfected of creating a voluntary committee or society to promote a particular concern or to accomplish a specific objective. This had been a favorite device since
the early days of his ministry, and his whole career might
almost be written in terms of his connections with various missionary, reform, and humanitarian societies. He first resorted
to this method of procedure when, in a blaze of indignation
following the slaying of Alexander Hamilton by Aaron Burr,
he decided that dueling was "a great national sin" which must
be stopped. Even on the floor of Congress, he declared in his
call for the formation of a society to put an end to the national
disgrace, "powder and ball" have been substituted for "delib-
eration and argument."[16]

Essentially a technique for co-operative action devised by the Free Churches of England, the voluntary society had been seized upon by Beecher and by others as a perfect instrument by which the American churches could exert their influence upon public opinion, effect reforms, meet humanitarian needs, and carry on extensive and far-reaching missionary and educational activities. At the turn of the century, local societies for the promotion of a host of causes—missions, education, peace, temperance, Sabbath observance, tract distribution, manual labor institutes—had begun to appear, and within a relatively brief period the local, state, and regional societies were replaced by organizations national in scope, such as the American Bible Society (1816), the American Colonization Society (1817), the American Sunday School Union (1824), the American Temperance Society (1826), the American Home Missionary Society (1826), the American Education Society (1827), the American Peace Society (1828), the American Seamen's Friend Society (1828), the American Tract Society (1828), the American Anti-Slavery Society (1833), and others too numerous to mention. "One thing is becoming daily more evident," a letter to Beecher in 1830 reported, "that the grand influence by which the church has been advancing with matchless success and triumph in the last forty years" is the result of the work done by these "voluntary associations of Christians."[17]

Such voluntary societies, organized by individuals within the churches but without any definite structural relationship to the denominational bodies, had several advantages. For one thing, they could be formed as need arose and they provided a channel for concentrated and concerted effort. More important, action did not need to be delayed until a corporate decision could be reached by a church or a denomination. A few interested friends could take the initiative and then, through the society they had created, could proceed to enlist broader support for their cause. Not only this, but such societies provided the necessary state-wide or nation-wide organization so essential to effective strategy and successful action. Equally advantageous was the fact, which Beecher had observed in connection with the operations of the Connecticut Bible Society, that through such voluntary societies the interest and active participation of members of other denominations could be secured for the particular objective being sought. "We are succeeding remarkably well in the county," Beecher had written in 1811, "in getting subscribers to the Connecticut Bible Society. . . . Churchmen and Democrats, Christians and men of the world, all fall into the ranks on this occasion. The thing is the most popular of any public charity ever attempted in Connecticut."[18]

In his campaign to save the establishment, Beecher was not oblivious of the advantages to be gained through the utilization of voluntary societies. From the beginning of the campaign the initiative had been taken by a small minority— Dwight at first providing the leadership and then Beecher moving in as the commander in the field. An "association of gentlemen" to publish a periodical was one of Beecher's ventures, and the Domestic Missionary Society for Connecticut and Vicinity was another. The latter came into being as a result of a sermon he had preached on "Building of Waste Places," in which he had pointed out that there were many parishes in Connecticut which were "lying waste," being without a resident Congregational minister as a result of the privilege which had been extended to dissenters to divert their tax money from the support of a worship which they did not approve. But the practical effect was, by neglect, to create in these destitute parishes "a brood of infidels, heretics, and profligates—a generation prepared to be carried about, as they have been, by every wind of doctrine, and to assail, as they have done, our most sacred institutions." Unless men of good will throughout the state band together and by uniting their resources provide a ministry in "the waste places," Beecher was sure that "the deep-laid foundations of our civil and religious order" will be overturned and "all our blessings" will "perish in the flames."[19]

The most important of the societies which Beecher fostered during this period, however, was the Connecticut Society for the Reformation of Morals. This society was initially conceived by Beecher, after he had become aroused by the tippling at ordinations, simply as an instrument for the promotion of temperance, but before it was formally organized in 1812 he had come to recognize its larger utility. He noted that the opposition to the Standing Order included all "the Sabbath-breakers, rum-selling, tippling folk, infidels, and ruff-scuff generally." Thus, it seemed clear to him that if the rough-scuff could be turned into temperate observers of the Sabbath, they would automatically cease to be a threat to the establishment. Furthermore, since such a society would "tend to awaken the attention of the community to our real state and danger," would tend to "be a rallying point for all good men," would determine "what needs to be done and the means of doing it," and would associate "the leading minds of the laity with us in council," it would be an ideal instrument for political action "to preserve our institutions." And that is just what it became.[20]

The curious feature of Beecher's activity is that—an ardent defender of a state-established church—he was to become by a perverse quirk of fate one of the major architects of the voluntary system in American religious life. The setting up of voluntary churches was never the end he had in view. He was out to save the establishment. But his very endeavor to preserve the old order led him to adopt and perfect the methods which were to enable the voluntary churches to survive and to make their influence felt. One of the most remarkable phases of his father's whole career, Charles Beecher was later to remark, was that period when "we see him, on the one hand, making Herculean efforts to uphold the system of Church and State, and, on the other, lavishing almost superhuman energies in laying the foundations of the voluntary system."[21] It was only after disestablishment had taken place and the Congregational churches of Connecticut had moved out into the main stream of American religious life, that Beecher recognized the full significance of what he had been doing.

IV

The Old Calvinists of New England in adopting the methods and techniques of voluntarism were wiser than they realized. They had come to revivalism by a roundabout path, but their instinct had been sound. They were now living in a democratic society, and revivalism in religion, as Adolf G. Koch has pointed out in his book *Republican Religion,* is the "counterpart or republicanism in politics."[22] In both the *élan vital* is democracy, freedom, discussion, persuasion, conviction, faith. In a democracy everything yields to the supremacy of public opinion; even constitutional guarantees are ultimately worthless without its support. And public opinion, if it is to be dependable, must always be grounded on personal conviction. Personal conviction, in turn, is of the essence of revivalism, for revivalism is nothing less than the seeking and securing of a verdict by a direct appeal to the minds and hearts of men. It is a quest for conviction, decision, commitment. In a democratic society, there can be no substitute for revivalism, in the best sense of the word. It was both necessary and inevitable, therefore, that American churches, if they were to make their influence felt, should take on all the characteristics of well-organized missionary societies. The responsibility for a political and social order determined by public opinion, as well as the responsibility for their own continuing institutional life, now rested directly upon the churches. It was a responsibility they could evade only at their peril.

Equally important, in a democratic society, was the restoration of church discipline, the doing away with lax practices with respect to the admission of church members, and the replacement of the "halfway covenant" with the older principle of a converted membership. To be sure, "it was no more possible now than it had been in the Puritan days to determine with precision who were the truly regenerate, or in whom conviction was thorough and sincere."[23] Yet, while a line could not be drawn that would be in any sense absolute, a reasonable approximation of the ideal of a church of convinced believers could be achieved, and this made all the difference in the world. For, a large part of the secret of the influence of religion in American life, as Tocqueville was later to observe, was to be found in the undisputed hold which the churches, as disciplined communities, had upon their members.[24] Convinced believers, conforming to the rigorous standards of the church and at the same time discharging their responsibilities as citizens in a free society, became something more than mere leaven in the larger community. Leaven is much too passive a figure to describe their role. They constituted a dynamic and aggressive force and were largely able to shape society to conform with their understanding of Christian truth and morality. The recognition of this fact, already demonstrated by other American denominations, was an important element in Beecher's great discovery. Under his leadership, New England Congregationalism—the last of the major American denominations retaining the "right-wing" point of view—capitulated to the dominant pattern of American religious life. The Congregationalists joined ranks with the "New Side" Presbyterians in seeking both a converted membership and a converted ministry; with the Baptists who from the beginning had rejected the birthright principle and were now flourishing throughout the country; with the Methodists who, with their "restricted membership and close-knit discipline," were winning the West; and by so doing, the Congregationalists once again began to play an influential role in the shaping of American culture.

No less important than revivalism and church discipline were the voluntary societies which were frankly interdenominational. As extrachurch agencies, the voluntary societies were explicitly designed to overcome the disadvantages of the denominational system and to provide an opportunity for Christians to unite in matters of common concern. One of the things which struck Beecher most forcibly, when the churches were disestablished in Connecticut, was the new feeling of solidarity which developed among Christians of all denominations as a consequence. Hitherto, the "sects"—Baptists, Methodists, Episcopalians, Strict Congregationalists—had "complained of having to get a certificate to pay their tax where they liked" and had aligned themselves politically with the forces of "infidelity." Now, he noted with elation, the repeal of the church rates had removed "the occasion of animosity between us and the minor sects," and, as a result, "the infidels could no more make capital with them against us." Indeed, the situation was now quite the reverse. The other denominations "began themselves to feel the dangers of infidelity, and to react against it, and this laid the basis of co-operation and union of spirit." From this time forward, released from the jealousies and antagonisms engendered by a state connection, the churches of Connecticut were to display in large measure that sense of common faith and of common responsibility in joint undertakings which was to become so characteristic of Protestant Christianity in the United States. Beecher, of course, was not the person to allow the shared concerns of Christians of the various denominations to be dissipated in ineffective sentiment. Ever a general who kept larger ends in view, he regarded the voluntary societies as heaven-sent means of uniting the resources of all the churches behind every good cause. Practically all the major societies enlisted his propagandist and promotional skill, and of all the New

Englanders, he was the most important figure in "the benevolent empire."[25]

Voluntarism in American religious life had come to terms with the two perennial problems of religious institutions—discipline and flexibility, authority and freedom. On the one hand, there were the voluntary churches, disciplined communities of convinced Christians organized into six or seven major denominations, self-governing and self-supporting, and perpetuating themselves by an active evangelism. On the other hand, through voluntary societies fashioned by individuals within the churches to meet specific needs, an instrument was created by which the resources of all the denominations could be brought to bear in a particular area of common concern. Nor did the organization of a new agency for co-operative activity need to wait until a majority of Christians was ready to act. Quite the contrary. The initiative in forming the voluntary societies always came from a small minority of the concerned, who then proceeded to win larger support for the enterprise they had fostered. As consciences became awakened to new needs, new agencies were created to meet them—the Y.M.C.A. and the Y.W.C.A., the Student Volunteer Movement and the Society of Christian Endeavor, the W.C.T.U. and the Anti-Saloon League, the Open and Institutional Church League and the Society of Christian Socialists, and a vast array of orphanages, asylums, hospitals, academies, colleges, and social settlements organized on a similar basis. These were the typical instruments of "Protestant Action" in a free society where religious uniformity had disappeared and where the churches were completely on their own.

V

It was not until disestablishment forced the Congregationalists of Connecticut to return to the early Congregational pattern of voluntary, gathered churches that Lyman Beecher's efforts to rally the people to the support of true religion and good morals became fully effective. The immediate effect of disestablishment was to make the churches dependent upon what Nathaniel W. Taylor was to call the "zeal and labors" of the ministry. Denied their former sources of support by the outcome of the election and forced to rely wholly "on their own resources and God," says Beecher, "the ministers were united, and had been consulting and praying." The result of their consultations and prayers soon became apparent. The laggards fell into line, and, reports Beecher with ill-concealed delight, "revivals now began to pervade the state."[26] Years later, Henry K. Rowe was to comment that "voluntarism is so obvious a principle, as it is exhibited among the American churches, that its significance is overlooked." Actually, he continued, it is one of the most "revolutionary principles adopted by modern ecclesiastical organizations."[27] Beecher made no such mistake. He may have been "wise only after the event," as Sidney E. Mead has observed, but "he was very wise."[28] Cut loose to stand or fall by their own efforts, subject to "that moral coercion which makes men work," the churches were roused from their lethargy, compelled to assume responsibility both for their own institutional life and for the moral and spiritual life of society, and were able to exert by "voluntary efforts, societies, missions, and revivals" a deeper influence than ever before. This amazing outcome, contrary to all his expectations, constituted the very heart of Beecher's great discovery.

CHAPTER V

THE GREAT CENTURY: The
Voluntary Churches Demonstrate Their
Strength and Effectiveness

Measured by geographic extent and the effect upon mankind as a whole, the nineteenth century was the greatest thus far in the history of Christianity. K. S. LATOURETTE[1]

New England was facing in two directions during the initial decades of the nineteenth century. The sailing captains of the coastal areas had discovered the islands of the Pacific and the teeming cities of the storybook lands which lay beyond, while the children of the New England uplands had discovered the rich farmlands to the west and were moving in a great migration across the Hudson.

I

The seaboard Yankees had long felt the lure of the sea. Fishing, whaling, shipping, and trading offered a welcome alternative to a meager livelihood won from thin and stony soil. "Local forests furnished oak for timbers and boards, fir for masts, pitch for turpentine and tar; fields yielded hemp for rope: and mines iron for anchors and chains. . . . All along the northern coast . . . were busy shipyards where, to the music of hammer and saw, rose splendid sloops and schooners—swift and beautiful—big enough to sail any sea and sturdy enough to weather any gale. By the middle of the eighteenth century, New England was launching seventy new ships every year."

At first the Atlantic was the highway of the hardy Yankee mariners, but following the Revolution they extended their voyages to the Pacific. The year after the surrender of Cornwallis, *The Empress of China* had sailed to Canton, and before the Constitutional Convention had completed its work at least nine voyages had been made by New England captains to the Far East. "In the year of Washington's inauguration the ships from Salem plowed the waters of the Indian Ocean. Before he delivered his 'Farewell Address,' warning his countrymen against foreign entanglements, American captains were at home in the ports of China, Java, Sumatra, Siam, India, the Philippines, and the Ile de France."[2]

The sea breezes which carried the New England ships around the Horn to the distant lands of the East also brought back reports of strange people and stranger customs. Popular interest in the faraway heathen thus evoked was more deeply stirred when the curios which had begun to appear in captains' parlors were followed by one of the heathen themselves— Henry Obookiah, a young Hawaiian. Brought to New Haven in 1809, Obookiah "represented his whole unfortunate race— and the heathen millions in general. His presence spurred missionary efforts. When he was converted, he symbolized what Christianity could and must do. A little later someone wrote of him that 'he appeared as one redeemed from the cruel bondage in which millions of the heathen, and all who are ignorant of God, may be found.' "[3] A profound and widespread interest in foreign missions was aroused.

The opening of the Pacific trade had coincided with the Second Great Awakening, and the new religious spirit kindled by the revivals impelled some of the more ardent and adventuresome of the youthful New Englanders to dedicate themselves to carrying the gospel to the ancient lands of the Orient. The year was 1810 and the society which was organized to undertake their support was the American Board of Commissioners for

Foreign Missions. Scarcely two decades before, a young Baptist cobbler-preacher, his concern awakened by the reading of Captain Cook's *Voyages,* had set out for India under the auspices of the newly formed English Baptist Missionary Society (1792). Three years later, in response to the urging of the trail-blazing Carey, the English Congregationalists, Presbyterians, and Evangelicals established the London Missionary Society. It was out of these two currents of interest—in England and America—that the modern foreign missionary enterprise was born—a movement which was destined to write one of the most amazing chapters in the history of the expansion of Christianity. The Free Churches of English-speaking Protestantism had come of age, and had taken the world as their parish.

But New England had not only discovered the world of distant ports and non-Christian peoples beyond the seas; she had discovered the broad expanse of fertile acres to the west of her hill country outposts. Her children were on the march and were carving out an empire in the hinterland of the American continent. "So great was the movement of New England people into New York State that the inhabitants of New York and New England seemed to Timothy Dwight, in 1821, substantially one people, 'with the same interests of every kind inseparably united.' In 1820 this shrewd observer estimated that from three-fifths to two-thirds of New York's increase of population from 1790 to 1820 had originated from New England. Others have estimated that from 1790 to 1820 southern New England alone sent 800,000 of its people to other sections of the country."[4] Northern New England contributed even more heavily to the westward march of younger sons for whom the overtilled western New England uplands had little to offer as an inducement to remain. As the concern of those at home supported the labors of missionary sons on the islands of the Pacific and the Asian mainland; so the concern of fathers and mothers followed the sons and daughters who took up the westward trek.

As early as 1787 the Connecticut General Association began sending missionaries to the new settlements which were springing up to the north and the west, and this action was followed in 1792 by the creation of a Committee on Missions of the General Association, whose work was financed by a special collection taken in the churches, including contributions from one Baptist and two Episcopal congregations. Six years later, in 1798, the home missionary activities were further consolidated and extended by the organization of the Missionary Society of Connecticut. The work of the Connecticut Society was almost immediately supplemented by the organization of other missionary societies on a local, state, or denominational basis, as well as by the formation of Bible, tract, and educational societies. The great impetus to the home mission enterprise, however, came in the years immediately following the close of the War of 1812, when the tide of migration to the West swelled to vast proportions and when the end of hostilities made it possible for Americans to forget Europe and to face the problems of their own hinterland. "The Christmas present which the American people received in December, 1814 (the Treaty of Ghent)," James Truslow Adams has written, "was nothing less than almost a precise century of time in which to concentrate solely upon their own problems of organizing their government and society and of the physical conquest of the continent, with scarce a thought of the Old World." The shift of attention which then occurred was reflected in the home missionary activity of the churches, and by the eighteen twenties national organizations had come into being to co-ordinate and direct the expanding effort to claim the West for Christ.[5]

The home missionary interest was to be a continuing concern of the American churches throughout the nineteenth century, and it found its most eloquent expression in Lyman Beecher's *Plea for the West* and in Horace Bushnell's *Barbarism, the First Danger*. Recognizing clearly that the character of America was to be determined in the vast region which stretched beyond the mountains, Bushnell wrote that the great task was "to fill this great field with Christian churches and a Christian people." "Home missions," he declared, had become "the chief, the all-important work," "the first and sublimest Christian duty which the age lays upon us."

> We have the future in our charge, and we mean to see the trust faithfully fulfilled. : . . . To present to mankind the spectacle of a nation stretching from ocean to ocean, across the broad continent; a nation of free men, self-governed, governed by simple law without soldiers or police; . . . a religious nation, blooming in all the Christian virtues; the protector of the poor; the scourge of oppression; the dispenser of light; and the symbol to mankind of the ennobling genial power of righteous laws and a simple Christian faith—this is the charge God lays upon us; this we accept, and this by God's blessing we mean to perform.[5]

Catharine Beecher voiced the common conviction when she wrote: "If we gain all we are aiming at in Foreign Missions, and the *West* is lost, all is lost."[6] The West was not lost, and a strong base for the world mission of the churches was made secure.

II

The shape of things to come was spelled out in central and western New York—the "Burned-over District" as it was called during the first half of the nineteenth century when the fires of the spirit swept over the area again and again. Here were concentrated the greatest efforts of the missionary and tract societies; and here, when the churches had been established, the societies were to find their greatest continuing support. Here the Plan of Union between the Congregationalists and Presbyterians was initially placed in operation, and here the techniques of the earlier frontier revivalists of Kentucky and Tennessee were systematized and put to more disciplined use by Charles G. Finney. In brief, as Whitney R. Cross has pointed out, the "Burned-over District" provides an almost perfect case study of the westward transit of New England culture and serves as a representative sample of the patterns by which the American churches sought to meet the religious needs of areas which were moving rapidly from a frontier to a mature agrarian or partially urbanized society.[7]

Drawing the major portion of its population from the New England hill country—chiefly from Vermont and the Berkshires—the religious coloration of the new communities beyond the Hudson was largely determined by the religious complexion of the Yankee uplands. The western hills of New England were the stronghold of the religious enthusiasm which stemmed from the Great Awakening, and here were to be found the various denominations of a shattered Congregationalism which were to become the major churches of the Yorkers. At the head of the list were the Baptists and the Presbyterians (Congregationalists back home),* the former somewhat larger, the latter possessing a margin of advantage in the number of educated ministers. These were the two upper class denominations and were markedly similar in many respects. Behind them ranged a cluster of denominations, smaller and more "popular" in type, and yet by no means negligible numerically. They constituted the liberal wing of the New England churches—Freewill Baptists, Universalists, Christians (Unitarian Baptists), and Friends. The other major group was the Methodist, ranking in numbers but not in social prestige with the Baptists, and representing a non-Yankee infiltration into this predominantly Yankee area.

"All the purposefulness of Yankeedom," observes Cross, had been marshaled to see that the sons and relatives and neigh-

* The churches formed by Congregationalists in New York and regions to the west, prior to 1840, "usually joined the General Assembly at Philadelphia, but the energy and money which created them came primarily from New England." (*The Burned-over District*, 19.)

bors who had departed "should continue to walk straightly in the accustomed faiths,"[8] and into the new region the voluntary societies of the various denominations moved with a thoroughly systematized program of evangelism. The earliest missionaries who were sent were itinerants. Then, when they found a station able to provide a portion of local support, they settled down and continued their itinerancy into neighboring communities as time permitted and opportunity offered. Still later, when a degree of stability had been achieved throughout the area, the missionaries worked in single communities, with a portion of their salary being underwritten until the field could become self-supporting. While the missionary societies were supplying the clergymen, the tract and Bible societies provided the necessary literature, the Sunday School Union busied itself promoting the religious training of the children, and the educational societies maintained the supply of new ministerial personnel by providing funds to aid needy theological students.

For the most part, a spirit of harmony and co-operation prevailed among the various denominations. Back home, the overwhelming religious needs of the West made concerted action by all Christians of whatever persuasion seem imperative. Ministers of five different denominations in Philadelphia, in 1805, united to sponsor the publication in tract form of Henry Scougal's irenic devotional booklet, *The Life of God in the Soul of Man,* as an antidote to an excessive sectarian spirit. As late as 1825 it was still being reprinted, and—to use the words of the preface—by directing attention from "matters of doubtful disputation, about which the best and wisest men differ" to "matters of the greatest importance, about which all good and wise men must agree," it reflected accurately the temper of the time.[9] In 1801 the Plan of Union between the Congregationalists and Presbyterians was adopted; and Baptists, Methodists, and Reformed co-operated with Presbyterians and Congregationalists in the early interdenominational missionary, tract, Bible, and Sunday School societies. Even when the Baptists and Methodists set up their own denominational organizations in these fields, the action was motivated quite as much by a desire to supplement the interdenominational activities as it was by a desire to compete. A Baptist editor in 1826 applauded such denominational co-operation in the Bible and tract societies, asserting that it could now be announced, to those who cited the divisions among Christians as an excuse for not making a formal profession of faith, that the stumbling block had been removed to such an extent that it could no longer be charged against the Church of Christ. In similar vein, a Methodist editor in 1818 hailed "the united exertions of thousands of all denominations of Christians to spread the holy scriptures" which "savours much of the catholic spirit by which the friends of Christianity should be governed, and furnishes a pleasing prospect of the extensive triumph of evangelical truth."[10]

The conditions of frontier life in New York State also worked toward cordial relations among the various denominations. "School houses in completely rural vicinities often harbored Methodist service on one Sunday, Baptist, the next, and perhaps Presbyterian, the third. As often as not, the first church building in a town was erected by general subscription and shared on alternate Sundays by at least two sects."[11] Forced at the outset to share meeting places, the ministers tended to stress Christian piety without worrying overmuch about sectarian labels, and they co-operated in promoting seasons of enthusiasm, even though they competed for the adherence of converts afterward. Later associations of ministers were formed in the larger centers to act together as occasion called, interdenominational support was given to protracted meetings, and benevolent and reform movements cut across denominational lines. Rivalry there was, to be sure, but for the most part it was a friendly rivalry. If it did result in the overchurching of some areas, the fault lay quite as much in a failure to foresee that the rapid growth in population would not continue as in any excessive denominational zeal. Presbyterians and Baptists did entertain some reservations concerning the Methodists due to the lack of education and undisciplined emotionalism of the latter group. But, as Horace Bushnell was to point out, in the long run the Methodists could be counted as allies rather than foes. "If sometimes their demonstrations are rude and their spirit of rivalry violent," he observed, "still it is good to have such rivals for their labor is still ours; and when they have reached the state of intelligence they are after, they are sure to become effectually, if not formally, one with us. Therefore, let there be, if possible, no controversy with them; but let us rather encourage ourselves in a work so vast by the fact that we have so vast an army of helpers in the field with us."[12] On the whole, the churches reflected the casual attitude, so typical of evangelicalism, toward differences in polity and practice so long as genuine piety was to be found within them.

The only serious controversy was with the Universalists and other freethinkers who quite obviously threatened the very fundamentals of true religion as understood by the more conventional denominations and consequently were regarded as undermining morality and destroying the very foundations of society. The Universalists, for their part, were no less belligerent in their condemnation of the supposed evil fruits of traditional Christianity. Happily, there was no longer any thought of an appeal to the police power of the state. The conflict was limited to invectives exchanged in pulpit and press, the forum of open debate and personal conviction was the final court of appeal, and community life was not unduly disrupted.

As in New England, so in New York, the revival was the chief means by which men and women were introduced to the Christian life and church membership. Revivalism had demonstrated its effectiveness in reaching the unchurched during the colonial era, and now in the national period even the Old Calvinists of New England were discovering its usefulness as a means of maintaining and perpetuating their churches on a voluntary basis and were developing a new theology to undergird their practice. The winter of 1799-1800 was called the time of the Great Revival in central and western New York until this awakening was eclipsed by the more celebrated revivals associated with the name of Charles G. Finney. During the years between these two periods of heightened emotion and enthusiasm, however, there were scattered awakenings which rose to peaks of a more widespread interest in 1807-8 and again in the postwar years, 1815-20

III

Frequently a movement can be seen most clearly in the career of its outstanding leader. This is particularly true of Charles G. Finney, for he combined in his person and activities many of the tendencies which were to dominate the American religious scene for the next half century. At the age of twenty-nine Finney was a lawyer, and according to his own confession a sinful, worldly man. His own sense of guilt heightened by the knowledge that his fiancee was praying for him; and the attention of George W. Gale, pastor of the church he attended and where he led the choir, being focused upon him as "the one man who stood in the way of the conversion of many," Finney was plunged into an extended period of intense soul-searching, which was finally resolved when a vivid apprehension of God's love overwhelmed him. Finney had said that the great trouble with Christians was that they were not sincere; that "it was not possible to believe that he and others were on the verge of hell, and yet be so indifferent in regard to the terrific fact"; that if he were ever converted, he would be a Christian in earnest and "pull men out of the fire." It is not surprising, therefore, that his conversion should have brought to an end his legal career. Indeed, the following morning a man appeared in his office and said: "Mr. Finney, do you recollect that my cause is to be tried at ten o'clock this morning? I suppose you are ready?" And Finney replied, "Deacon B——, I have a retainer from the Lord Jesus Christ to plead his cause, and I cannot plead yours."[13]

Failing to secure scholarship aid to attend seminary, Finney undertook to pursue his theological studies under the direction of his mentor, George W. Gale, and began preaching expeditions into the neighboring communities. His success was immediate. He spoke, without mannerisms, in the simple language of everyday life, simply talking (as he said) about the things that the preachers preached about, but with a bluntness and directness that his audiences could not evade. With his "great staring eyes" and utter sincerity, multitudes in the remote hamlets felt the Lord's power. Late in 1825 he moved into the upper Mohawk valley. The village of Western was the first to respond, then "Rome was ignited from Western, and 'the explosion of Rome . . . scattered the fire over this region of country,' sending sparks to Utica, Boonville, Verona, and many other towns."[14] Finney was wanted everywhere at once, and the fame of the awakening made him a figure of national prominence.

The most famous of Finney's revivals occurred in Rochester during the winter of 1830-31. By that time much of the earlier crudity and sensationalism of his back-country campaigns had disappeared. "The exceptional feature," reports Cross, "was the phenomenal dignity of this awakening. No agonizing souls fell in the aisles, no raptured ones shouted hallelujahs. . . . The great evangelist, 'in an unclerical suit of gray,' acted 'like a lawyer arguing . . . before a court and jury,' talking precisely, logically, with wit, verve, and informality. Lawyers, real-estate magnates, millers, manufacturers, and commercial tycoons led the parade of the regenerated. The theatre became a livery stable. Taverns closed. An Institute of Practical Education, modeled on Gale's school at Whitesboro, planned to train the forty young converts heading for the ministry while they worked to support themselves." The other converts joined Presbyterian, Baptist, and Methodist churches almost indiscriminately. While Finney would tell a Universalist that he had no more religion than his horse, he also warned his converts not "to dwell upon sectarian distinctions, or to be sticklish about sectarian points."[15]

Finney had succeeded in combining the New England theology with a more disciplined form of the revivalistic techniques developed in the earlier frontier communities south of the Ohio River—measures definitely intended to provoke a religious awakening. The procedure, succinctly summarized by Finney, was to distract attention from the world, attract attention to religion, and present the claims of Christianity with telling power. The preaching was always direct, language simple, manner colloquial, repetition frequent, and delivery extemporaneous. There had to be sufficient novelty, insisted Finney, to get the public ear, and enough emotion to win a verdict. The ideas implicit in his preaching were largely those which Taylor and Beecher had hammered out in the course of the Second Great Awakening in Connecticut. Most important of all Finney won disciples among the clergy and especially among the young candidates for the ministry who spread the awakening in everwidening circles throughout the hills and valleys of the "Burned-over District." Other followers went west to Ohio and the territory beyond, and Finney himself moved to Boston and then to New York City, determined to capture that citadel for Christ. In 1835 Finney also went west, becoming professor of theology at Oberlin College in Ohio and dividing his time for several years between the college and his pastorate in New York.

The great task of the churches, separated as they were from the state and denied all powers of coercion, was not only to awaken faith and win recruits for their congregations; they were also faced by the necessity of inducing society at large voluntarily to recognize and to heed the obligations of the moral law. It was for this reason that the whole impetus of revivalism—particularly in New England and New York where there was an intense awareness of the responsibility of the churches for the moral foundations of society—was placed behind benevolent and reform activities. Converts, Finney declared, did not escape life; they began a new life "in the interests of God's kingdom." Working, he insisted, was quite as necessary as believing. The whole impulse of the religious life was thus directed into channels of charitable activity and of moral and social reform, and a high-powered, well-organized, well-financed system of voluntary associations or societies was created to make the impulse effective. But this organizational activity should not obscure the central conviction that as the life into which the Christian gospel led could be entered upon only by individual decision and faith, so the moral order could be made secure only by personal conviction. Lyman Beecher acknowledged that his second great mistake was his effort to "bring back the keeping of the Sabbath" by legislative action. "We tried to do it by resuscitating and enforcing the law. That was our mistake, but we did not know it then." We "got the victory. The thing was done." But "the political revolution that followed" brought it all to naught. Sabbath observance, he had learned, could be made secure in a democracy only by an inner check, not by external restraint.[16]

Typical of the Evangelical pattern of reform during the first half of the nineteenth century was the Washingtonian temperance movement. "This movement," says Gilbert Seldes, "was as personal as the Anti-Saloon League was impersonal. It required moral conversion, and it offered individual happi-

ness, invoking no law but the moral law, appointing no bureauc-
racy, and carrying on no lobby. This was the typical movement of the time, trusting to moral suasion, appealing to the
individual, and involving no compulsion."[17] And so it was with
other issues and with the voluntary associations which arose
to care for the wards of society and to carry out experiments
in communal living. The Sunday mail question did call forth
a demand for legislative action—a necessary tactic because
the mail was a government operation—but even this was resisted by many and voluntary action was enlisted, as an alternative, for the organization of boat and stage companies on
"the six day principle." The one great exception to the general
pattern was the antislavery agitation which definitely involved
an appeal for coercive action by the government, but it was
a form of coercion designed to set men free and the antislavery
campaign was based upon a summons to repentance—personal
repentance—on the part of each individual citizen for his share
in the perpetuation of the system of human bondage. The great
effort was to create a society knit together by voluntary obedience, a society of free men in which moral obligations were
clearly recognized and freely accepted.

IV

The story of the "Burned-over District" is the story of the
American West as a whole. Details varied, emphases differed,
but the basic pattern was much the same. The difference between the revivals in New York and the equally famous
awakenings of the trans-Allegheny region "is not a difference
in principle but a difference in the educational and general
culture level and outlook of the leaders and audiences."[18] Central and western New York had little active frontier "godlessness" to combat in marked contrast to some of the other frontier areas, and its settlers had a vastly greater degree of education and culture. Consequently, the Baptist farmer-preacher,

the Methodist circuit-rider, and the camp-meeting revival played a much more important role in the region south of the territory occupied by the westering New Englanders along the Great Lakes.

The self-supporting Baptist farmer-preachers who moved across the mountains from the Shenandoah and Piedmont regions of the South accompanied the initial wave of population into the newer territories. They "lived and worked," observed Theodore Roosevelt in *The Winning of the West*, "exactly as did their flocks . . . ; they cleared the ground, split rails, planted corn, and raised hogs on equal terms with their parishioners."[19] And the churches they formed waited for no help from missionaries sent over the mountains but proceeded to "raise up" additional preachers out of their own number to evangelize neighboring communities. Equally indigenous were the Methodist circuit-riders. "A Methodist preacher in those days," reports Peter Cartwright, "when he felt that God had called him to preach, instead of hunting up a college or Biblical institute, hunted up a hardy pony or a horse, and some traveling apparatus, and with his library always at hand, namely, Bible, Hymn Book, and Discipline, he started, and with a text that never wore out nor grew stale, he cried, 'Behold the Lamb of God, that taketh away the sin of the world.' In this way he went through storms of wind, hail, snow, and rain; . . . lay out all night, wet, weary and hungry; held his horse by the bridle all night or tied him to a limb; slept with his saddle blanket for a bed, his saddle or saddle-bags for his pillow, and his old big coat or blanket, if he had any, for a covering."[20] These Methodist preachers, as Horace Bushnell acknowledged, were "admirably adapted, as regards their mode of action, to the new west—a kind of light artillery that God has organized to pursue and overtake the fugitives that flee into the wilderness from his presence. They are prompt and effective in action, ready for all service, and omnipresent, as it were, in the field.

The new settler reaches the ground to be occupied, and, by the next week, he is likely to find the circuit crossing by his door, and to hear the voice of one crying in the wilderness, 'The kingdom of God is come nigh unto you.' "[21]

Augustus Longstreet, in his study of the Georgia frontier, has remarked that "the honest Georgian preferred his whiskey straight and his politics and religion red hot."[22] So it was in much of the region beyond the Allegheny Mountains, where frontier society was remote, raw, rough, and largely uncontrolled. Here physical manifestations of religious excitement, which tended to be frowned upon in the Yankee areas, were permitted and even encouraged. But the achievements, in terms of the genuine piety that was awakened and the moral order that was introduced as well as in terms of increase in church membership, were no less significant. It was a society, says Ralph Gabriel, "crude, turbulent, and godless," and "Evangelical Protestantism, more than any other single force, tamed it."[23]

All, to be sure, was not clear gain, either in New York, or in Kentucky. A price was paid for the extravagances of the revivalist tide, but this price was more than counterbalanced by the constructive results. As a recruiting technique in a society where 90 per cent of the people were outside the churches, revivalism proved exceedingly effective. "The churches . . . built by individual recruiting of membership on a purely voluntary basis—tripled their enrolled membership, relative to population," in the fifty years from 1800 to 1850.[24] In addition the churches succeeded in penetrating society and culture with an ethos which, whatever its inadequacies, was distinctly Christian, and the churches standing beside the courthouse on the village square came to be symbols of the common conviction that morals and good order rested upon religion. Even though "the flame of religious zeal burned with significant brightness only in the hearts of a minority," the generality of

the community believed that "if America were to be suddenly
bereft of its churches, moral collapse would result." Thus, "the
church building, the services within it, and all the self-denying Sabbath customs were symbolic expressions of a folk belief in an eternal and changeless moral order upon which society
rests," and the universal esteem in which the churches were
held is a measure of the extent to which they had effectively
penetrated the life of their society.[25]

V

To look outward merely from New England is to take too
parochial a view of events and activities which were in reality
but a phase of a much larger movement—a movement whose
achievements caused Kenneth Scott Latourette to describe the
nineteenth century as "the great century" in the history of
Christianity. Primarily a century of Protestant advance, the
nineteenth century derived its greatness for the most part
from the positive accomplishments of the free churches of
Great Britain, the United States, and the British dominions
beyond the seas. Only by a repetitive refrain of superlatives
could Latourette describe what had taken place.

Never before in a period of equal length had Christianity or any
other religion penetrated for the first time as large an area as it had
in the nineteenth century.

Never before had any religion been planted over so large a portion of the earth's surface.

Never before had Christianity, or any other religion, been introduced to so many different peoples and cultures.

Never before had Christianity, or any other religion, had so
many individuals giving full time to the propagation of their faith.

Never before had so many hundreds of thousands contributed
voluntarily of their means to assist the spread of Christianity or
any other religion.

Never before . . . had Christians come so near the goal of reaching all men with their message.

Never before had any other set of agencies pioneered in education for as many different peoples as did the Christian missions of the nineteenth century.

Never had the faith won adherents among so many peoples and in so many countries. Never had it exerted so wide an influence upon the human race.

"Measured by geographic extent and the effect upon mankind as a whole," he concludes, "the nineteenth century was the greatest thus far in the history of Christianity."[26]

As every schoolboy knows, the nineteenth century was the era when four centuries of expansion by European peoples and culture reached floodtide, and the major expansion which took place during the nineteenth century was from Great Britain and in the United States, in both of which Protestantism was dominant. This, in part, is an explanation of the remarkable achievements of Anglo-American Protestantism during those years, but only in part. This was its opportunity, but it was an opportunity which easily could have been lost. The important fact is that the expansion coincided with a new burst of spiritual life within the English-speaking churches with consequences no less momentous within the older centers of the Anglo-American life than on the expanding periphery. Nor should it be forgotten that, while the greatest revivals occurred in England and America, "awakenings" also were to appear among Continental Protestants, enlisting them as partners in the general evangelical advance.

It is difficult to systematize the scattered "awakenings" of the eighteenth century in which Evangelicalism was born. In part they represented a revival of Puritan "experimental" religion; in part they may be traced to Pietist influences from the Continent. It might be argued, with good reason, that the Evangelical Revival began in the American colonies, spread to England through the Wesleys and George Whitefield, and returned once again through Wesleyan converts to strengthen the new life that had come out of the Great Awakening. Whatever the direction the reciprocal influences actually took, it is clear that the Great Awakening of Frelinghuysen, the Tennents, Jonathan Edwards, and Samuel Davies in America was paralleled by a similar spiritual quickening in Great Britain. On both sides of the Atlantic the revival was in essence a great home missionary campaign which ultimately was to produce a concern for the last and the least in the most remote lands of the earth. In England "it was timed so as to catch the new barbarian invasions from within, the masses of laborers huddled in the warrens of the early industrial revolution, without roots or traditions or stake in society," and it was led by "a dignified Oxford don" who "found himself so consumed with the news of the Kingdom that he would force himself to preach in the fields or streets or wherever the people were."[27]

The significance of New England in this larger movement is that it provides a vivid illustration, particularly when viewed in the person of Lyman Beecher as a typical defender of the state church system, of the "moral coercion" which brought Evangelicalism to birth. The great light which dawned upon Beecher followed the overthrow of the Standing Order in Connecticut, and this seeming disaster, compelling the churches to depend upon their own efforts, in turn had awakened the latent energies of both ministers and people. As a consequence, revivals "began to pervade the state." Of course, they had actually resorted to revivalism in the preceding campaign to save the establishment, for it was only by the renewal of personal religious conviction that they could hope to avert what they regarded as hostile action by the state. In effect, from the moment disestablishment threatened, the churches were on their own.

Elsewhere in America most of the churches had long labored under the necessity of maintaining and perpetuating themselves as voluntary institutions, and it was among these churches that the Great Awakening had originated. They were confronted by the dual problem of recruiting church members and of making their influence felt in society without any governmental assistance. Lacking any formal coercion which would automatically bring the members of the community under the beneficent influence and discipline of the church and being deprived of any institutional authority in society, they were wholly dependent upon voluntary adherence and the power they might exercise through a godly public opinion. In neither instance could there be any alternative to personal decision and faith.

In England the relationship between voluntarism and Evangelicalism is not immediately so apparent. The situation there was more closely akin to the colonial awakening in New England under Jonathan Edwards, which was in part the product of the contagious influence of the awakening in the Middle Colonies and in part a response to a situation in which a large portion of the population remained unchurched or at best had but a nominal relationship to the church. In England a similar situation had been created by the influx of people into the new industrial communities and mining centers. Uprooted from their old homes and living amid indescribable squalor, these new city dwellers were the first casualties of the industrial revolution to irreligion. Seemingly oblivious to their responsibilities, too many of the clergy of the established church were content to rest upon the prerogatives they enjoyed by virtue of state support and were fearful lest any tampering with existing ecclesiastical arrangements destroy the "position" of Christianity in society. But the existing ecclesiastical arrangements— which permitted widespread nonresidence among the clergy and included a hopelessly outdated geographical distribution of parishes—were ill-adapted to the maintenance of Christianity anywhere in the land, and provisions for a religious ministry among the new urban masses were almost nonexistent. It was not simply that these people were unchurched; in one instance at least there was not even a church within the corporate limits to which they might relate themselves. "Since 1688," reports Halévy, "neither bishops nor parsons had given a thought to the need of adapting" the parish boundaries "to the increase of population and its altered distribution. Therefore the distribution of parishes was treated in the same fashion as the distribution of constituencies (for parliamentary representation)"—a condition which was not to be fundamentally altered until legislation for church reform was enacted in the middle decades of the nineteenth century. An extreme but by no means an isolated example of the situation was the parish of Marylebone, where a population of forty thousand had to be content with a village church accommodating at the most two hundred persons.[28]

If John Wesley ignored parish boundaries and preached in the marketplace and open field, it was due quite as much to the fact that the structure of the established church was so ill-suited to the actual religious needs of England as it was to the fact that complacent clergymen forbade him the use of their churches. Wesley was on his own no less than the voluntary churches in America, and ultimately he had to fashion churches of his own—in the form of classes and societies—for the people to whom he ministered. The free church system which had been thrust aside and rejected at the Restoration, only to win a partial toleration in the Glorious Revolution of 1688, won its ultimate victory in the Evangelical Revival and was to continue as the dominant feature of English religious life thereafter. The established church, while retaining some privileges, adjusted itself to the free church pattern and accepted its position as the church of only a minority of the people within the realm. Nor was the triumph of Evangelicalism itself restricted to the Methodist societies which were brought into being as a separate denomination by the revival.

The churches of the English Presbyterians, Congregationalists, Baptists, and even the Anglicans were profoundly penetrated and reconstituted by the Evangelical spirit and outlook. Throughout the nineteenth century, in England as in America, Evangelicalism was to be the vital religious force.

The free church motif held true in the far-flung outposts of the foreign mission enterprise as well as at home. Despite the fact that the missionary thrust in non-Christian lands accompanied and paralleled Anglo-American political expansion and economic penetration, "there was less direction and active assistance from the state than in any era since the beginning of the fourth century." The greatest extension of Christianity in history was carried forward almost exclusively by voluntary organizations supported by the gifts of private individuals. "As never before in its history, unless possibly in the first three centuries, the expansion of Christianity was not left to small professional monastic groups through the initiative of princes, but was by the support of large elements in the rank and file of its lay adherents." Subjected to the "moral coercion" exerted by the voluntary status of the church in society, "the entire body of Christians" was recognizing its responsibility for the spread of the faith.[29]

VI

Numerical gains and geographical extension, remarkable as they were, should not be allowed to obscure the greatest achievement of the free churches in "the great century"—the placing of a distinctly Christian stamp upon an entire culture. Paradoxically enough, during the very period when, as Latourette says, "the climate of opinion was increasingly against the automatic identity of membership in the community and the church," the influence of the church upon society was greatest.[30] Elie Halévy, the noted French interpreter of nineteenth-century England, has described the process as he observed it at work in English society. "During the eighteenth century England had been the scene of a great religious movement, unparalleled on the Continent. . . . This was the 'Methodist' or 'Evangelical' revival. . . . We shall witness Methodism bring under its influence, first the Dissenting sects, then the Establishment, finally secular opinion." Halévy explains this development in these words:

The religious bodies whose freedom was respected by the State were societies which, because they lacked the power of a legal coercion, were obliged to direct their efforts to the establishment of a powerful moral authority alike over their own members and over society as a whole. And their efforts were successful. They exercised the influence they sought. Not only did they encourage the growth in every sphere of a spirit of free association, and occasion directly or indirectly the mass of voluntary institutions both philanthropic and scientific so characteristic of modern England. They disturbed the torpor of the Government and even of the Established Church. They occupied themselves with the regulation of public morality, compelled the application of existing laws, revived laws which had fallen into abeyance, demanded new legislation. . . . The ruling classes watched the growth of this new power, whose nature they could not comprehend. . . . Had they understood the situation better, they would have realized . . . that the free organization of the sects was the foundation of social order in England. "England is a free country": this means at bottom that England is a country of voluntary obedience, of an organization freely initiated and freely accepted.[31]

Although Halévy understood what had happened, he never ceased to marvel that a minority group could so place its stamp upon the culture of English society as a whole.

The same process was at work in the United States. Here also was tried what has been called the great experiment of "applying Christianity directly to man and society without the intervention of the state.[32] Obviously in a democratic society, emphasizing government by discussion and free debate with a minimum of coercion, everything depends upon the efficacy of persuasion. And the persuasion was effective. The story has already been told in terms of the activity of the churches and the place they won for themselves and for religion in public esteem. But the full measure of their achievement in society as a whole can best be seen, perhaps, in terms of a single individual.

No one better illustrates the strength and pervasive power of the culture which the free churches had nurtured and established in American life than Abraham Lincoln. No churchman in any formal sense, Lincoln nonetheless possessed—and expressed with "a simplicity and dignity rarely equalled"—a sensitivity of conscience, a depth of religious insight, and a sure grasp of the essentials of the Christian faith which makes him one of the great modern representatives of Christian statesmanship. While his faith was to be deepened by bereavement and his war experience, it was by no means something which had come to him only late in life. "I was early brought to a living reflection," he said, "that nothing in my power whatever . . . would succeed without the direct assistance of the Almighty— but all must fail." As a true child of Protestantism, he affirmed: "I have often wished that I was a more devout man than I am."[33] From the very moment he left Springfield, Lincoln's speeches reflect the essential integrity of a faith long held and unconditionally accepted.

On the curiously meandering journey from Springfield to Washington, Lincoln made clear his confidence that the will of God would be done and that justice would be effected according to the purposes of a moving, if inscrutable, providence. At Indianapolis he told the assembled citizens that he was "a mere instrument, an accidental instrument," of a great cause. Two days later he spoke a few cryptic words to the state legislature at Columbus. With six states already having withdrawn from the Union, he assured the legislators that "there is nothing going wrong" and that "this is a most consoling circumstance."

All that is required is "time, patience, and a reliance on that God who has never forsaken this people." "I fear that the great confidence placed in my ability is unfounded," he told the people of Steubenville. "Indeed, I am sure it is." But, "nothing shall be wanting on my part, if sustained by God and the American people." To the state assembly at Albany he said: "While I hold myself, without mock modesty, the humblest of all individuals that have been elevated to the presidency," yet "I have a more difficult task to perform." Nevertheless, he continued, "if we have patience, if we restrain ourselves, if we allow ourselves not to run off in a passion, I still have confidence that the Almighty, the Maker of the Universe, will through the instrumentality of this great and intelligent people, bring us through this as he has through all the other difficulties of our country."[34] Finally, when Washington was reached, he made clear in unmistakable terms his firm adherence to two basic tenets long inculcated by the free churches of America— namely, that God's will shall ultimately prevail and that "honest inquiry and discussion of the whole people into God's will" is "a surer organ of perception than any ecclesiastical functionary."[35] "Why should there not be a patient confidence in the ultimate justice of the people?" he asked in his inaugural address. "Is there any better hope or equal hope in the world? In our present differences is either party without faith of being in the right? If the Almighty Ruler of Nations, with his eternal truth and justice, be on your side of the North, or on yours of the South, that truth and that justice will surely prevail by the judgment of this great tribunal of the American people." "Suppose you go to war, you cannot fight always; and when, after much loss on both sides, and no gain on either, you cease fighting, the identical old questions as to terms of intercourse are again upon you." There is "no single good reason for precipitate action. Intelligence, patriotism, Christianity, and a firm reliance on Him who has never yet forsaken this favored land, are still competent to adjust in the best way all our present difficulty." And then, with words reshaped from a suggestion by Seward into an eloquent expression of his own spirit, he concluded the address:

I am loath to close. We are not enemies, but friends. We must not be enemies. Though passion may have strained, it must not break our bonds of affection. The mystic chords of memory, stretching from every battlefield and patriot grave to every living heart and hearthstone, all over this broad land, will yet swell the chorus of the Union, when again touched, as surely they will be, by the better angels of our nature.[36]

This was the theme of all Lincoln's subsequent utterances— a simple faith in the living God, a humble submission to his will, a constant readiness to follow the divine leading as God shall make it known through honest inquiry and open discussion, and an unfaltering confidence that—whether we recognize it as such or not—God's will is being done and his purposes fulfilled even in the midst of evil and disaster. "In the present civil war," he wrote to John Hay in 1862, "it is quite possible that God's purpose is something different from the purpose of either party; and yet the human instrumentalities, working just as they do, are of the best adaptation to effect his purpose. I am almost ready to say that this is probably true; that God wills this contest, and wills that it shall not end yet." To a visiting Congressional delegation in the same year, he said that he believed that God "will compel us to do right in order that he may do these things, not so much because we desire them as that they accord with his plans of dealing with this nation. . . . I think he means that we shall do more than we have yet done in furtherance of his plans, and he will open the way for our doing it. I have felt his hand upon me in great trials and submitted to his guidance, and I trust that as he shall further open the way I will be ready to walk therein, relying on his help and trusting in his goodness and wisdom." As Lincoln spoke, James

F. Wilson reports, his air of dejection disappeared. "Sometimes it seems necessary," Lincoln observed as the delegation was about to leave, "that we should be confronted with perils which threaten us with disaster in order that we may not get puffed up and forget him who has much work for us yet to do." In similar vein a year later Lincoln told another group of visitors: "Amid the greatest difficulties of my Administration, when I could not see any other resort, I would place my whole reliance in God, knowing that all would go well, and that he would decide for the right."[37]

It was Lincoln's Second Inaugural Address, however, that was destined to become the immortal expression of his religious faith. "Seldom," writes Carl Sandburg in commenting upon it, "had a President been so short-spoken about the issues of so grave an hour."[38] But never had a President been able to speak with more directness and simplicity to the essential meaning of the struggles of men.

On the occasion corresponding to this four years ago, all thoughts were anxiously directed to an impending civil war. . . . Both parties deprecated war; but one of them would make war rather than let the nation survive; and the other would accept war rather than let it perish. And the war came. . . .

Neither party expected for the war the magnitude or the duration which it has already attained. . . . Each looked for an easier triumph, and a result less fundamental and astounding. Both read the same Bible, and pray to the same God; and each invokes his aid against the other. It may seem strange that any men should dare to ask a just God's assistance in wringing their bread from the sweat of other men's faces; but let us judge not, that we be not judged. The prayers of both could not be answered—that of neither has been answered fully.

The Almighty has his own purposes. . . . If we shall suppose that American slavery is one of those offenses which, in the providence of God, must needs come, but which, having continued through his appointed time, he now wills to remove, and that he gives to both North and South this terrible war, as the woe due to those by whom the offense came, shall we discern therein any departure from those divine attributes which the believers in a living God always ascribe to him?

Fondly do we hope—fervently do we pray—that this mighty scourge of war may speedily pass away. Yet, if God wills that it continue until all the wealth piled by the bondman's two hundred and fifty years of unrequited toil shall be sunk, and until every drop of blood drawn with the lash shall be paid by another drawn with the sword, as was said three thousand years ago, so still it must be said, "The judgments of the Lord are true and righteous altogether."

And then, with words strikingly reminiscent of the magnanimity of the concluding paragraph of his First Inaugural, Lincoln brought his message to a close:

With malice toward none; with charity for all; with firmness in the right, as God gives us to see the right, let us strive on to finish the work we are in; to bind up the nation's wounds; to care for him who shall have borne the battle and for his widow and his orphan—to do all which may achieve and cherish a just and a lasting peace among ourselves, and with all nations.[39]

Over and beyond the formal utterances which revealed the depth and reality of his understanding of the more profound implications of the Christian faith, Abraham Lincoln exhibited in his conduct of the government during the war years the self-restraint which was the crucial ingredient in the social philosophy of Evangelicalism and the indispensable virtue in a democracy. Lincoln believed in the principle of constitutional government, in the principle that the public official is subject to and restrained by a written law whose authority is superior to the authority of an office no matter how exalted. And Lincoln conceived his vocation as President to be the preservation of that principle in America. He was seeking "to protect and defend a supreme law that was no longer supreme"—a Constitution whose provisions for the orderly determination of public policy had been openly defied. In the crisis confronting the nation, Lincoln found himself compelled, by the necessity for quick decisions and rapid action, to transgress the letter of the law, to ignore the limitations restricting his authority, and to seize almost unlimited dictatorial powers. Yet Lincoln "did not become a dictator." Like Oliver Cromwell, who in a similar crisis sought repeatedly to devise some instrument for a constitutional exercise of power, Lincoln "accepted freely and completely the restraint of what was for him the ultimate law"—an inner check, the nature of which was determined by his religious faith. During the years of conflict, says Ralph Gabriel, this inner check "set the limits which governed the policy of the President, when he pioneered in the exploration of that vague constitutional domain known as the war powers. In his meticulous adherence to these self-imposed limits when he was possessed of overwhelming authority, Lincoln personified the American ideal of the autonomous, self-determined, free individual."[40] It was an ideal, to be sure, which was not exclusively American, but it was distinctively Protestant and Evangelical, and the effectiveness of the restraint it imposed made possible a return to the normal pattern of a free society at the close of hostilities.

The great significance of Lincoln is that he bears witness, in his person and in his faith, to the extent to which the free churches had shaped American culture. The true greatness of "the great century" is that the culture that had been created could itself produce so great a Christian as Abraham Lincoln. The ideals, the convictions, the language, the customs, the institutions of society were so shot through with Christian presuppositions that the culture itself nurtured and nourished the Christian faith. So complete was the penetration of the culture that an Abraham Lincoln—lacking even a nominal formal relationship to a church—was enabled to reflect accurately and to exemplify profoundly the basic insights of the Christian faith. In a very real sense, however, the very success of the free churches in this respect was ultimately to be an important factor in their undoing. For the strength and vigor of the culture which the churches had brought into being led men to discount the importance of the churches and to neglect the springs from which the power and vitality of the culture had been derived. While faith could be nurtured by the culture apart from the churches, the Christian character of the culture could not be maintained apart from the churches. When churches became complacent and satisfied with the achievements of the past and failed to enlist an active concern for the renewal of spiritual life in the personal experience of individual men and women, the distinctively Christian character of the culture began to be dissipated and its vigor and vitality tended progressively to diminish.

CHAPTER VI

THE CITY AND THE CHURCHES:
The Resourcefulness of the Churches in Meeting a New Challenge

What shall we do with our great cities? What will our great cities do with us? These are the two problems which confront every thoughtful American. For the question involved in these two questions does not concern the city alone. The whole country is affected, if indeed its character and history are not determined, by the condition of its great cities. LYMAN ABBOTT

We must save the city if we would save the nation. JOSIAH STRONG.

If religion fails in America, it will fail most colossally in the cities. H. K. ROWE[1]

On March 4, 1829, Andrew Jackson rode into Washington to take the oath of office as President of the United States. A horny-handed son of the soil, Jackson was the symbol of a triumphant agrarian democracy. The settlement of the West had shifted the balance of power in national life, and the day of the back-country farmer had arrived. But even as the oath of office was being administered, signs were multiplying that the triumph of agrarian democracy was not to be of long duration. New economic forces were in the saddle, and the lure of the city was beginning to cast its spell over young men of spirit and ambition. A strong townward drift was setting in. The tariff of 1828—embodying Henry Clay's ideas of economic nationalism—had given powerful impetus to the thriving industrial communities along the Atlantic seaboard which had come into existence during the years from 1807 to 1815 when American buyers had been cut off from British factories. The Erie Canal, pushing its way westward from 1817 to 1825, left in its wake booming commercial and manufacturing centers, Rochester alone having grown 512 per cent during the decade of the twenties. Scarcely had "Clinton's ditch" linked the Great Lakes and the Atlantic, when ground was broken for the Baltimore and Ohio Railway and the ganglia of the iron horse began reaching out to create a new economic system. "With the swift expansion of the national market, textile mills in New England roared louder, blast furnaces in Pennsylvania flamed higher," and "all over the Middle West, crossroads hamlets grew into trading towns, villages spread out into cities, cities became railway and industrial centers."[2]

By the time of Jackson's inauguration, New York City had already become a metropolis of sufficient magnitude and influence for Finney to regard it as the citadel which at all costs must be captured for Christ, and New York was doing no more than set the pace for the growth of Boston, Philadelphia, and Baltimore. The most astonishing urban growth, however, was in the Old Northwest. Almost overnight Cleveland, Columbus, Cincinnati, Detroit, Indianapolis, and St. Louis became scenes of significant commercial and manufacturing enterprise. But Chicago was the lustiest child of them all, a fabulous infant multiplying its population sevenfold during the forties and fourfold during the fifties. Established in the open prairie in 1833, by 1860 Chicago had become the principal rail center of Middle America and was well on its way to becoming the "hog butcher of the world." Thus, during the years which lay between the inauguration of Jackson and the election of Abraham Lincoln, the center of gravity in American life was shifting from the rural countryside to the new urban communities. "When Lincoln was inaugurated, the capital invested in industries, railways, commerce, and city property exceeded in dollars and cents the value of all the farms and plantations between the Atlantic and the Pacific."[3]

On the industrial growth of the pre-Civil War period, the war itself had "the effect of a hothouse." Military needs, currency inflation, and repeated increases in the protective tariff combined to produce a booming industrial economy. But even the wartime advances paled in comparison with what followed. "Backed by a friendly federal government, businessmen bestirred themselves to meet the heavy demands levied by the rapidly peopling West and by the necessities of the prostrate South, while they vigorously developed new markets in the North. Many circumstances contributed to the success of their efforts: brilliant industrial leadership, inventive genius, abundant capital (largely from abroad), the country's unmatched physical resources, the wide extension of methods of mass production, and a plentiful supply of cheap labor."[4] In 1800 there had been only six cities in the United States with more than eight thousand inhabitants. By 1860 this number had risen to 141, and by 1890 to 143. Cities grew so fast that it was difficult to keep track of them. During the three decades from 1860 to 1890, the population of New York, Philadelphia, and Baltimore more than doubled, Kansas City and Detroit grew fourfold, San Francisco and Memphis fivefold, Cleveland sixfold, Chicago tenfold, Los Angeles twentyfold, and Minneapolis and Omaha fiftyfold or more. "There is a city of thirty-five thousand added to Chicago, and one of fifty thousand added to New York, every year," reported Josiah Strong in 1887. And Samuel Loomis confessed in the same year that the cities farther west, "springing up and growing great and splendid as it were in a night, are the marvel of the world. We behold with wonder such places as Minneapolis, St. Paul, and Kansas City, towns that had not been heard of twenty years ago, selling their corner lots at Broadway prices."[5] In the country as a whole, the proportion of townspeople rose from a sixth of the population in 1860 to more than a third in 1890. Nor did the tempo diminish thereafter. By 1950 one-fourth of the total population lived in twelve urban areas of a million or more persons, whereas the farm population had dwindled to less than one-sixth of the total.

I

"Evangelizing a procession" is a phrase which has been aptly used to describe the major task of the American churches from the very beginning of their existence. Unlike the situation in Europe where stable societies developed at not too infrequent intervals and where people "stayed put" for extended periods of time, the American people have never settled down and the churches have always had to deal with the problems implicit in a constantly moving population. Consequently, the churches have never been able to relax their evangelistic and church extension activities in order to consolidate gains already won. During the colonial period, there was a continuous migration of settlers into newly opened territories beyond the tidewater regions, and in the half century following the adoption of the Constitution this migration became a moving sea of humanity flooding over all of Middle America. Throughout this whole area, from the valley of the Hudson and the slopes of the Alleghenies to the great plains beyond the Mississippi, the American churches displayed a remarkable capacity to match the pace of settlement with a religious ministry, planting new churches and bringing the emerging agrarian society under the influence of Christian truth.

No sooner had the churches demonstrated their ability to establish the Christian faith as a vital force in the new communities of the westward marching frontier, than the movement of population to the cities began. Now the churches were confronted not only by a continuing westward march but also by a large-scale redistribution of population within the older regions. Extensive sections of New England had a smaller population in 1850 than at the beginning of the century, yet the total population of the region was increasing. People were not only going west, they were moving from the hilltop villages and the back-country farms to the new mill towns of the valleys. Nor was New England unique in this respect. A large part of central and western New York had reached its peak of settlement by 1835 or shortly thereafter, and in these sections of the state a continuing decline of population set in as the communities along the Erie Canal began to draw upon the hinterland for hands in the mills and clerks in the stores. A similar pattern was repeated elsewhere, following the initial wave of settlement. No less dramatic than the seemingly endless procession moving west, the influx of people into the cities presented the churches with an equally great responsibility and an equally compelling challenge.

The primary problem posed for the churches by the migration to the cities was a missionary one. They were now faced with the necessity of duplicating among the new urban populations the achievements of the churches among those who had created the farm and village civilization behind the receding frontier. At the outset, a major portion of the new urban inhabitants came from the farms and villages where the churches had been most effective in shaping the life of the community, but their move to the city created the problem which always arises when people are pulled up by their roots and transplanted in a completely different environment. The initial effect of such a move, as Charles Loring Brace of the New York Children's Aid Society pointed out in 1872, was to weaken the religious ties. The subtle coercion of habit and emotional association as well as of community pressure which served to bind the individual to the church in the old home was removed, with the result, reported Brace, that the transplanted Christian often became "indifferent." And, he continued, the "moral ties are lessened with the religious."[6] As on the frontier, so in the cities, new churches had to be established to minister to the swelling population, and strenuous efforts had to be made to reclaim the folk from the villages and farms who tended to backslide in the urban environment.

The churches did not long delay initiating a powerful counteroffensive to meet the problems arising from the new migration to the cities. The Finney revivals, after his opening campaign, were primarily directed to this end, as were those of Dwight L. Moody later in the century. City mission societies began to be organized as early as 1816 in the major cities of the Atlantic seaboard. Predominantly lay organizations, voluntary and interdenominational in character, these pioneer societies conformed to the traditional American pattern of creating extrachurch agencies to meet particular needs. At first the societies devoted themselves almost exclusively to the distribution of tracts, Bibles, and the evangelization of the poor, but following the Civil War they began to be replaced by voluntary denominational societies and "church extension" rather than direct evangelistic work became their major concern. Thus the activity of the societies was confined increasingly to the establishment of mission churches, and work with individuals was left to the institutions fostered by the societies and to other specialized agencies.[7]

Important as were the city mission societies, the great instrument of the urban counteroffensive of the churches was the Young Men's Christian Association. The first Y.M.C.A. had been organized by a "dozen youthful salesmen in a London dry goods store in 1844" to improve "the spiritual condition of young men engaged in the drapery and other trades by the introduction of religious services among them." Deeply influenced by the writings of Charles G. Finney, these young men sought to create a society, as one of them recorded in his diary, by which they might "spread the Redeemer's Kingdom amongst those by whom they are surrounded." The head of the firm was converted and he supported the organization with "his presence and his purse." Quarters were rented in a nearby coffeehouse, and the London Association was launched on its career of seeking to reach young men as soon as they arrived in the city and to hold or win them to the Christian faith. This, to be sure, was not the first organization of this type to be formed, but it was the most successful and it was the one destined to endure.[8]

In the United States there had been a similar interest in the young men who were coming to the cities. During the eighteen thirties, "young men's societies for religious improvement" had sprung up in many of the rapidly growing urban centers, but most of them failed either to prosper or to endure, lacking an effective and attractive pattern of organization for enlisting the interest of young men in religious activity. This latter need was supplied in 1851 when visitors to the Great Industrial Exhibition held at the Crystal Palace in London brought back information on the "aims, methods, and excellences" of the London Y.M.C.A. In December, the Boston Y.M.C.A. came into being, expressing its hope to become

a social organization of those in whom the love of Christ has produced love to men; who shall meet the young stranger as he enters our city, take him by the hand, direct him to a boarding house where he may find a quiet home pervaded with Christian influences, introduce him to the Church and Sabbath School, bring him to the Rooms of the Association, and in every way throw around him good influences, so that he may feel that he is not a stranger, but that noble and Christian spirits care for his soul.

"The Rooms of the Association" were equipped with suitable reading matter, including newspapers from the towns and villages of rural New England. Prayer meetings, Bible classes, an employment bureau, and a lodging house register were integral parts of the program. Active membership was restricted to members in good standing of the orthodox evangelical denominations, but an associate membership was provided for young men of good moral character as a means of introducing them to Christian influence. The success of the Boston organization was immediate and served as a powerful stimulus elsewhere. By 1860, as a result of active promotional effort, no less than 205 local Associations had been formed throughout the country.[9]

While the Y.M.C.A. was explicitly designed as "a mission of the evangelical churches to young men," the religious fervor of the youthful members led them to extend their Christian witness to the community at large. They volunteered to care for the sick in the hotels and lodging houses; they collected funds and dispensed aid to the destitute; they gave dinners to the inmates of almshouses; and they sponsored "ragged schools" for indigent boys and girls. But the larger share of their energy was channeled into evangelistic activity. Mission Sunday Schools were established; tracts and Bibles were distributed; rescue mission work was carried on in blighted areas; and young men were sent out "to preach on street corners, at the wharves, in neighborhood fire-houses—wherever they could gather an audience." During the summer months many Associations held services in tents pitched in conspicuous places, while during the winter they sponsored "interdenominational revivals aimed at interesting men who would attend a meeting in a public hall but could not be induced to enter a church." The great "businessmen's" or "prayer meeting" revival of 1857-58 grew out of the noonday prayer meetings of the New York Y.M.C.A., and was carried forward by the other Associations throughout the country. Through his connection with the Chicago Y.M.C.A., Dwight L. Moody was introduced to organized evangelistic work and was induced to forsake his business activities and devote himself wholly to revivalism, quickly becoming the single most influential person in the entire Y.M.C.A. movement. Throughout the remainder of the century, the Y.M.C.A., as the most immediately available interdenominational agency at the local level, provided the major leadership in initiating and promoting community-wide revival campaigns. In essence, the Y.M.C.A.'s were the "flying artillery of Zion," regarded as an "integral part" of the program of the churches, reflecting the nonsectarian spirit so characteristic of nineteenth-century Protestantism, and charged with the specific responsibility for preaching the gospel to the great unchurched masses of the urban centers. These Associations, declared a speaker in 1859, constitute a "lightarmed, chosen, consecrated, fleet of foot, and trusty band sent out to reconnoiter and open the way for salvation to follow."[10]

The course of the Association movement was temporarily deflected by the Civil War. Membership was greatly depleted as the young men of the nation were drawn into the ranks of the opposing armies. Rapidly shifting gears, delegates from local Y.M.C.A.'s met in New York and established the United States Christian Commission—a committee of twelve members —which was charged with the responsibility of extending the work of the Y.M.C.A. to the young men in uniform. "Agents" or "delegates" were sent out by the local Associations for a tour of duty in the camps or on the battlefields. Volunteering for a limited period of service without compensation, the delegates held "meetings for prayer, singing, and exhortation"; distributed tracts, Testaments, and hymnbooks; cared for the sick and the wounded; wrote letters home for those unable to write for themselves; operated diet kitchens to supplement the army's hospital equipment and supplies; and in other ways sought to mitigate the horrors and discomforts of war.[11]

Scarcely had the smoke cleared from the battlefields when the churches once again directed their attention to the problems of the city. In the autumn of 1865 the United States Christian Commission was reconstituted as the American Christian Commission, an organization designed to marshal the Christian forces of the nation for peacetime activity in meeting urban religious needs. The Commission sought to develop a systematic plan for urban missionary endeavor based on a thorough study of religious conditions in the major population centers. The difficulties encountered by the Protestant churches in the cities of the land, the *Circular of Inquiry* asserted, were due to "want of knowledge of their moral condition; lack of organization of the wealth, piety and labor which exist there; need of experimental knowledge of the best agencies and how to perfect organizations already formed; and want of trained, tried, permanent laborers in the various spheres of city labor." The first act of the Commission, therefore, was the appointment of two secretaries "to collect information concerning mission work in cities." Their report the following year, giving the results of a personal investigation in thirty-four cities, was the first significant survey and analysis of Protestant work—both evangelistic and philanthropic—in urban America. "No mission field," the report concluded, "is more necessitous, none more easily accessible, none which appeals to so many interests of the Christian patriot and philanthropist as this in our very midst."[12]

During the sixties and seventies, the conventions of the American Christian Commission popularized its central concern and acquainted the rank and file of the churches with the critical nature of the problem. "These assemblies discussed the necessity for thorough district visitations of the poor, the use of churches for humanitarian purposes, the formation of Christian associations, lay preaching, open-air preaching, the rescue of social outcasts, and the promotion of Christian union." One of the most valuable contributions of the Commission was made by its department of foreign correspondence, which assembled literature detailing the "experience developed in European societies and institutions," most notably in Great Britain and Germany. This information was made available through the monthly publication of the Commission, *The*

Church at Work, and thus provided helpful suggestions for coping with problems which were now beginning to become acutely disturbing to many thoughtful Christians.[13]

As a result of the agitation carried on by the American Christian Commission new agencies and activities sprang up to supplement the work of the Y.M.C.A. The Young Women's Christian Association made its appearance in 1866, winning the eloquent and influential support of Dwight L. Moody. Typical was Moody's action at the Pittsburgh Convention of the Commission in 1867. In a speech before the convention he had explained the dire need for concerted action among young women as well as young men, and he immediately proceeded to translate his words into deeds by organizing the women of the city into an Association. Under Moody's influence, the Pittsburgh Association was designed to operate a wide range of mission enterprises and thus a pattern was established that was to be reproduced in other Associations. The postwar years also witnessed a resurgence of city mission societies devoted largely to "church extension," and of interdenominational "rescue missions" which like the Y.M.C.A. often provided lodging, recreational facilities, and employment services. Addressing their efforts primarily to the social outcasts, the "rescue missions" sought first to supply immediate material needs. "This we believe to be the Biblical way of reaching the heart," it was asserted. "Till the cravings of hunger are satisfied, we cannot develop the moral nature." Less successful were the efforts of the Commission to persuade the denominations to establish orders of deaconesses or sisterhoods for professional work in the church, although numerous schools to prepare women for Christian service did come into existence and thus laid the groundwork for the strong deaconess movement which developed after 1885. The concern of the Commission that laymen be trained for efficient Christian service began to be met through laymen's institutes conducted by the Y.M.C.A. and by independently organized lay colleges and Bible schools. Stephen H. Tyng, however, ran counter to the general intention when he described his Home of the Evangelists as providing "a short cut to the ministry." An instrument for the training of volunteer lay leadership, which arose independently of the Commission but which enjoyed its hearty support after the Commission had been organized, was the Young People's Society of Christian Endeavor, founded by Francis E. Clark in 1861. It sought to equip and prepare young people for effective Christian work in and through their churches by providing them with a society of their own in which they could develop their talents and abilities and at the same time deepen their devotion and increase their understanding of the Christian faith. Conspicuously missionary in interest and displaying the full enthusiasm of youth, the Christian Endeavor societies gave the older leaders real grounds for optimism. "Fair as the moon, clear as the sun, terrible as an army with banners," declared Graham Taylor, "are the 600,000 youth who are looking forth from the Christian Endeavor societies of our churches, as an enlisted, sworn, disciplined force ready for active service on the field."[14]

The interest of the American Christian Commission in trained lay workers was aroused by the need for adequately equipped personnel to implement the program of what was called Home Evangelization or House-to-House Visitation. Too many of the churches, Moody observed at the 1868 convention, had become victims of a fashionable Christianity which was content to depend upon "opera-singing in the churches" to entice people to their services. Actually, the masses of people were not interested in "opera-singing" and consequently they were being neglected. "Christian people," another speaker assured the convention, "were beginning to realize the startling fact that the Gospel was not presented to every creature." Class lines, it was insisted, must be obliterated and the churches must reach out to people where they live. This, of course, required house-to-house visitation and necessitated lay effort. The New York state convention in the same year suggested to pastors, "especially those in our more densely populated communities, that they seek out and employ all such talent in their congregations as they shall believe to possess qualifications for this important and pressing work."[15]

The Congregationalists, as a denomination, had been the first to make a serious effort to carry out a program of home evangelization. The National Council in 1865 had recommended that every local church adopt the program, and in the same year the Massachusetts Congregationalists created a Committee on Home Evangelization and appointed a full-time secretary to promote the effort. Other state associations and churches of other denominations followed the Massachusetts example with varying degrees of success.[16] But it was not until the American branch of the Evangelical Alliance, which had been organized in 1867 to represent the common interests of the evangelical churches, made community-wide house-to-house visitation the central feature of its activity that the program was applied on any large scale.

Under the vigorous leadership of Josiah Strong, the Evangelical Alliance had addressed itself to the problem of winning the nonchurchgoing masses of the cities. It was Strong's conviction that the churches had generally lost the personal touch and hence had been largely shorn of their power. A "personal, living, love-convincing touch" between the churchgoer and the nonchurchgoer, he asserted, was conspicuously lacking.

Christian men, instead of going personally to those that know not God, think to discharge their obligations by making a check for this and that *institution*, which stand as their representatives in Christian work. Christian influence has now become largely *institutional* instead of personal, and, therefore, largely mechanical instead of vital. The common response to the divine command is not, "Here am I, send me," but "Here is my check, Lord, send some one else,"

—and many forget to offer the check as a substitute. The average Christian today is hiring his Christian work done by proxy—by societies, institutions, the minister, the city missionary. . . .

Christians must go to the multitude, must search them out in the workshop and the home . . . must go not once as a census-taker, but repeatedly, to establish friendly relations, to acquire a personal influence, to study the temporal and spiritual needs of the family and do all possible good.

To remedy this situation, Strong proposed that all the churches of a particular city unite and pool their lay personnel to make possible a monthly visitation of each family within the city. "Observe," he commented, "how this house-to-house visitation in the name and spirit of Christ will . . . do much to neutralize the evil effects of the constant moving. . . . The family is followed with Christian influence and found by another visitor, who helps to reunite church ties." By 1889 the Alliance program—"founded on two propositions: first, that there is necessity for the co-operation of Christian forces; and second, that there is a necessity for securing a systematic and continuous watchcare over every part of every community"—had been put into operation in some forty cities.[17]

II

Those from the hinterland accounted for only a part of the population flowing into the cities. The other part came from abroad. A small current at first, the tide of immigration from Europe became a torrent and then a flood as the century advanced. During the forties and fifties, the incoming tide was made up mostly of Irish, Germans, and Scandinavians; but after the Civil War, Hungarians, Bohemians, Poles, and Italians began to appear at the ports of entry, and by the turn of the century when immigration swelled to almost a million persons annually, the eastern and south Europeans accounted for by far the larger portion of the new arrivals. By 1880, 80 per cent of the population of New York City was foreign born or children of foreign-born parents; and 87 per cent of the people of Chicago, 78 per cent of St. Louis, and 60 per cent of Cincinnati had their immediate antecedents abroad. The concentration of the foreign born was even greater in some of the smaller cities, such as Passaic and Paterson, New Jersey, or Lawrence and Fall River, Massachusetts.

These new Americans constituted a much more difficult missionary problem for the churches than did the older American stock. The older Americans as they came into the cities brought with them memories of earlier religious emotions and loyalties which needed only to be rekindled. The immigrants from abroad, however, came for the most part from a quite different religious tradition, and they were isolated from the existing churches as well as from the community at large by language and cultural barriers. But if the evangelization of the foreign born was more difficult, it soon came to be regarded as a much more urgent task. As the tide of immigration increased, the nature of its impact upon American life became more evident. As Father Francis X. Talbot, former editor of the Jesuit weekly *America,* has pointed out, a "distinctly Protestant culture" had been created in the United States, which gave "complexion to the country, entered our legislation, sociology and economics," was "the basis of our commerce and industry, and, in fact, . . . formed a great part of the American people."[18] To many thoughtful people during the latter decades of the nineteenth century, this whole social order, embodying the ideals and moralities of evangelical Protestantism, seemed in danger of being completely subverted by the new arrivals. Charles A. Beard, in describing the consequences for American society of the incoming tide of cheap labor recruited abroad by the agents of American industry, commented: "Not since the patricians and capitalists of Rome scoured the known world for slaves— Celts, Iberians, Angles, Gauls, Saxons, Greeks, Jews, Egyptians, and Assyrians—to serve them, and then disappeared themselves under a deluge of strange colors, had the world witnessed such a deliberate overturn of a social order by masters of ceremonies" as occurred in some of the American cities.[19]

The most apparent, if perhaps the most superficial, threat to the accustomed pattern of life was the challenge to two of the most distinctive moralities fostered by the American churches —Sabbath observance and temperance. Strangers to the deeply-rooted Puritan tradition of Sabbath observance, the new arrivals spread consternation by their desecration of the Lord's Day. Equally alarming to members of Protestant churches who had long since been enlisted in the temperance cause was the attitude of the immigrant groups toward the "liquor question." In 1873 the editor of a brewer's journal hailed the growing influence foreign-born citizens were beginning to exert. "The future," he wrote, "is ours! The enormous influx of immigration will in a few years overreach the puritanical element in every state in the Union."[20]

Of even greater concern to the churches was what seemed to be a serious threat to the most deeply cherished principles and institutions of American democracy. Unversed in the practice of democracy, without experience in urban living, handicapped by language barriers, and increasingly illiterate as the century advanced, the poverty-stricken peasants of Europe who crowded the cities became the prey of the political machine. The political boss was a curious mixture of good and evil—in part the exploiter of the poor and in part their protector and benefactor, serving as a buffer between the rich and the socially disinherited, and providing "an avenue by which the humblest could get his grievances before the municipal government." But the total effect of the flagrant corruption to which the party managers resorted was seriously to demoralize and undermine the entire democratic process. Perhaps, as has been suggested, this was the price which had to be paid to avoid "riots and revolutions," but it was a price which aroused the apprehensions of many churchmen.[21]

Disturbing as were the opportunistic levies of the city bosses on the body politic, an even more disturbing concern arose on quite another level. The tension over Sabbath observance and temperance was but a symptom of a more deeply running conflict. Throughout its history, America had been Protestant—culturally, politically, and religiously. The newer immigration was predominantly Roman Catholic. And, as Elie Halévy was to observe, "Catholicism and Protestantism represent opposite and mutually exclusive views of church government and Christian dogma, indeed of religion and life as a whole."[22] Apart from the folk moralities, the aspect of Roman Catholicism which aroused the most deeply-seated apprehension was its supposed antidemocratic political philosophy.

Both "logically and theologically" as well as "historically and pragmatically," Roman Catholicism seemed to most nineteenth-century Americans to constitute a definite threat to what had become regarded as sacred constitutional principles. Historically and pragmatically, the evidence seemed clear enough. Memories of past ecclesiastical tyranny, of massacres and burnings, had not grown dim, and "the belief that Catholicism" was still "hostile to what were deemed fundamental American principles" seemed plausible enough to freedom-loving people "because the Vatican was in active alliance with every reactionary and antidemocratic force in Europe during the forty years after Napoleon." Logically and theologically, the evidence appeared to be equally clear. As Henry Steele Commager has pointed out, from a logical point of view Roman Catholicism seemed to be "in conflict with many principles of the American political system . . . . Thus the *Papal Syllabus of Errors* of 1864 pronounced it an error to assert that 'it is no longer expedient that the Catholic religion shall be held as the only religion of the State, to the exclusion of all other modes of worship' or 'that the church ought to be separated from the state and the state from the church.' " Equally dismaying was the papal encyclical of November 1, 1885, in which Leo XIII condemned as contrary to Christian and natural law the principle that

as all men are alike by race and nature, so in like manner all are equal in the control of their life; that each one is so far his own master as to be in no sense under the rule of any other individual; that each is free to think on every subject just as he may choose.

"In a society grounded upon such maxims," the encyclical continued, "all government is nothing more or less than the will of the people," and from this flows the erroneous opinion that "princes are nothing more than delegates chosen to carry out the will of the people." It also logically follows from the initial premise "that the most unrestrained opinions may be openly expressed as to the practice or omission of divine worship, and that everyone has unbounded license to think whatever he chooses and to publish abroad whatever he thinks." Thus, the demand for religious liberty, Leo declared, "is the same thing as atheism," while the assertion of the right of the freedom of the press is a dangerous and pernicious doctrine. "The liberty of thinking, and of publishing, whatsoever each one likes, without any hindrance is not in itself an advantage over which society can wisely rejoice. On the contrary it is the fountain-head and origin of many evils." In a closing exhortation, the faithful were urged "to make use of popular institutions" in order to rectify the lamentable situation where these erroneous opinions held sway and "to bring back all civil society to the pattern and form" advocated by the Holy See.[23]

To the extent to which the faithful in America were ready to heed papal admonitions, the fears of many Americans concerning Roman Catholicism as an antidemocratic force in the United States would seem to have been justified. Actually, however, the political beliefs of very few American Catholics were determined by the official definitions of the Vatican. Liberal democracy was still exerting its charm over the minds and hearts of men, not least among those to whom America had beckoned as a land of hope and promise. Far more serious was the attrition in terms of religious allegiance which occurred as a consequence of the removal of these new Americans from their homeland to a completely different environment. Like their urban neighbors who had come from the rural areas, by far the larger part of the immigrants were both unchurched and religiously indifferent. This spiritual need rather than any immediate threat to American political institutions was the great and pressing problem with which the churches were primarily concerned.

The basic requirement in an approach to the immigrant groups was a ministry in their own language, and this the churches sought to provide as soon as any particular nationality group began to arrive in any significant numbers. Thus the Baptists, who were ultimately to carry on a ministry to twenty-one different nationality groups in as many different languages, began work among the Germans in 1846, the Scandinavians in 1848, the French Canadians in 1853, the Poles and Portuguese in 1888, and the Italians in 1894. Congregationalists, Presbyterians, and Methodists developed a ministry among these same foreign-language elements in the population, and among the Bohemians, Hungarians, Slovaks, Rumanians, and other less conspicuous groups as well. The recruiting of a "native ministry" was haphazard at first, but as an increasing number of converts were secured training institutes were organized, and within a surprisingly short time foreign-language departments were founded in the theological seminaries. Thus, the Baptists established a German department at Rochester in 1858, Swedish, Danish, and Norwegian departments at the Morgan Park seminary in Chicago in 1871, a French department at Newton in 1889, and an Italian department at Colgate in 1907. The Congregationalists provided courses and professors for the Germans and Scandinavians at their Chicago seminary, and for the Slavic groups at Oberlin. The Presbyterians varied the pattern somewhat by establishing two separate theological seminaries for the training of a German-speaking ministry, a procedure followed by the Congregationalists in the founding of their French Protestant College at Lowell, Massachusetts. "So ample were these facilities," writes Abell in his study of urban Protestantism, "that by 1900 a body of clergymen ready to meet all calls for independent or assistant pastorates had come into existence." Five years earlier the Congregational Home Missionary Society had reported that the once "greatest desideratum—trained Congregational pastors—to supply these churches of foreign tongues, is now supplied in a degree almost beyond our power to use, through the Oberlin and Chicago Theological Seminaries, whose well-equipped graduates stand ready to enlarge the field of our missionary service wherever the means are at the command of this society to employ them."[24]

Much of the missionary activity among the immigrants was carried on by local churches through home visitation and provision for special Sunday School classes and worship services. In other instances, mission centers were established which developed into foreign-language churches. In time these tended to become bilingual and ultimately many of them were assimilated into the existing denominational structure of American Protestantism as English-speaking congregations. A still greater number of these churches, within two or three generations, were left to dwindle and die as their members completed the process of adjustment to American life and found a place for themselves in the older churches. This was less true among the German and Swedish churches of the various denominations, but until they frankly became English-speaking congregations they were largely dependent upon new immigration for their continued existence.

The greatest successes of this foreign-language missionary

endeavor were won among the Germans, Italians, and Scandinavians. While it is true, as Kenneth Scott Latourette has affirmed, that "no large movements of Roman Catholics to Protestantism occurred," his concluding comment that "the size of most Protestant congregations gathered from Roman Catholic immigrants was small, the growth of such congregations was unimpressive, and many of the converts who were made were unstable in their faith" would seem to be unduly pessimistic.[25] If not spectacular, the results of the work among immigrants from nominally Roman Catholic lands were by no means meager. Accurate statistics, of course, are not to be had, but there are indications which give ample evidence that results were not completely negligible. The prominence of such Protestants as LaGuardia, Pecora, and Poletti in the political life of New York State is one such indication, and an examination of the lists of students in a typical Protestant theological seminary during recent years reveals such names as Morreale, Fattaruso, Scipione, Haddad, Apra, Ramirez, Lewno, Rybnicek and many more. Nor are the O'Briens and the O'Haras absent. A study of local congregations would reveal many members with similar antecedents. Actually, as soon as the language barriers were removed, assimilation into the general body of Protestantism began to take place.

On the other hand, much of the activity of the older Protestant denominations among the immigrants was "not for the purpose of gaining converts" but arose from "the desire to be helpful to strangers, and to assist them in making a successful adjustment to their new surroundings."[26] Out of this concern grew extensive programs of "Christian Americanization" or "Christian Friendliness." The women of the churches were enlisted to go into the homes of the immigrants to teach them English, to help them prepare for naturalization examinations, to show them how to cook the food available in American stores, and especially to relieve the loneliness so many of them experienced in a strange land. Such service was not designed to secure proselytes, being simply one phase of the expanding humanitarian activity of the churches.

III

The task of the churches in the growing metropolitan areas, in terms both of ministering to delinquent Protestants and of reaching the newer arrivals from abroad, was complicated by the fact that people did not stay put once they had come to the city. Changing labor demands and better economic opportunities encouraged migration from city to city, and within a particular urban center there was a constant movement of population from the center to the periphery. Factories, warehouses, and commercial establishments encroached upon residential areas, and as neighborhoods grew older and housing deteriorated the more economically secure moved to newer residential sections on the outskirts, making room in their former communities for those who had more recently arrived in the city. In such a situation, the churches faced a perplexing problem. One alternative was for a church to follow its congregation, moving each time the neighborhood changed. Thus the First Presbyterian and the First Baptist churches of Chicago moved four or five times during the first century of their existence. Another alternative was for a church to stay where it was and attempt to draw its members from a distance. Still another alternative was to adapt the ministry of the church to a new constituency. The final alternative was unimaginatively to eke out a dwindling existence which was little more than a lingering death. Many of the churches did go out of existence. A still larger number perhaps elected to follow their congregations. "When the Civil War ended nearly a half-hundred important congregations had already deserted lower New York, and soon after Bostonians were leaving historic meeting houses for sumptuous edifices in Back Bay." This solution, of course, left unsolved the critical problem of providing a ministry in the areas that had been deserted. On the other hand, it did reduce the by no means inconsiderable task of establishing and equipping churches in the outlying areas into which great numbers of people were moving. By 1880, however, the development of the "institutional" church movement marked the beginning of "an heroic effort on the part of courageous Christians" to adapt the ministry of the church to changing communities and thus "to stem the tide of church removals." Even before the eighties, Episcopalians and Congregationalists had been experimenting with educational, recreational, and social service activities as a means of avoiding the death or removal of their inner city churches, but it was only in this latter decade that the new trend became a definitely self-conscious movement.[27]

An institutional church was defined by Edward Judson as

an organized body of Christian believers, who, finding themselves in a hard and uncongenial social environment, supplement the ordinary methods of the gospel—such as preaching, prayer meetings, Sunday School, and pastoral visitation—*by a system of organized kindness*, a congeries of institutions, which, by touching people on physical, social, and intellectual sides, will conciliate them and draw them within reach of the gospel.

Thus the distinguishing mark of an institutional church was its effort to adapt its program to the needs of the neighborhood in which it was located. If "it finds that the people living around it have in their homes no opportunity to take a bath, it . . . furnishes bathing facilities." If they "have little or no healthful social life, it . . . opens attractive social rooms and organizes clubs." If, "they are ignorant of household economy," the church establishes cooking schools and sewing classes. If they have access to few books and periodicals, "in the church they find a free reading room and library." If they lack education, "the church opens evening schools and lecture courses." The objective was to keep the church building occupied at all hours every day, and never to permit it to be "dark and deserted, like many of our costly sacred edifices that are in use on Sunday and perhaps one or two week nights, and the rest of the time are tenanted by mice, silence, and gloom."[28]

Among the outstanding institutional churches, Saint Bartholomew's Protestant Episcopal Church in New York City may be regarded as typical. Its program was so large and varied that a yearbook of three hundred and fifty pages was required to describe the activities, but probably the program was little more extensive than that of several of the others—Saint George's and Judson Memorial in New York, the Jersey City Tabernacle across the river, and the Baptist Temple and Bethany Presbyterian in Philadelphia. At Saint Bartholomew's over eight thousand meetings of various types were held each year, the average number of gatherings on Sundays being nineteen and on weekdays twenty-four. Sunday services were conducted in German, Swedish, Armenian, Turkish, and Chinese as well as in English. Evangelistic services were held each night in the year and drew an aggregate attendance as large as one hundred and twenty thousand annually and resulted in some five thousand conversions in a decade and a half. There were clubs for men, boys, girls, mothers, and children. Membership in the Girls' Evening Club entitled one to

the use of the club-rooms and library; access to the large hall every evening after nine o'clock, to the physical culture classes, lectures, talks, entertainments, discussion class, glee club, literature class, English composition class, the Helping Hand Society, Penny Provident and Mutual Benefit Funds; the privilege of joining one class a week in either dressmaking, millinery, embroidery, drawn-work, system sewing, or cooking, and also by paying a small fee, the privilege of entering a class in stenography, typewriting, French, or book-keeping.

There was also a girls' club boarding house and a working girls' summer home. Excellent medical clinics treated twenty thousand patients each year. An employment bureau found jobs for two to three thousand persons annually. A loan association, providing small sums of money at low rates of interest, had total loans and receipts of almost a million and a half dollars over an eight-year period. A tailor shop provided work for the temporarily unemployed.[29]

The growth of the institutional churches was little less than phenomenal. By 1900 the Baptist Temple in Philadelphia, whose evening classes were to father a university which included theological, medical, and law schools as well as undergraduate instruction, had become the largest congregation in America. Saint George's, which had been left stranded with only six families, within twenty years became the largest Protestant Episcopal Church in the nation with more than five thousand members, one third of whom were German born. The Congregationalists discovered that the average institutional church of that denomination had "precisely six times as many additions on confession of faith as the average non-institutional church," while the two institutional churches among the twenty-three Baptist churches of Cincinnati and vicinity received 64 per cent of all the additions by baptism to the churches of the association. Josiah Strong remarked, however, that such a comparison between the two types of churches was hardly fair to the institutional churches, "because they are generally located in the hardest fields, where churches working on the old lines have utterly failed, many having died and many having run away to save their lives."[30]

By 1894 the time seemed ripe to the leaders of the movement for organized advance. "A number of churches, having experimented for several years with some of the new methods, have reached results which encourage us to believe that the burning question, 'How to reach the masses,' is practically solved," they declared. "What we now need is co-operation and aggressive action on the part of these churches." The result was the organization of the Open or Institutional Church League, dedicated to advancing the cause of "open church doors every day and all the day," and of "a ministry to all the community through educational, reformatory, and philanthropic channels, to the end that men may be won to Christ and his service." The league was a potent factor in multiplying institutional churches and by the turn of the century a leader of the movement was able to list one hundred and seventy-three, acknowledging that some may have escaped his attention. In addition scores of other churches in industrial communities had adopted parts of the institutional program.[31]

Viewed from another angle, the institutional church was not simply an instrument of evangelism, it was one phase of the vast humanitarian activity in which the churches were engaged. The consciences of ministers and laity alike had been awakened by the extremes of urban poverty and squalor, and all city missionary activity was, in effect, institutional. The scores of missions which had resulted from the agitation of the American Christian Commission and which were multipled through the stimulus provided by the Convention of Christian Workers, "though basically rescue institutions, developed in many instances elaborate educational and philanthropic features." The same was true of the work of the Salvation Army, which served as a recruiting agent of the churches among the most neglected elements of the population during the last decade of the century. The humanitarian concern also found expression through another type of institution, which in some instances quite explicitly disavowed any distinctly religious work. These were the "social settlements," planted in slum areas by churches, colleges, seminaries, and independently organized groups of citizens. "Like the institutional church, the settlement went beyond the 'mission' in attempting to root itself permanently in the community," and it was dedicated to providing a complete range of social services. Once again, the idea and the pattern of organization was a British importation, this time from Toynbee Hall, being brought to America by Stanton Coit and Jane Addams. No similar movement of the period enlisted greater popular enthusiasm and by 1905 there were over seventy church-related settlements in the United States.[32]

During the decades following the Civil War, the cities had become the new frontier of the American churches. There, "where the races meet and fuse, where the rivalries and antagonisms of trade and industry provoke the clash of classes and the contradictions of races, where life is lived under the urge of the struggle for prestige and power," it was believed were to be found "the problems of America's future." "We must save the city," declared Josiah Strong, "if we would save the nation." Whatever the final outcome was to be, it is clear that the churches had been displaying amazing resourcefulness in their attempt to reach and to claim the urban inhabitants for Christ.[33]

CHAPTER VII

THE END OF AN ERA: The Last of the Great Revivalists

The passing of the religious revival from the American scene has deprived our churches . . . of what has been for at least a century the one most familiar means of recruiting the ranks of members, both young people and lapsed adults. We have been faced therefore with the necessity of finding some other means of winning and holding members to the churches. WILLARD L. SPERRY[1]

The death of Dwight L. Moody during the last days of 1899 marked the end of an era, for Moody was the last of the great revivalists. For more than a century, revivalism had been the chief means by which the voluntary churches had maintained and perpetuated themselves. Through stated "seasons" of spiritual quickening the unchurched were reached, faith was awakened, church membership replenished, and the influence of Christian truth as a vital force in society made secure. But the noble succession of Edwards and the Wesleys, of Whitefield and the Tennants, of Lyman Beecher and Charles G. Finney had now come to an end. After Moody the decline of revivalism was headlong and precipitate. He had "no direct descendants" and those who sought to be his successors inherited "only the debris" of a once "great estate."[2]

I

A towering figure in the American religious scene during the last half of the nineteenth century, Moody more than any other single individual determined the religious climate of the country in the immediate postwar decades and he stood near the center of almost every agency devised by the churches to implement their task. His great success was as a lay evangelist, but he had an equal talent for putting men to work. God's purpose, he insisted, was not only "to make men good, but to make them good for something," and he made sure that those who came under his influence should have ready at hand appropriate channels for Christian service. "Every man has his own gifts," he said. "Some start things; others can organize and carry them on. My gift is to get things in motion." And get them in motion he did. Operating on the principle that "it is better to get ten men to work than to do ten men's work," he provided the major share of the impetus to a host of organized activities, almost all of them related in one way or another to the Y.M.C.A. of which he was the chief "evangelist, organizer, financier, and statesman." Although he consistently refused to accept professional responsibilities and rarely consented to hold elective office, preferring to put other men to work, Moody was the decisive influence in determining the nature of the "Y" program, the chief fund-raiser for the movement, the principal recruiter of personnel, and the major factor in the winning of significant popular support. In similar fashion the United States Christian Commission, the American Christian Commission, the International Sunday School Association, the Student Christian Movement, the Northfield conferences, the Student Volunteer Movement, the Y.W.C.A.—all enlisted his active participation and benefited from his contagious enthusiasm. But Moody was primarily an evangelist and the one end of all his varied activities was the winning of people to Christ.[3]

Moody had come to Chicago in 1856 as a young shoe salesman of nineteen and almost immediately he launched out on his career of religious work. During the preceding two years which he had spent in Boston, under the gentle leading of his Sunday School teacher, he had experienced conversion and after more than a year's probation had been admitted to church membership. He had also been active in the newly established Boston Y.M.C.A. and when he arrived in Chicago he immediately joined forces with the group of young men from the First Baptist Church who had organized a Chicago Association three years before. With characteristic vigor and enthusiasm, he soon was one of the leaders of the noonday prayer meetings which sparked the "businessmen's revival" of 1856-57 in Chicago, and with the hearty support of John V. Farwell—"another farm boy well on the way toward earning the title of 'merchant prince' "—Moody extended the activities of the Chicago Association in the direction of mission and Sunday School work.[4] His first venture was to rent four pews in the Plymouth Congregational Church which he filled each Sunday with young men whom he invited as his guests. Soon he was recruiting children for the Sunday School, and shortly thereafter he and his Y.M.C.A. friends organized a school of their own in "the Sands," an area of saloons and gambling dens. In the meantime, in typical "Y" fashion, he spent his evenings collecting provisions for needy families or conducting open-air services in the Court House Square.

The decisive turn in Moody's life came in 1860 when, having accumulated sufficient savings to support himself for a time, and the North Market Sunday School having grown to large proportions, he determined to devote his full time to city mission work. The outbreak of the Civil War, however, diverted him temporarily from this course, and he became one of the first Y.M.C.A. "delegates" or "agents" to be sent to the camps and battlefields under the auspices of the United States Christian Commission. At the close of hostilities, Moody returned to Chicago to become "librarian and agent" and for a time president of the Chicago Y.M.C.A. As a result of his labors the first Y.M.C.A. building in Chicago was erected, and when it burned three months later, he is reputed to have had funds for a new building in hand almost before the last embers of the old one had been extinguished. During these years Moody's skill as an evangelist was growing, and he was beginning to gain national recognition as a result of his addresses at Y.M.C.A., American Christian Commission, and Sunday School conventions. His real stature as a national figure, however, dates from his amazingly successful visit to Great Britain, 1873 to 1875. Not since Wesley, the newspapers reported, had the British Isles witnessed such a revival. In London alone 2,530,000 came to hear him. In Scotland he had enlisted university students, among them Henry Drummond and George Adam Smith, as his assistants. The great outpouring of people was an astonishing phenomenon, totally unexpected, gaining momentum only after the most inauspicious beginnings, and it was reported by the press in sensational terms while even the most staid of the clergy acknowledged the beneficent results.[5]

Moody's return to America in August, 1875, was front-page news and the occasion for extended editorial comment. The *New York Herald,* in a five-column article, reported:

> The arrival here on Saturday of Messrs. Moody and Sankey, the great evangelists, who like the apostles of old have turned the world upside down, has created no little stir in the community. . . . When they landed on British soil they were unknown, unhonored, and unsung. But now every movement they make is a matter of interest to two continents, every word they utter, almost, will be read in the ends of the earth.

"They have achieved a popular success abroad," an editorial of the preceding day commented. Now the American people are waiting "to see what these famous apostles will do" at home.[6]

What Moody was to do, now that he was back home, did not long remain undisclosed. The crucial position of the mushrooming cities in American life had been repeatedly emphasized at the conventions of the American Christian Commission, and Moody was now determined to do his best to win them to

Christ. "Water runs down hill," he observed, "and the highest hills are the great cities. If we can stir them, we shall stir the whole country."[7] The campaign began in Brooklyn in October, moved on to Philadelphia, and then he returned to New York for the spring months. The following year Chicago and Boston were his objectives, and the autumn, winter, and spring of 1877-78 he devoted to campaigns in the smaller cities of New England.

Once again Moody met with "unexpected success," great numbers being unable to gain admittance to the meetings, even in Philadelphia and New York where he spoke in halls which could accommodate ten thousand people. Moody himself was mystified by the response. "I am the most overestimated man in this country," he confided to a friend. "By some means the people look upon me as a great man, but I am only a lay preacher and have little learning. . . . Brooklyn every Sunday hears a score of better sermons than I can preach." The newspapers were equally at a loss to account for the thousands who braved mid-winter storms "to attend religious meetings in such a cheerless auditorium as the 'Hippodrome.' " They could find nothing "exciting or sensational" in his sermons; appeals to fear and future torment were notably absent; the audiences were "singularly calm and still" and no "physical excitement" was apparent. The *New York Times,* acknowledging that Moody had "little rhetorical power, less culture, and no learning," found the secret of his appeal in the fact that "his unusual earnestness and simplicity keep all hearers enchained." The *Chicago Times-Herald* described him as "rough, honest, sincere, without frills, consistently simple, and grandly in earnest." "A plain man reaching plain people by his very plainness and cultivated people by the power of his sincerity of belief," Moody, the *Chicago Tribune* noted, "has not the remotest suspicion of cant in his talk."[8]

Whatever the reasons for his success—the careful planning

and organization which preceded and accompanied his meetings, the singing of Sankey, the mood of the time, his own genuine earnestness and sincerity—Moody was not satisfied with
the results. For one thing, in these large-scale, intensive campaigns there was scarcely time to put the converts to work. But
basically Moody distrusted large gatherings and spectacular
numerical gains unless followed up with extensive personal
counsel and guidance. His interest was in the individual. The
full value of his work, he felt, was not being realized because
it was so largely dissociated from the churches. Persons whose
lives had been touched, too often were left without pastoral
oversight and unrelated to any sustaining Christian fellowship.
If lapses were to be prevented and if continued spiritual growth
was to be encouraged, he was convinced that this situation
must be remedied. Consequently, in the fall of 1878 Moody
changed his procedure. From large, intense, centralized, and
relatively brief campaigns in different cities, he now turned
to a more protracted mission which would be closely identified
with the churches. His plan was to spend a year, except for the
summer months, in a single city; and, in addition to services
in a centrally located auditorium, to give a considerable portion of his time to individual churches "where, as men were
turned to Christ," he could immediately place them under the
care of the pastor. This was the course he followed for the
next three years in Baltimore, St. Louis, and San Francisco.[9]

It was during these years also that Moody made his first
appearance on a college campus, an event of great consequence
for the future of the Student Christian Movement. In 1876
Moody had been persuaded by President McCosh, much
against his better judgment, to speak at Princeton, and his sermons had kindled what was reported as the most remarkable
revival of religious interest in the history of the institution.
Two years later similar results were reported at Yale, where
Moody had finally consented to speak after an invitation signed

by five hundred students had convinced him that they really wanted him to come. Despite these two experiences, Moody remained reluctant to accept invitations to speak before college audiences. Deeply conscious of his own intellectual limitations, he was certain that there were other men much better qualified than he to bring Christ's message to the students. Even in later years at the Northfield student conferences, Moody was always reticent about assuming any central place in a program which he explicitly designed to feature what he called "acceptable college speakers." It was only after the increasing number of requests to speak before college groups were reinforced by petitions from the students themselves that Moody agreed to participate in a work for which he felt himself so singularly ill-equipped, but in which he succeeded in recruiting for the Christian cause the "first minds" of the college campuses, among them John R. Mott, Robert E. Speer, Sherwood Eddy, and Charles Foster Kent. Although the effort had been viewed by him with grave misgivings, the Student Volunteer Movement which grew out of the Northfield Conference of 1886 was Moody's greatest single triumph. An even one hundred of those present at the conference that year volunteered for foreign mission service, and before a year had elapsed the number had grown to more than two thousand as the delegates carried their contagious enthusiasm back to the institutions from which they had come.

By the time Moody returned from his second extended visit to the British Isles (1881-84), where he had repeated his earlier success, winning an enthusiastic reception from students at Cambridge and Oxford and sending Grenfell to Labrador, he was deeply saddled with many new responsibilities. The Chicago Avenue Church which had grown out of the old North Market Street Mission, the two Northfield schools which he had established in 1879, as well as the Chicago Evangelization Society which he had organized to train young women for Christian service, all made increasing demands upon his time

and energy. In addition, he continued to assume heavy responsibilities in connection with the Y.M.C.A., giving a considerable amount of time now both to the student work and to the
securing of financial support for various phases of the total
Y.M.C.A. program. Nor were these varied responsibilities to
diminish, for he soon was engaged in broadening the scope of
the Evangelization Society to include training for general lay
leadership, and the Student Volunteer Movement and the
Y.M.C.A.'s world service program were both to claim a major
portion of his attention.

These numerous and in some instances burdensome obligations unquestionably account in large part for Moody's return
to his earlier pattern of short, intensive evangelistic campaigns. Because of increasing institutional responsibilities he
could not afford the time for more than a brief stay in any one
city, and consequently after 1884 he began responding to more
invitations but restricted the length of time that he would be
present. On the other hand, this shift of method and the di-
version of time and energy into other channels was indicative
of a deeper shift taking place in Moody's thinking. Dissatisfied
with the results he had been achieving in his meetings, he was
beginning to experience some misgivings which caused him to
re-examine the entire strategy which he had been pursuing.

Somewhat earlier he had begun to recognize that evangelistic meetings were not always appropriate or effective. "There
are many ways of reaching young men," he confessed to a
meeting of Y.M.C.A. secretaries in 1879:

. . . I would recommend a gymnasium, classes, medical lectures, social receptions, music, and all unobjectionable agencies. These are
for week days. We do not want simply evangelistic meetings; I
have tried that system in Association work and failed, so I gave up
the Association and became an evangelist.

But now it was becoming apparent that the audiences he was
addressing as an evangelist were largely composed of Chris-

tians and the inquiry meetings were increasingly dominated by those who wished to testify to their past Christian experience. More and more Moody was becoming convinced of the necessity for a personal rather than a mass approach. The monthly house-to-house family visitation program of the Evangelical Alliance appealed to him strongly and received his hearty support. It was primarily to provide trained lay visitors for the implementation of this program that Moody expended such prodigious efforts in the face of innumerable obstacles, during 1888 and 1889, to transform the Evangelization Society into a coeducational Bible Institute. An additional urgent motivation was Moody's increased appreciation of the need for trained Sunday School teachers. The times were changing and large segments of the urban population no longer possessed the background of religious instruction which the earlier arrivals had brought with them from the countryside. "Thirty years ago," he said,

pretty much everybody believed that the Bible was true. They did not attack it or question it. They believed that the Lord Jesus Christ by dying on the cross had done something for them, and that if they received him they would be saved. And my work was to bring them to a decision to do what they already knew they ought to do. But all is different now. The question mark is raised everywhere, and there is need for teachers who shall teach and show the people what the gospel is.

And Moody was also becoming increasingly impressed with the importance of general education. Student work and the Northfield schools received a progressively greater portion of his time. Of the latter, he was to remark: "They are the best pieces of work I have ever done." Yet he by no means regarded education as the answer to his central concern for the redemption of men. "This country," he said in 1896, "is not lacking in regard to education," for "a good education has been put within the reach of the poorest." But, he continued, "of what use is knowledge alone, mere knowledge? It has no spiritual or moral power."

Until the heart is made right all else will be wrong; for out of it are the issues of life. . . . No amount of secular education can change its character. What is needed is a new heart, a knowledge of the true and living God.

The old evangelism had run its course. What was needed and what Moody was seeking was a new evangelism which would reach men with the compelling power which the old evangelism had displayed in an earlier day.[10]

II

"The most notable thing to the detached observer," in the years following Moody's death, was "the remorseless falling off of revivalism," not only in numbers, but "in dignity and passion." The decline in numbers had set in during Moody's lifetime, but the vulgarity and tawdriness of the professional breed of evangelists came largely after his death. The reasons for the decline in the quality and effectiveness of revivalism are not difficult to identify. Changes in the intellectual climate, the spread of education, the loss of homogeneity in the population, the dwindling of the number of the explicitly un-churched, the distractions and diversions as well as the increasing tempo of city life—all combined to make it more difficult to secure the attention and to create the community pressures which are indispensable to revivalism.

In a sense everything which has interested the American and occupied his thoughts, everything which has given him pleasure and withdrawn him from the pursuit of sanctity; everything which has fed and clothed and prospered him and removed him from the shadow of fear, has helped . . . to make the work of the evangelist harder.

But these changes of circumstances alone do not account for the degeneration which occurred in what had been a noble tradition.[11]

The seeds of disintegration were inherent in the nature of revivalism itself. This fact has been clearly demonstrated by Sidney E. Mead.[12] Two things are required of a revivalist. First of all, he must reduce the complex and highly ambiguous situation in which an individual finds himself to a simple choice between two clear-cut alternatives. Second, he "must appeal to the masses of the people, and theological issues must be put in terms simple enough for common apprehension." As a result of these two pressures, the tendency of the revivalist was to oversimplify theological issues and the ultimate result was to render the faith devoid of content. This tendency was more or less successfully resisted by the greater revivalists. For, while they spoke the language of the common man, they were men of the people in the deeper sense of being acutely sensitive to the profoundly felt needs, anxieties, dilemmas, and yearnings of the human spirit. But where this sensitivity was lacking the "flight from reason" was both headlong and inexorable.

A third pressure inherent in revivalism is the temptation to stress results and to justify whatever produces them. Here the consequences involve both faith and practice. Thus Finney justified his "new measures" on the ground that they were effective in securing conversions, and Daniel D. Williams has described how for a later generation of revivalists "the ultimate standard for judging every doctrine and every practice of Christianity was . . . ; Will it help or hinder the salvation of men?"[13] A pragmatic test thus became the criterion of truth and the justification for even the crudest of methods. Finally, revivalism, with "its emphasis, at least by implication, that man can somehow save himself through choice," tended to affirm man's responsibility for his own moral and spiritual condition and to deny the traditional acknowledgment of dependence upon God for one's salvation. Ultimately the unaided effort of the human will came to be regarded as sufficient to gain divine grace, and the self-sufficient individual emerged in the drama of redemption as the captain of his own soul.

The fading of revivalism as a dynamic movement and its consequent externalization and institutionalization has been vividly described by H. Richard Niebuhr. The miracle of grace became a human possession, with clearly defined and institutionalized procedures by which it might be appropriated. "Mapped, motorized, and equipped with guard rails," the hazards and uncertainties of the road to redemption were removed. The new birth—"the dying to the self and the rising to new life," with its ambiguities and anxieties, its suddenness and its slowness, its joy and its pain, its assurance and its doubt—was stylized into a "conversion which takes place on Sunday morning during the singing of the last hymn or twice a year when the revival preacher comes to town." Some still found new life and the reality of a Christian experience by following the prescribed ritual, but for many the life had departed from the whole procedure. It was no longer so much "the road from the temporal to the eternal, from trust in the finite to faith in the infinite, from self-centeredness to God-centeredness," as it was "the way into the institutional church or the company of respectable Christian churchmen who keep the Sabbath, pay their debts promptly, hope for heaven and are never found drunk either with sensual or with spiritual excitement."[14]

The final degeneration and degradation of what had been a respected and respectable religious institution can be seen in Billy Sunday and his professional imitators. Shorn of intellectual content and increasingly barren spiritually, revivalism in his hands became more and more simply "the business of creating fervor and frenzy." A thoroughgoing pragmatist, the campaigns of the ex-ballplayer were completely calculated and wholly theatrical. Persuaded that the end justifies the means, almost anything was permitted that was good for a headline in the morning paper. Striving for results that were increasingly difficult to secure, Sunday was driven to greater and greater extremes, and his antics and efforts to attract attention and draw a crowd became ever more grotesque and sensational. As the sensationalism increased, the effectiveness of his campaigns progressively declined; and this in turn led to even more frenzied efforts to provoke a response. Before he was through, the great mass of church people had been alienated and revivalism had been brought into complete disrepute.

Moody, on the other hand, had resisted the tendencies within revivalism toward disintegration with considerable success. It is true that theologically he was uninformed. His intellectual interest was slight and the doctrinal content of his preaching was notably deficient, and his revivals were calculated and contrived. Yet his great good sense kept him from making "preachableness" the sole criterion of truth and caused him to respect in large measure the judgment of scholars. His specific task as an evangelist, Moody felt, was to pull the trigger, not load the gun; and if the theology of the bright young men with whom he surrounded himself was superficial, it was quite as much the fault of the theologians to whom he referred them as it was to his own obvious theological deficiencies. Moody's ecumenical spirit and irenic temper also kept him from pursuing any divisive or separatist course which would have involved a break with the Christian community at large, while his essential sanity and healthy-mindedness kept him for the most part from employing the more bizarre and sensational methods. And lastly, his single-minded love of God and for humanity kept him from being satisfied with any superficial evidences of success. Actually, Moody's distrust of purely emotional conversions led him to shift the burden of his preaching from a stress upon the sufficiency of simple belief to an emphasis upon the necessity for thoroughgoing repentance, even though the change resulted in a greatly reduced number of converts. "He was just as earnest, as vigorous, as impressive as before," R. W. Dale reported. "People were as deeply moved. Hundreds went into the inquiry room every night. But the results, as far as I can learn, have been inconsiderable." On the other hand, Moody does illustrate the intellectual weakness of the revivalist movement, and in a certain sense he was a pragmatist. But it was a pragmatism in which ethical rather than numerical considerations were determinative. When the theology of Henry Drummond came under attack as heterodox, Moody found it quite impossible to remonstrate with his good friend and colleague, because Drummond seemed to him to be "so much better a Christian than I am."[15]

The measure of Moody's full stature is revealed by his recognition that the era of the older revivalism had clearly passed, and he began casting about for some other means of introducing people to the Christian life and of winning and holding them for the Christian church. Just before Moody's death, Charles M. Sheldon reported that he remarked that "his only regret in going up higher was that he would not be here to see what he himself called the new evangelism, which would be different from his own, but for which the race is waiting." By this, however, Moody did not mean that there could be any substitute for "the plain, old-fashioned, unadulterated gospel." "People say the old gospel has lost its power," he confided to a member of his family near the end of his career, but "I have not found it so." Methods might change, techniques might vary, but "the world," he asserted, "still hungers for the same message."[16]

III

The most promising alternative to revivalism as an evangelistic device for the recruiting of church members on the basis

of sound Christian experience was the Sunday School. The
monthly family visitation plan of the Evangelical Alliance had
many distinct values in a highly mobile urban situation, but it
had to be related to something, preferably to a smaller, more
intimate, and more informal group than the church itself and
specifically to a group in which the inquirer might find instruction, fellowship, and opportunities for service. The Sunday
School with its organized classes was ideally equipped to meet
this need. The interdenominational house-to-house visitation
proved to be little more than a sudden flame which flickered
out after a year or two of earnest effort, but the Sunday Schools
had already largely perfected their own methods of visitation
and enlistment.

"When the war is ended," Moody had suggested to his friend
and fellow Christian Commission "delegate" from the Chicago
Y.M.C.A., B. F. Jacobs, "let's give our strength to Sunday
School work." This they had done with striking results. For
forty years the missionaries of the American Sunday School
Union had been busy establishing Sunday Schools for the children of the nation, but now city, county, state, and national
conventions of Sunday School workers were to supplement the
pedestrian efforts of the missionaries and bring to the movement a burst of enthusiasm and eager devotion. The promotion
of these conventions by enlisting the vigorous leadership developed by the Y.M.C.A. behind them was the "work" Moody
had in mind. In characteristic fashion, Moody gave himself
without stint to the Sunday School cause, traveling incessantly
in its behalf, speaking at conventions, serving on committees,
helping to organize local units, furnishing ideas, and awakening enthusiasm and devotion, but Jacobs was the real architect
of the movement. A real estate operator who was described by
one of his friends as a "steam-engine of a man," Jacobs pursued the indispensable organizational work with a relentless
singleness of aim. He was the strategist who kept the various
denominations working together harmoniously, and he was

largely responsible for the efficient county convention system which provided the real strength of the movement. Within less than a decade, mass Sunday School conventions, crowded with ardent and enthusiastic workers, had become one of the most conspicious features of American church life. "To attend a convention revealed to the local worker his chosen cause operating on a larger field, broadened his fellowship, inspired him to new effort," and at the same time acquainted him with new methods and supplied him with a measure of training. Keyed to evoke the ardour and zeal of those in attendance, the conventions not infrequently became the occasion for a revival in the city in which they were held.[17]

The convention system largely determined the lay and popular character of the new instrument of the churches which was being fashioned, but two other innovations were scarcely less significant and both indicate the tremendous drive and vigor of the movement. The first was the Uniform Lesson Plan adopted, at the insistence of Jacobs, by the National Convention of 1872; the second was the establishment of "normal" classes and teachers' institutes. The uniform lessons had many advantages. They unified the existing Sunday Schools, and, being printed in the denominational journals as well as in a good portion of the daily press, did much to publicize and popularize the Sunday School movement as a whole. Moreover, "next Sunday's lesson" became a bond between members of different churches and contributed greatly to the strengthening of a common Protestant sentiment throughout the nation. But, above all, the uniform plan facilitated lesson preparation. In Boston, New York, Buffalo, Cleveland, and Chicago, some "eight to twelve hundred teachers" were soon gathering "every Saturday afternoon . . . to study the uniform lesson." The teachers' institutes, on the other hand, were designed for prospective teachers and sought to equip them, before they assumed Sunday School responsibilities, with the tested methods of effective Bible teaching. Initiated by John H. Vincent in 1865, when a weekly institute began meeting in Chicago, the institute idea soon swept across the country, awakening tremendous popular response, and giving birth in due time to the Chautauqua movement.[18]

The popular enthusiasm for the Sunday School, the widespread support it enjoyed, and the leadership of conspicuous ability it had enlisted, combined to make it an ideal instrument to replace the older evangelism as a recruiting technique for the churches. Definitely evangelistic in purpose from the beginning, the Sunday School required no readjustment of aims and objectives to fit it for the new importance which was now assigned to its activities. Curiously enough, however, the Sunday School was devoted almost completely to work with children and this situation began to change only during the last two decades of the century. Classes for adolescents began to be introduced during the eighties, partly as a result of the influence exerted by the Y.M.C.A. which was conducting Bible classes for this age group with considerable success, and during the nineties classes for adults became a central concern.

Many influences converged to encourage the expansion of the Sunday School to include adults. The popularity of the teachers' institutes and the Chautauqua movement had demonstrated the existence of a widespread interest in adult education, and the phenomenal success of William Rainey Harper's American Institute of Sacred Literature, organized in 1889, was added confirmation of the fact that large numbers of people were definitely interested in Bible study. The Institute, directed by a "Council of Seventy" leading Biblical scholars, was soon enrolling ten thousand students annually in its correspondence courses and, like the Chautauqua movement, stimulating the formation of local study groups. The most decisive influence, however, was the demand for a new method of reaching the unconverted and the unchurched. The answer to this need was the organized class.

For several years an occasional strong Bible class for adults was to be found—several in Washington, D.C., one at the Central Presbyterian Church in Rochester, New York, and a few scattered elsewhere. But adult classes did not begin to appear in any large numbers until the advent of the organized class during the nineties, and the organized class was of a different character for it was designed quite explicitly to serve as an instrument of evangelism by the simple expedient of putting each member of the class to work in an endeavor to win others for Christ and the church. "Each one win one" was a typical slogan and was clearly indicative of the spirit of the movement as a whole.

The organized class idea was originated by Marshall A. Hudson of Syracuse, New York, in 1890. Noting the crowd of young men who regularly gathered outside the First Baptist Church, he determined "to gain them by setting them at work for others." Those who responded to his invitation were organized as a class, with their own officers, the name "Baraca," and an inner circle—"the secret service"—who were pledged to pray secretly each day for "the unconverted members of the class" and "at a suitable time to speak to those for whom they are praying." The class grew rapidly, the idea spread to other communities, and in 1895 the Philathea classes for women were established. By 1913 the World-Wide Baraca-Philathea Union, with its national conventions, numbered more than nine thousand classes with a membership of nearly one million in churches of thirty-two different denominations. Similar in character were other nationally organized classes—the Agoga and Amoma classes, the Drexel Biddle classes, the Bereans, the Gleaners, the King's Daughters, the Wesley Bible classes, and the Loyal Movement (Sons, Daughters, Men, and Women) which alone numbered some four thousand classes by 1912 in eleven different denominations. Not the least important were the numerous strong locally organized classes, gathered about a striking personality whose name was frequently given to the class, the membership of which in many instances ran into the hundreds. By 1903 the promotion of adult work was well under way in the state Sunday School Conventions, and two years later the International Association established an adult Department which by 1908 was issuing Certificates of Recognition for having fully met the International Standard of Organization to as many as six thousand new classes each year. A red button with a white center was given to the members of each class to remind them that "the chief business of this movement is the winning of souls to Jesus Christ."[19]

Adult Bible Class parades, sponsored by the multiplying Adult Bible Class Federations, became the dramatic feature of the Sunday School conventions. At San Francisco in 1911, the parade was headed by a platoon of mounted police and ten thousand men were in the line of march, each with a Bible in hand, carrying banners, and singing hymns and official delegation songs. At Washington the year before, Congress adjourned to witness the parade, and the Colorado delegation greeted the reviewing stand with a "yell" composed for the occasion.

> Colorado is big, Colorado is great,
> We are the only centennial state;
> We have gold in our mines; we have silver galore,
> We have money in banks and goods in our stores;
> But the brightest assets in our glorious state
> Are the workers for God that our Sunday Schools make.

Workers for God they were, and very effective workers in many ways. The parades, with their songs and yells, may seem unduly adolescent to a later and more sober generation, but at the time they were quite in keeping with the typical expressions of enthusiasm and group morale, whether in politics, the

fraternal orders, or college life. In spite of much that was superficial, these young men and women of the organized classes
constituted a potent force in the life of the churches.[20]

IV

The decline of revivalism could scarcely be regarded with
equanimity by the churches nor could its demise be lightly
dismissed. For more than a century, revivalism had been the
chief means upon which the voluntary churches depended for
their continued existence, and it is not surprising that cries of
alarm were raised and frenzied efforts were made to perpetuate
it as a method for reaching the unchurched portions of the
population. But, for good or ill, revivalism had lost its effectiveness and was rapidly coming into disrepute. The churches, on
the whole, responded to this new situation with imagination
and resourcefulness. By the close of the century, the techniques of a new evangelism had been largely perfected and
were being utilized with considerable success. Of the specifically urban devices, the institutional church and the Y.M.C.A.
were the most effective, the latter alone having been reporting
from two thousand to thirty-five hundred "hopeful conversions" each year.[21] Moreover, both the "rescue mission" and
the specialized ministry to foreign-language groups had displayed evidence of real strength, and this was also true of the
Christian Endeavor societies. The primary reliance, however,
was upon the Sunday School with its "Decision Days" for adolescents and its organized classes for adults. Vigorous and
strong, enjoying popular support and the ablest leadership of
the community, the Sunday Schools entered the new century
bright with the promise of greater things to come.

CHAPTER VIII

PRINCES OF THE PULPIT: The
Preachers and the New Theology

We do not nowadays refute our predecessors, we pleasantly bid them good-bye. GEORGE SANTAYANA[1]

Henry Steele Commager speaks of the last decade of the nineteenth century as the great "watershed" in American life. During these ten fateful years modern America came to life, seemingly almost overnight. To go back beyond that decade is to find oneself in an almost unfamiliar world in which Indians still roamed their ancestral hunting grounds and homesteaders could still take up land on the frontier. Behind the frontier a farm and village civilization largely reigned supreme. City life to the majority of the people still constituted an alien world, known only at a distance, and susceptible of romantic treatment at the hands of literary hacks. Stereotypes of "hayseed" and "city slicker" bore witness to the gulf which still existed between the old and the new America. By 1890 all this was changed. The Indians were couped up in reservations, the cheap land of the frontier was gone, the isolation of the hinterland had begun to disappear with the advent of the automobile, and the cities with their telephones and electric lights, their factories and slums, their robber barons and political bosses, their transient and propertyless inhabitants had become the dominant feature of American life. The slow pace of the older era had given way to the rapid tempo of the modern age.[2]

In religion the final decade of the nineteenth century was no less decisive as a time transition between the old and the new. While it is true that any break with the past is somewhat blurred and the continuity of the old with the new and the new with the old is never completely severed, nevertheless from the perspective of more than half a century the nineties emerge as the years when religious leaders pleasantly bid good-by to their predecessors. Even a cursory reading of their sermons makes it apparent that the preachers of the nineties, at least the more influential among them, belong to the twentieth rather than to the nineteenth century. The topics they selected and the assumptions upon which they proceeded still constitute the larger portion of the common pulpit fare of the contemporary churchgoer. Like the novels of the period, the sermons can be read today without the feeling that they are unduly "dated." They are, to be sure, somewhat more ornate in literary style and definitely more sentimental in expression than contemporary sermons, but still not markedly different in spirit or presuppositions. On the other hand, when one goes back another decade or two, he enters a world in which the preaching seems obtrusively and almost immodestly personal in its urgent demands. There is a difference in language, of course, but the real distinction is in mood and in the understanding of the nature of the Christian faith.

I

In many respects the decade from 1890 to 1900 may be regarded as the great age of the American pulpit. It was a time when sermons were not infrequently front-page news, and those of some of the more prominent of the clergy were regularly syndicated nationally in their entirety. The preachers themselves, so Bryce informs us, were regarded as "first citizens" and exercised "an influence often wider and more powerful than that of any layman." Not since Abraham Lincoln, he observed, had there been a man "so warmly admired and so widely mourned" as Phillips Brooks.[3] What was true of Brooks was true only to a slightly lesser degree of the whole galaxy of stars who shared with them a national and in some instances even an international reputation—Russell Conwell, George A. Gordon, T. DeWitt Talmadge, Washington Gladden, Lyman Abbott, Newell Dwight Hillis, Frank W. Gunsaulus, Charles M. Sheldon, Charles A. Parkhurst, Josiah Strong, Graham Taylor, and a host of others whose fame was more regional than national. Henry Ward Beecher had just died, and Dwight L. Moody—somewhat ill at ease in the new religious climate—was still pursuing his vigorous course in support of the numerous enterprises which had enlisted his concern.

The Americans of the nineties were living in what seemed to them to be the best of all possible worlds. The traditional hopefulness of a new people in a new world which had been kept within reasonable bounds by the arduous toil involved in subduing a continent and winning a living from the soil had now given way to an almost completely unbridled confidence, complacency, and cheerfulness. As the century moved toward its close in a burst of technological and industrial expansion, American experience seemed ample evidence for the belief that "though the ascent of man may be slow it is also sure." Looking back, Bryce reported, the men and women of the nineties could see "human nature growing gradually more refined, institutions better fitted to secure justice, the opportunities and capacities for happiness larger and more varied"; and looking ahead they saw "a long vista of years stretching out before them, in which they will have time enough to cure all their faults, to overcome all the obstacles that block their path." All contrary evidence—the recurrent scandals and corruption of municipal politics, the increasing labor strife culminating in the Haymarket riot and the Pullman strike, the manipulation of the markets by speculators, the Panic of 1893, the descent of Coxey's Army on Washington—yielded in the end, even among the most sensitive, to the sanguine temper of the time, which regarded present evils as tolerable because they were "transitory" and "removable as soon as time can be found to root them up."[4]

The striking thing about the men who now dominated the American pulpits is the way in which they all—in their several and, to be sure, diverse ways—reflected the common mood of the time. This was true even among the most conservative of the evangelicals who did not hesitate to adopt that most utopian and optimistic of all proposals—"the evangelization of the world in this generation." The most typical expression of the new temper, however, was what was already being called the New Theology. Even an ostensible archconservative like Talmadge found much of the New Theology eminently preachable but succeeded in cloaking his departure from the faith of the fathers by a curious blending of profuse Biblical allusions with figures of speech derived from the marts of trade.

While an occasional scientist and novelist ran counter to the prevailing mood of self-congratulation and questioned the optimistic conclusions which were being derived from the doctrine of evolution, few members of the clergy were either alert enough or perceptive enough to grasp the more somber implications of the new "sciences" of personal and social behavior. In spite of all that their creeds affirmed concerning the depravity of man and the divine decrees, many of the preachers now eagerly embraced a contrary gospel which sanctified the "natural" man, substituted sentiment for the more rigorous demands of justice, and rejoiced in the pleasant doctrine of the liberty of men to will and to choose the good. In a sense, it is not surprising that this should occur. A century of revivalism with its progressive simplification of the faith and its tendency to move in a Pelagian direction had largely dismantled the intellectual defenses of historic Protestantism, and the process was hastened by the impact of "romanticism" upon the later evangelicalism. To the extent that theology survived in American Protestantism, its most characteristic insights had been effectively emasculated. Horace Bushnell, Mark Hopkins, and the other "neo-romantic" evangelicals had done their work well. "The hardness of Calvinism had been softened. The old fear of God had relaxed. Love had been substituted for discipline."[5] The humanity of Christ as the great exemplar in whose steps all might aspire to walk had been asserted, and the divinity of man was implicitly affirmed. Thus, the theological vacuum left by revivalism was already being filled, well before the nineties, by an emphasis that was quite in keeping with the popular mood of complacent and self-confident optimism.

The New Theology was essentially a culture religion with a single fundamental theological idea—the doctrine of the Incarnation, interpreted in terms of divine immanence and a superficial understanding of the notion of evolution. By means of this doctrine, Christ was identified with what was conceived to be the finest cultural ideals, the noblest cultural institutions, and the best scientific and philosophical thinking. The most significant feature of the New Theology, therefore, was its lack of normative content. It was compatible with every conceivable social attitude, with whatever stream of secular thought one might wish to support and consecrate, with whatever system of values might seem good in the light of one's own personal predilections. Thus, in the words of John Herman Randall, the New Theology represented "a pretty complete acceptance of the world, the flesh, and the devil" and became largely "an emotional force in support of the reigning secular social ideals" which offered "no independent guidance and wisdom" to the Christian believer.[6]

In many ways, because the culture was recognizably Christion, the New Theology was recognizably Christian, not only in language and lingering emotional loyalty, but—with certain notable exceptions—in moral attitudes and practices. On the other hand, men of differing temperaments and differing backgrounds did hold differing opinions as to what constituted the best of the cultural "goods," and thus they were led to select as of primary importance in the economy of Christ differing aspects of the existing culture. While the essential unity of basic assumptions should not be obscured, it is important to note the diverse tendencies of the New Theology in terms of the practical aspects of the religious life. The differences were not always great and in the last analysis not highly significant, but in their very variety they help us understand the problem which later was to plague the churches.

Both the essential unity of these presuppositions and the diversity of the practical implications of the New Theology can be clearly seen in terms of four of the outstanding preachers who blazed the way for the practitioners of the pulpit arts during the nineties—Phillips Brooks, Henry Ward Beecher, Russell Conwell, and Washington Gladden. All four had been born in the first half of the century, had served a varied apprenticeship during the days of the Civil War, and—with the exception of Beecher who died in 1887—had reached the height of their influence and public acclaim in the final decade of the century. Partly because of the influence they exerted, but even more because they were representative men who made explicit tendencies which were already widespread, these four men accurately reflect the major lines of division which were to develop within a common acceptance of the tenets of the New Theology.

II

Phillips Brooks was a true prince of the pulpit in almost every sense of the word. Endowed with a commanding stature, a compelling personality, and great eloquence, Brooks was by far the most attractive and the most widely loved of the preachers of the New Theology. An abundance of natural vigor coupled with an innate gentleness of spirit and cheerfulness of temper gave to his preaching a quality of winsomeness and serenity which was tremendously appealing to the comfortable and enlightened folk of Back Bay Boston, Harvard Yard, and the other cultural oases of the East and Middle West. For twenty-two years, after his call to Boston in 1869, Phillips Brooks spoke to crowded congregations in the Romanesque elegance of Trinity Episcopal Church on Copley Square, achieving an international reputation that has rarely been equaled.

Sunday after Sunday, with never-failing charm and power, Brooks laid before the worshippers his simple faith in the spirit of man as the candle of the Lord, revealing God in human life. "Only a person can truly utter a person," he declared. "Whoever has in him the human quality, whoever has the spirit of man, has the candle of the Lord." Even "a poor, meager, starved, bruised life, if only it keeps the true human quality, and does not become inhuman, and if it is obedient to God in its blind, dull, half-conscious way becomes a light. . . . There is no life so humble that, if it be true and genuinely humble and obedient to God, it may not hope to shed some of his light." Only the man who willfully denies his own nature, who steadfastly refuses to acknowledge the beauty and the glory of life, and fails utterly to respond, in reverence and devotion, to the mystic summons of goodness and purity which rises forever within his heart, remains an unlighted candle.[7]

Enthusiasm for humanity, then, was the key to Brooks' gospel and the theme of all his sermons. "From the very beginning of the Bible, at the very creation, the grand note of centralness of man is struck."

The animals wait for man to name them. . . . The forest waits to catch the color of his light; the beasts hesitate in fear or anger until he shall tame them to his services, or bid them depart. The earth under his feet holds its fertility at his command and answers the summons of his grain or flower seeds. The very sky over his head regards him, and what he does upon the earth is echoed in the changes of the climate and the haste or slowness of the storms.

But man is not only a lord of creation; he is a child of God, with his deepest desires in harmony with the eternal purposes of God. "The ultimate fact of human life," Brooks declared in an address before the Evangelical Alliance, "is goodness and not sin." Religion, therefore, "is the highest reach of our human life."

There is nothing in religion, there is nothing in Christianity, which has not its roots in human nature and in the fundamental affections of mankind. Utterly swept out of our thought must be any old contradiction between the graces of the gospel and the natural affections; the natural affections reach upward and when they find the God who has been in them from the beginning, then they are the Christian graces. . . .

Believe in yourselves and reverence your own human nature; it is the only salvation from brutal vice and every false belief. . . .

An optimist is a believer in the best, and any man who believes that anything less than the best is the ultimate purpose of God, and so the ultimate possibility of God's children, has no business to live upon the earth. . . .

And of this one can be sure, God "has not forgotten and never will, and never can forget or curse, the least or most unworthy of his children."[8]

The fundamental structural support for Phillips Brooks' faith was his supreme confidence in the power of the culture itself to nurture the natural Christian graces which were resident in every human heart. "I do not know how a man can be an American, even if he is not a Christian, and not catch something with regard to God's purpose as to this great land." The most impressive feature of American life, to him, was "the effort of men to do outside the churches and outside Christianity that which the churches and Christianity undertake to do." In the imperfection of the church, "the spirit of the world feels the desire of the things the church means, and tries to do them . . . in another way."

What mean all the secular, all the studiously irreligious, all the even blasphemous attempts at education and the development of character? What mean the efforts of philanthropy that studiously disown anything except political economy as the impulse from which they work? . . . What do they mean except that that which Christianity intends the human heart desires, and where the Christian church is incompetent . . . , the great human impulse, which is the divine impulse, desires character and philanthropy and political purity, and seeks after them in its own way? . . . Shall we not dare to rejoice that that which the church cannot do, that which the church does not do, in any feeblest, in any falsest way, is attempted by the heart of man?

This confidence in the power of culture—"the spirit of the world"—was the secret of Brooks' broad churchmanship. The organized church played only an incidental role in the fulfillment of God's purposes—useful to the extent that aspiration was awakened and devotion kindled but scarcely indispensable. Indeed, by limiting its vision, by affirming the priority of special revelation, and by positing a tension between itself and the world, the organized church served to hinder as much as to advance the cause of truth. Humanity itself, not any organized body of believers, is God's instrument, and through humanity itself he effects his purposes. This is the true church, embracing the whole of mankind, the entire family of God. It is a church without organization, discipline, or ritual, but a church in which "the great human impulses" lead men to do "Christian work in the spirit of Christ" even when they "studiously" or "vehemently" disown him.[9]

The great human impulses, however, did not lead Brooks to espouse any program of social reform. Basically this was because he shared in the prevailing satisfaction with the times and did not believe that contemporary society stood in need of any real reform. A natural aristocrat, Brooks was firmly of the conviction that there should be no leveling of the classes. Inequalities were both inevitable and desirable.

There can be no doubt, I think, whatever puzzling questions it may bring with it, that it is the fact of privilege and inequalities among men for which they do not seem to be responsible, which makes a large part of the interest and richness of human existence. . . . I believe that the more we think, the more we become convinced that the instinct which asks for equality is a low one, and that equality, if it were completely brought about, would furnish play for the lower instincts and impulses of man.

Education, wealth, and social position were gifts of God which involved responsibilities which must not be ignored; while poverty, though scarcely a positive blessing, had its own special virtues and sources of happiness. Excessive poverty, of course, should command the charitable concern of the more fortunate, but happily it did not exist to any great extent in America. "Actual suffering for the necessities of life, terrible as it is, is comparatively rare." The only word to be spoken to the laboring classes was the same word to be spoken to the upper classes—the injunction to "live worthier and nobler lives." By so doing, workingmen will not only conquer their enemies within but will contribute to the solution of the great problems of society. These problems "will get settled somehow," Brooks firmly believed, "and things will be juster than they are today," for there is a natural harmony which in the end will bring all diverse interests into perfect accord, so that each individual will be able to make—in freedom and originality—"his appointed contribution to society."[10]

Possessing no real intellectual interest, the length and breadth of the "incarnational theology" of Phillips Brooks was spelled out in the essentially mystical affirmation of faith in the goodness and nobility of men as children of God, living together harmoniously in an interesting and enriching inequality. Untroubled and serene in his faith, Brooks never undertook to refute the doctrines he quietly discarded. Even when charges of heresy were leveled against him, he refused to be drawn into controversy and answered his critics with calm and unruffled silence. The attempt to give systematic expression to the full implications of the central affirmation embodied in his sermons was left to his friend and neighbor across the Square, George A. Gordon, minister of Old South Church.

Gordon was dismayed by what he regarded as the essentially untheological character of the New Theology. Primarily an attitude or emotion which had been called forth by a new understanding and appreciation of the nature of the world, the New Theology, Gordon pointed out, had not as yet been reduced to an intellectually disciplined and defensible system of thought. As a result, even those who were its most ardent advocates were frequently involved in confusions and contradictions. "For all thinking men who are in any measure open to the new light and spirit of our time," he declared, the old theology "as an adequate interpretation of the ways of God with men, or even as a working philosophy of life, is forever gone," and has left a vacant throne. "Thus far nothing equally elaborate and commanding has arisen to take its place."

> The absence of a theology giving intellectual form and justification to the better sentiment of the time is abundantly visible in our ministry. Among almost all our effective preachers the sympathies are modern; but in the greater number the theology is either ancient or non-existent. . . .
>
> One looks almost in vain for books giving an elaboration into coherent and commanding form of the new ideas by which men are living. The new ideas lie in our life with the most confusing and provoking miscellaneousness. . . .

Gordon, perhaps, was reacting to his own earlier confusion. At the time of his installation as minister of Old South Church in 1884, the *Christian Union* had commented: "He is neither old school nor new school, Calvinist nor Arminian, Bushnellite nor

Parkite. He is equally ready to realize the possibility of verbal inspiration in one passage and to reject it in another; equally ready to admit the possibility of redemption after death and to refuse to assert it dogmatically." In the next few years, however, Gordon was captivated completely by Phillips Brooks and his own confusions and uncertainties began to recede. Setting himself to remedy the obvious deficiency of his older colleague, he published *The Christ of Today* in 1895, but a more concise statement of his "reasoned apologetic" may be found in an address, "The Theology for Today," which he gave at the fiftieth anniversary celebration of the Plymouth Church in Brooklyn, November 11, 1897.[11]

With Brooks, Gordon affirmed that "the incarnation is the center of all sane theology," for "man at his best can alone give us God at his best." The fundamental harmony between the impulses of men and the intentions of God, he contended, was amply evident in the experience of the race. This belief "is not founded upon sentiment; it is not the product of benevolent dreamers; it is not held blindly in spite of human nature, the movement of history, the spirit of the New Testament, the order of the moral world, the heart of the universe." Quite the contrary. The hopeless outlook of the older theology was due to "limitation of vision," looking out upon only "the part, the utmost part, the wretchedest part, and not upon the magnificent whole." The ground of hope, theologically stated, is "the perpetual coming of the Christian God in the life of mankind," for all that is "deepest in human nature, in human society, in human history, in the course of the world, in the on-going universe, makes for the seeker after righteousness," and "righteous character, and nothing else, is salvation." While salvation is the gift of God in the sense that the very structure of life fosters righteousness, it is by no means an unmerited gift. For, in the end, righteous character "is the achievement of the personal will" and "can be won, in the deepest sense, only by the soul for itself."[12]

While Gordon acknowledged the agony and anguish which frequently accompany the upward quest, he hesitated to identify God completely with the course of history, and was more willing to admit the extent of man's present imperfection; yet it is difficult to see where his interest in a coherent theological formulation of the new ideas associated with the sympathies, emotions, and practical outlooks of "this new and greater day" represented any marked advance from the unsystematized sentiments of Phillips Brooks. It was the same gospel in more academic dress. Superficial as many aspects of the gospel of Phillips Brooks now seem, even in terms of Gordon's more consistent intellectual formulation, it did have the very real merit of stressing those qualities of gentleness, serenity, nobility of character, and worthiness of living which, within the context of a Christian culture, may rightfully be regarded as aspects of a mature Christian faith. If the foundation was missing, the superstructure did exhibit large elements of Christian truth. The rather ambiguous tribute of one of his biographers, however, is not altogether unjust: "Phillips Brooks' supreme contribution to this country was himself."[13] And with that tribute, emphasizing as he did the importance of personality, Phillips Brooks would have been content.

III

Henry Ward Beecher, pastor of Plymouth Congregational Church in Brooklyn from 1847 to 1887, was described by Phillips Brooks as "the greatest preacher of America and of our century." Certainly he was the most conspicuous and influential minister of his day. His showmanship was rivaled only by that of T. DeWitt Talmadge of the neighboring Central Presbyterian Church and he consistently reached a far larger audience than Brooks. His sermons, delivered to crowded congregations in an unadorned tabernacle accommodating three thousand people, were printed in many newspapers and were collected at the close of each year for publication in book form. His views were also made known through innumerable addresses, lectures, and essays on current issues of every sort, and especially through editorials in the two influential journals, the *Independent* and the *Christian Union,* which for extended periods of time were his personal organs. But Beecher's influence derived primarily from his own dynamic and magnetic personality and the publicity which surrounded his whole spectacular career.[14]

In many respects Beecher was the most typical representative of the preachers of the New Theology. More than anyone else, he established the pattern and set the fashion, and in his ministry of more than fifty years one can see the newer point of view unfolding. He was a child of revivalism who wanted to get results, and he early discovered—as had his father—that to be secured they must be pursued with singleness of aim, without any quibbling over the finer points of doctrine. His method was to find a truth upon which his hearers could all agree, and then to press it home with an intense personal application and appeal. "The first time he tried this method, seventeen men were awakened." It was, said Beecher, "the most memorable day of our ministerial life. The idea was born. Preaching was a definite and practical thing. . . . Preaching was only a method of enforcing truths, not for the sake of the truths themselves, but for the results to be sought in *men*." For the next few years Beecher expended himself in intense revivalistic efforts, traveling through the State of Indiana from camp meeting to camp meeting, and preaching one spring in Indianapolis seventy successive nights in an effort to kindle an awakening.[15]

During his seminary course, lacking an appetite for systematic theology and displaying no capacity for serious theological thinking, Beecher was uncertain as to his message and consequently was not even sure about his call to preach. But one "blessed morning," he later reported,

. . . it pleased God to reveal to my wandering soul the idea that it was his nature to love man in his sins for the sake of helping him out of them; that he did not do it out of compliment to Christ, or to a law, or a plan of salvation, but from the fullness of his great heart; . . . that he was not furious with wrath toward the sinner, but pitied him—in short, that he felt toward me as my mother felt toward me to whose eyes my wrong doing brought tears, who never pressed me so close to her as when I had done wrong. . . . Time went on, and next came the disclosure of a Christ ever present with me—a Christ that was never far from me, but was always near me, as a companion and friend, to uphold and sustain me. This was the last and best revelation of God's Spirit to my soul.

This was to be his message—God's "nature to love man in his sins for the sake of helping him out of them" and Christ as an ever-present spiritual influence. "I was like the man in the story," Beecher remarked in describing his experience, "to whom the fairy gave a purse with a single piece of money in it, which he found always came again as soon as he had spent it. I thought I knew at least one thing to preach. I found it included everything."[16]

Beecher also found that his conception of God as love included some things which were not orthodox. It led him ultimately to question, among other things, the notion of everlasting punishment. "If I thought God stood at the door where men go out of life ready to send them down to eternal punishment, my soul would cry out: 'Let there be no God!' My instincts would say: 'Annihilate him!'" At the moment, it led him to regard sincerity as the true test of a man's life.

I made up my mind distinctly that . . . I would never engage in any religious contention. I remember riding through the woods . . . where I had such a sense of the love of Christ, of the nature of his work on earth, of its beauty and its grandeur, and such a sense of the miserableness of Christian men quarrelling and seeking to build up antagonistic churches . . . that I sat in my saddle, I do not know how long . . . , saying audibly, 'I will never be a sectary.' I remember promising Christ that if he would strengthen me and teach me how to work I would all my life long preach for his kingdom and endeavor to love everybody who was doing that work. Not that I would accept others' beliefs, not that I would embrace their theology, not that I would endorse their ecclesiastical organizations; but whatever their instruments might be, if they were sincerely working for the kingdom of Christ I would never put a straw in their way and never strike a blow to their harm. By the grace of God I have kept that resolution to this day.

As a consequence, the question, What do you believe? was ruled out of order in Beecher's church. "What Mr. Beecher held and this church holds on this subject, I hold no less earnestly," declared Lyman Abbott, Beecher's successor in the Plymouth pulpit.

We do not ask what men believe . . . , what they think about decrees or foreordination. I think we would even let a man join us who believes in limited atonement and special election; he might be as heretical as the old-time Puritans, and we would not close the door on him. . . . Some of us believe in infant baptism, and some do not; some believe in universal salvation, some in conditional immortality, and some in endless punishment; some are liberal and progressive, and some are conservative: we do not ask what they think on these questions. The one thing that holds us together is this: we all love Christ as our Saviour; we all acknowledge him as our Master; we all follow him as our Leader; we all bow down to him with absolute allegiance as our Lord.

The one thing demanded was loyalty to Christ, but how he would save or where he would lead was left to the individual to decide. "I will exercise my own rational judgment in determining what he said: I will exercise it on the Gospels as freely as I exercise it anywhere else." What Christ meant to Beecher himself was never wholly clear. At the close of his life, he left an unfinished manuscript life of Jesus, and his sons undertook to finish it for him. "They found in his sermons," reported Abbott, "enough of description of Christ's life to complete the work, with one great exception." Beecher had never ventured to preach upon "the passion and death of Christ upon the cross." Christ was an unseen friend, a spiritual presence, a noble example, a king of love, "a man of such purity, wisdom, beneficence, that men believe that he came from above to translate heavenly life and love into earthly conditions," but Christ as truth was subject to individual preferences and feelings, and above all to the pragmatic test of the revivalist. "I gradually formed a theology by practice," he was to declare in 1882 "—by trying it on, and the things that really did God's work in the hearts of men I set down as good theology, and the things that did not, whether they were true or not, they were not true to me."[17]

During his first years in the Brooklyn pastorate, Beecher's sermons were chiefly evangelistic in emphasis, but during the fifties he began to preach more and more on political questions —"moral issues" as he called them—and he rapidly moved to the fore as a power in Republican party politics. By 1862 Beecher was insisting that "it is the duty of the minister of the gospel to preach on every side of political life. I do not say that he *may*; I say that he *must*." Thereafter, the practice of relating religious truth to every "topic of the times" which involved "the welfare of men" was a characteristic feature of his ministry. In sermons and addresses he discussed the problems of emancipation, Reconstruction, immigration, the currency, taxes, a standing army, women's rights, Civil Service reform, local party politics, municipal corruption, free trade, pacifism, presidential candidates, and even urged that public libraries and picture galleries be open on the Sabbath. "A man," he admitted, "may preach politics too much. A man may do it foolishly . . . , but that is no reason why they should not be preached upon." On the whole, however, his influence was scarcely in the direction of moderation.[18]

After the Civil War, Beecher became increasingly interested in intellectual questions and this concern was to become the third note in his preaching. As a result of the never-to-be-forgotten spectacle of his father—"the most eminent clergyman of his day"—being subjected to the indignity of defending himself "for believing that a man could obey the commandments of God," Beecher had early acquired a distaste for what he regarded as orthodox Calvinism. This emotional reaction against the major theological expression of the traditional faith combined with the fundamental indifference of evangelicalism to doctrinal questions, left him open to respond eagerly and gladly to the new intellectual currents which were beginning to arise. By 1872 Beecher was warning the theological students at Yale of the "danger of having the intelligent part of society go past us."

There is being now applied among scientists a greater amount of real, searching, discriminating thought . . . to the whole structure and functions of man . . . than ever has been expended upon it in the whole history of the world put together. More men are studying it, and they are coming to results, and these results are starting, directly or indirectly, a certain kind of public thought and feeling. . . . And if ministers do not make their theological systems conform to facts as they are; if they do not recognize what men are studying, the time will not be far distant when the pulpit will be like the voice crying in the wilderness. And it will not be "Prepare the way of the Lord," either. . . . The providence of God is rolling forward in a spirit of investigation that Christian ministers must meet and join. . . . You cannot go back and become apostles of the dead past, drivelling after ceremonies and letting the world do the thinking and studying.

Beecher was referring, of course, primarily to the new theories concerning the evolution of man and society which were beginning to be popularized. If not actively hostile as yet to traditional Christianity, Beecher was at least indifferent to the older doctrinal controversies and had long been accustomed to test his own beliefs by the way they made him feel, and the new scientific conclusions made him feel very good. They were exactly suited to his own innately optimistic temper. "I am a cordial Christian evolutionist," he later announced. "Man," he declared, "is made to start and not to stop; to go on, and on, and up, and onward, steadily emerging from the controlling power of the physical and animal condition in which he was born and which enthrall him during his struggle upward, but ever touching higher elements of possibility, and ending in the glorious liberty of the sons of God."[19]

The implications of Beecher's new faith were summarized in an article, "Progress of Thought in the Church," which appeared in the *North American Review* for August, 1882. Religion, he now insisted, is natural. Believing is more natural than unbelieving, and this was especially true in America, where man's inherent religious nature was reinforced by widespread education and "domestic common sense." "Scoffing infidelity" is quite "uncongenial to the temper and good sense of Americans of native birth and of American education." Americans "may applaud intelligent doubt which refuses the weeds which have been bound up in the sheaves of theology," but "rational reverence" and "aspiring ideality" will "forbid the American mind to join in wasting skepticism." There is "an ineradicable belief" among American parents that "Christian morality is the safe road from childhood to manhood, and that the qualities enjoined by Jesus are indispensable to success in life." Thus the family itself serves as "a bulwark against infidelity" and "the household is a church." In similar fashion the other institutions of American society contribute to that moral elevation, the fostering of which is the sole legitimate function of the organized church. Since the new spirit of enlightenment has begun to pervade the churches themselves, they are moving away from the "superstition and credulity" which suggests that they occupy a distinctive place in society and are beginning to recognize that their existence can be justified only in terms of their "usefulness" as "organized centers of influence for morality, for education, and for public spirit."[20]

Not only was religion to be regarded as natural and as supported and sustained by the structure of society; it was to be defined solely in terms of "disposition and conduct." In the name of reason and intellectual respectability, reason and intellect were to be sacrificed to sentiment. "There is a growing conviction," said Beecher, "that great-heartedness is more akin to the Gospel spirit than dogma or doctrine." Common sense tells us that doctrine is of little consequence if the results are good. Men are to be "judged by the work which they perform, and not by the tools which they use." Then, shifting ground, he informed the reader that doctrines do make a difference and that reason is important, for false doctrine drives people away from the church and false reason hideously disfigures the method of creation and the scheme of redemption. "The dread of Darwinian views is sincere . . . . But have men considered what a relief they will be from some of the most disgraceful tenets of theology? Are they content to guard and defend a terrific scheme which sullies the honor, the justice, and the love of God, against a movement that will cleanse the abomination and vindicate the ways of God to man?" When "the creeds of the past era have passed away" they shall be replaced with "the creeds of a new era."

These will differ not alone in their contents from former doctrinal standards, but they will differ in the very genius and method of construction. Our reigning creeds begin with God, with moral government, with the scheme of the universe, with the great, invisible realm beyond. These are the weakest places in a creed, because the matters they contain are least within the reach of human reason. . . . The creeds of the future will begin where the old ones ended: upon the nature of man, his condition on earth, his social duties and civil obligations, the development of his reason, his spiritual nature, its range, possibilities, education . . . , man as an individual, man social and collective; and from a sound knowledge of the nature of the mind, developed within the scope of our experience and observation, we shall deduce conceptions of the great mind—the God idealized from our best ascertainments in the sphere within which our faculties were created to act with certainty of knowledge. Our creeds will ascend from the known to the unknown, which is the true law and method of acquiring knowledge.

Two months later, in a paper read before the Congregational Association of New York and Brooklyn, Beecher made the point concerning the importance of right belief even more vigorously. "The chapters of the Westminster Confession of Faith concerning decrees, election, reprobation . . . , I regard as extraordinary specimens of *spiritual barbarism*. . . . I hold it to be a monster, and not a master of love, that is there portrayed." This idea of God "stands in the way of thousands. It has turned more feet into the barren ways of infidelity than any other single cause."[21]

Beecher's act which followed the reading of his paper on "Spiritual Barbarism" was quite in keeping with the whole tendency of his career. He submitted his resignation from the Congregational Association and joined what was to be a growing number of clergymen who disowned any denominational affiliation. Beecher believed that the Christian minister should be "the freest of all free-thinkers" and he had made the Plymouth pulpit a "free" pulpit. "It does not require bravery to be brave in Plymouth pulpit," said his successor. "He who stands here can speak on the labor question, on Biblical criticism, on theological and ethical problems, on any phase of any theological or ethical problem, and the church, whether it agrees with him or not, will say, Speak, if you speak your own convictions. . . . It does not take courage to speak freely on this platform. A man would have to be a hero in cowardice to be a coward here." But a free pulpit of his own was not enough for Beecher, and for the last five years of his life he went his way unfettered even by the tenuous ties of Congregationalism—a free man with obligations to no one but himself.[22]

Sentimental, exuberant, egotistical, self-indulgent, and inconsistent as he was, Beecher became an early victim of the "debunking" school of biographers. Emphasizing with Phillips Brooks the importance of "personality" in the pulpit, he exhibited himself with much less restraint. His tastes, while no less expensive than those of Brooks, were more spectacular, including as they did a passion for driving fine horses and carrying uncut gems in his pockets. His sense of propriety was conspicuously poor. "Henry Ward Beecher's Opinion of Pears' Soap" was the heading of one of the earliest "testimonial" advertisements.

> *Cleanliness* is next to Godliness. Soap must be considered as a means of *grace* and a clergyman who recommends *moral* things—should be willing to recommend soap.
>
> I am told that my commendation of *Pears'* soap has opened for it a large sale in the *United States*.
>
> I am willing to *stand by every word in favor of it, I have ever uttered*. A man must be fastidious indeed who is not satisfied with it.

The advertising ethics of his own papers were subjected to criticism, and he was forever hailing the most recent as the best—including phrenology—with uninhibited enthusiasm. But in his own day, Beecher's great warmheartedness, genuine charm, and natural spontaneity enabled him largely to transcend the consequences of his foibles—including the unpleasant publicity occasioned by "the great divorce scandal"—and his popularity remained undiminished to the end.[23]

The great significance of Beecher, writes one of his biographers, is that he was "barometer and record" of the changes that were taking place. "He was not in advance of his day, but precisely abreast of his day." He stood forth as "a prodigious figure, not by blazing a path in any wilderness, but by the fact that his inner experience was identical with that of millions of his fellow countrymen. His gift was merely that he was articulate while they were not." By being their voice, by giving them the kind of preaching they wanted to hear, he became the most conspicuous and successful of the princes of the pulpit. Russell Conwell and Washington Gladden, each in his own way, were his successors. But the true succession was in Plymouth pulpit itself, through Lyman Abbott to Newell Dwight Hillis, both of whom reflected Beecher's uncritical and unquenchable optimism. Abbott, after Beecher himself, became the foremost popularizer in America of the essential compatibility of religion with the new scientific conclusions concerning the nature and destiny of man and human society, and Hillis sang the tune with even more sanguine assurance.

Better times are coming. Good will is taking the place of hate. Even labor and capital are becoming better friends. Peace is going to succeed war. Wealth is becoming the almoner of universal bounty. Statesmen are trying to right the wrongs of the oppressed. . . . Literature is sharpening arrows against injustice. Eloquence is redoubling its power. The galleries are being made beautiful, and are standing open by day and night for all the people. Never were the libraries filled with wiser books; the press is sowing the land with the good seed of wisdom and knowledge. God is abroad, and like his sun, his love shines on the evil and the good, on the just and the unjust. For centuries the democracy of Jesus has slowly leavened the people, but the time is not far off when with one accord every knee shall bow, and every tongue confess that Jesus Christ is Lord, to the glory of God the Father.

Abbott's preaching, like Beecher's, was topical rather than expository or textual, and it betrayed the editorial style developed during his career as a journalist. But Hillis represents the final degeneration of this tradition, for he was reduced to delivering essays on timely topics in which he would celebrate the virtues of war one Sunday and the virtues of peace the next, and would extol the aggressive acquisitiveness of the business entrepreneur the week after he had lifted a paean of praise to the simple life as exemplified in Thoreau. Hillis, probably as much as anyone else, was responsible for Moody exploding with one of his rare caustic remarks: "I'm sick and tired of this essay preaching . . . , this 'silver-tongued orator' preaching. I like to hear preachers and not wind-mills."[24]

IV

Russell H. Conwell, minister of Philadelphia's Baptist Temple, had led a varied career after his return from the Civil War. After a brief period in a law office, he became a successful newspaper publisher, and then, for the sake of his health, went abroad as an immigration agent for the State of Minnesota, seeking to lure settlers for Minnesota farmlands from the Old World by recounting the glowing opportunities for advancement to be found in the New World. Returning to Boston, he entered the publishing business once again, married a wealthy woman, and undertook to revive a run-down church in Lexington, Massachusetts. This latter venture led to his ordination, the decision to devote his full time to the ministry, and the call to Philadelphia in 1882. The Philadelphia church had a small, struggling congregation, heavily burdened with debt, but within ten years under Conwell's leadership it had a new home—the Baptist Temple—and was well on its way to becoming the largest and most famous "institutional" church in America, with a university and three hospitals numbered among its more notable progeny. The most familiar figure of the Chautauqua circuit, Conwell toured the country with his famous lecture, *Acres of Diamonds,* delivering it no less than six thousand times with total earnings, including royalties from its sale in printed form, of eight million dollars.[25]

While perhaps not the foremost clerical exponent of Andrew Carnegie's "Gospel of Wealth," Conwell was at least its chief and most conspicuous evangelist. Among the many clergymen who sanctioned the single-minded pursuit of financial gain, Conwell distinguished himself by the intensity of his fervor and his almost obsessive preoccupation with the theme. In this, he was simply focusing attention upon one item in Henry Ward Beecher's varied assortment of homiletical goods. Conwell idealized the culture and the society in which he lived no less than the others, but he was more rigidly selective in his choice of what seemed to him to be the secret of its abundant promise of continued growth and progress.

During the post-Appomattox years, Beecher had fallen in line with the prevailing satisfaction with the American economic millennium. With Phillips Brooks he had affirmed that poverty was practically nonexistent in America, but what was more significant he identified whatever poverty did exist with sin. "There may be reasons for poverty which do not involve wrong," he declared, "but looking comprehensively through city and town and village and country, the general truth will stand, that no man in this land suffers from poverty unless it be more than his fault—unless it be his sin." "Even in the most compact and closely populated portions of the East, he that will be frugal, and save continuously, living every day within the bounds of his means, can scarcely help accumulating." A few years later, in the midst of the great strike of 1877, Beecher denounced the railroad workers for not being content with the current wage rates.

It is said that a dollar a day is not enough for a wife and five or six children. No, not if the man smokes or drinks beer. It is not enough if they are to live as he would be glad to have them live. It is not enough to enable them to live as perhaps they would have a right to live in prosperous times. But is not a dollar a day enough to buy bread with? Water costs nothing; and a man who cannot live on bread is not fit to live. What is the use of a civilization that simply makes men incompetent to live under the conditions which exist?

If poverty is largely the product of sin, the obverse is equally true. Prosperity is ordinarily an indication of virtue. "Generally," said Beecher, "the proposition is true, that where you find the most religion, there you will find the most worldly prosperity—in communities, I mean; not in single persons." While stock frauds and corporate swindles might bring temporary riches to a few, these represent a threat to any permanent prosperity which must forever rest upon sound morality.[26]

The benefits which accrue from wealth were rehearsed by Beecher in a sermon on "The Deceitfulness of Riches." While warning young men of wealth's incidental temptations, he described in glowing terms the power of riches to further the cause of morality, culture, civilization, and Christian missions. With all this at stake, he concluded, we must not "inveigh against riches" or "warn young men against becoming, or desiring to become, rich." To the contrary, every encouragement should be given them and no obstacle should be placed in their way. Everyone should have full opportunity to gain wealth. There is a natural inequality in life, but there should be no inequality of opportunity. "No government has a right to thrust a strong man down to the level of weakness" and conversely it would be wrong "to force a weak man up to the level of a strong." What we need in this country, Beecher's *Independent* had asserted, are "all the Jay Cookes we have and a thousand more."[27]

To Conwell this was an intoxicating gospel and it became the lodestar of his ministry and the constant burden of his sermons. In his hands, however, it became even more crass and materialistic. The recognition of the inevitable inequality of talent and ability gave way to the conviction that anyone could get rich and ought to get rich. "I say that you ought to get rich, and it is your duty to get rich." "To secure wealth is an honorable ambition, and is one great test of a person's usefulness to others," he said over and over again.

Money is power. Every good man and woman ought to strive for power, to do good with it when obtained. Tens of thousands of men and women get rich honestly. But they are often accused by an envious, lazy crowd of unsuccessful persons of being dishonest and oppressive. I say, Get rich, get rich! But get money honestly, or it will be a withering curse.

There are things "sweeter and holier and more sacred than gold." But "the man of common sense also knows that there is not any one of those things that is not greatly enhanced by the use of money. . . . Love is the grandest thing on God's earth, but fortunate the lover who has plenty of money." It is absurd for a man to say, "I don't want money," for that is simply saying, "I do not wish to do any good to my fellowmen."[28]

No man need be a victim of circumstance, Conwell assured his congregation repeatedly. "Seek and ye shall find, knock and it shall be opened unto you." Success is not restricted to a chosen few. There are acres of diamonds everywhere for those perceptive enough to see them. "Almost any man should be able to become wealthy in this land of opulent opportunity," he declared in one sermon. "How many in this house tonight are poor people, living up to your income, with your Saturday's wages hardly covering your bills, who might just as well have been able to have drawn your check for a half million of dollars for any good cause had you chosen right or had you chosen right things at the right time?" was his question in another sermon. "Jesus said: 'Ye ought to have done these things, but ye ought not to have left undone the other things.' That is, you ought not to have spent all your time on that which was of the least consequence and left untouched that which was of the most." Success has no secret. "Any normal young man . . . is equipped fully to climb to the very heights of life." All that is needed for success is virtue—virtue defined in terms of pluck, determination, and alertness to one's opportunities.

The message I would like to leave with the young men of America is a message I have been trying humbly to deliver from the lecture platform and pulpit for more than fifty years. . . . And the message is this: your future stands before you like a block of unwrought marble. You can work it into what you will. Neither heredity, nor environment, nor any obstacle superimposed by man can keep you from marching straight through to success, provided you are guided by a firm, driving determination, and have normal health and intelligence.

"Keep clean, fight hard, pick your openings judiciously, and have your eyes forever fixed on the heights toward which you are headed," was the simple formula. Beyond this, one should seek the aid of that "mysterious potency shaping the forces of life, which if we would win we must have in our favor." Through prayer even those obstacles over which we have no control can be forced to yield.

There come to us all, events over which we have no control by physical or mental power. Is there any hope of guiding those mysterious forces? Yes, friends, there is a way of securing them in our favor or preventing them from going against us. How? It is by prayer. When a man has done all he can do, still there is a mighty, mysterious agency over which he needs influence to secure success. The only way he can reach that is by prayer.

"Men who have tried it," a kindred spirit reported, "have confidently declared that there is no sleeping partner in any business who can begin to compare with the Almighty."[29]

Wealth, of course, was a means not an end, and its purpose was to do good. A man holds the wealth he acquires as a steward of the Lord. "The good Lord gave me my money," John D. Rockefeller told the members of the first graduating class of the university to which he contributed so liberally, "and how could I withhold it from the University of Chicago?" Conwell, like Rockefeller, was a good steward to a superlative degree, pouring his money without stint into the blossoming enterprises of the church. Doing good included supporting the church, providing opportunities for the ambitious to secure an education, and creating and maintaining facilities for the care of the sick. But no sympathy was to be wasted on the poor. "In this life a man gets about what he is worth" and "the world owes a man nothing that he does not earn." "The number of poor who are to be sympathized with is very small," Conwell believed, and "to sympathize with a man whom God has punished for his sins, thus to help him when God would still continue a just punishment, is to do wrong, no doubt about it." Unfortunately, "there are some people who think that to be pious they must be very poor and very dirty," but "they are wrong." I, for one, said Conwell, "don't want to see any more of that kind of God's poor," for "when a man could have been rich just as well, and he is now weak because he is poor," you can be sure that "he has done some great wrong."[30]

At the beginning of Conwell's ministry, he believed that the church stood at the center of every man's drive for success, exhorting him to struggle and strive and aiding him with the resources of unseen power. Later he came to the conclusion that the ministry of the church must be supplemented by classes organized to provide specific skills and abilities for those who aspired to climb the ladder of wealth and power. When these classes developed into a full-fledged educational institution and as Conwell came more and more under the influence of the new science with its notion of progressive evolution, the importance of the church receded.

If the dream of the scientist or the belief of the theologian is ever realized; if the mind is to rule matter . . .; if everything psychological, geological, and astronomical is to be as plain to the mind of man as it is to the mind of God—and this is the logical sequence of continuous progress—then it appears to me, judging from history, that it will be accomplished by the aid of institutions of learning as much as by prayer and sacrifice.

But his basic convictions concerning the interrelationship of Christianity, morality, wealth, power, and social usefulness remained unchanged. Bishop Lawrence of Massachusetts summarized both the formula and the confident hope in a few well-chosen words. "In the long run, it is only to the man of morality that wealth comes. We believe in the harmony of God's universe. We know that it is only by working along his laws natural and spiritual that we can work with efficiency. . . . Godliness is in league with riches. . . . Material prosperity is helping to make the national character sweeter, more joyous, more unselfish, more Christlike."[31]

The doctrine of stewardship was grounded initially in a simple gratitude to God for his mercies, and the economic virtues of diligence, thrift, honesty, and sobriety arose as a rigorous moral discipline designed to redeem God's bounty to his service. But in the hands of Conwell and Lawrence these fundamentally ascetic convictions were exaggerated and perverted into a philosophy which sanctified the workshop materialism of the rising American industrial order. It is true, as Ralph Gabriel has pointed out, that Conwell was one of a "minority who strove to play the role of steward to the Lord to the full extent of their ability," but Daniel Drew, "master fleecer of the lambs and founder of Drew Theological Seminary," was a more typical expression of the spirit upon which Conwell conferred divine approbation. "For American Protestantism as a whole," Gabriel continues, "the gospel of wealth ... was a sign of decadence," a particularly glaring illustration of the general surrender to the spirit of the times.[32]

V

The gospel of wealth did not go unchallenged within the churches. The siren song of a society that had stumbled upon easy money was persuasive and convincing, but there were rebels among the clergy who refused to bow their knees to Baal. It was not that they ran counter to the common belief that everything would turn out all right in the end. They too for the most part, were happy believers in a new day that was about to dawn, but they were more sensitive than many of their clerical colleagues to present evils which were being dramatized for them by the rising tide of labor unrest. Among these early advocates of the "social gospel," there was no one more prominent and influential than Washington Gladden.

In 1876 Gladden published a slender volume, *Being a Christian and How to Begin,* which has been called the first book of the social gospel movement. Although the book dealt with the general nature of the Christian faith rather than with any of the specific economic and political issues with which the movement was later to be chiefly preoccupied, it did insist that Christianity was to be primarily defined in ethical terms. Being a Christian, Gladden wrote, was not to be confused with submission to certain outward rites, nor with an acceptance of a body of dogma, nor with an emotional mystical experience. To be a Christian means simply to follow Christ—"to accept as the ruling axiom of ethical conduct the command that a man shall love his neighbor as himself"—and the way to begin is just to begin. All disturbing questions of ability and inability, of election and condemnation, can be laid to one side.[33]

At the time, Gladden was minister of the North Congregational Church of Springfield, Massachusetts, having recently resigned from the editorial staff of the *Independent* because he considered its advertising policy not entirely honest. In 1882 he was called to the First Congregational Church of Columbus, Ohio, where he remained until his death thirty-six years later. Although Gladden was a distinguished and nationally famous preacher, he exercised his greatest influence through his writings. He had begun his literary career while pastor of a church at North Adams, Massachusetts, becoming a regular contributor to several journals and publishing the first of the thirty-eight books which were to come from his pen. *Plain Thoughts on the Art of Living* was the title of his first book, and during the succeeding years the "art of living" in an industrial society was to be the theme he constantly expounded in book after book—*Working People and Their Employers, The Christian League of Connecticut, Applied Christianity, Tools and the Man, The Cosmopolis City Club, Social Salvation, The Church and Modern Life*. At the same time he carried on a running skirmish in defense of the conclusions of the more recent Biblical scholarship, insisting that it was the duty of the minister to inform the people concerning the findings of the historical critics so that obstacles might be removed and the way cleared for a proper understanding of the nature of Christianity. *Burning Questions, Who Wrote the Bible?, How Much Is Left of the Old Doctrines? Present Day Theology* were some of the books by which he sought both to disarm the obscurantists and to hold the allegiance of the skeptics.

In a certain sense it may seem curious to regard Gladden as a successor to Henry Ward Beecher, but surprisingly enough many of the leaders of the social gospel acknowledged their debt to the illustrious preacher from Brooklyn. They shared the common faith of the New Theology, of course, but Beecher's rugged economic individualism would scarcely seem to suggest the humanitarian concern of the social gospel. Nevertheless, they were indebted to Beecher in two vital respects. First, true to the tradition of his father and of Charles G. Finney as well, Beecher had emphasized the duty of the preacher to discuss political and social issues. In addition to this Beecher was supremely confident that God's will could and would be done on earth. What this meant in terms of the social gospel can clearly be seen in the comment of Beecher concerning the contrast between his views and those of Dwight L. Moody. In 1875 Moody had urged Beecher to join him in evangelistic work. "We two, working together," said Moody, "could shake the continent as it never has been shaken before." Beecher, in refusing to leave his pulpit, is reported to have commented: "Mr. Moody and I could not possibly work together in such a mission. He believes that the world is lost, and he is seeking to save from the wreck as many individuals as he can. I believe that this world is to be saved, and I am seeking to bring about the Kingdom of God on earth." Beecher may have oversimplified Moody's point of view and the remark may be entirely apocryphal, but a fundamental difference between the two men did exist, and Beecher's emphasis on the Kingdom of God as a present historical possibility was eagerly appropriated by the more socially sensitive who came under his influence. To

Gladden, Beecher—in spite of his economic and social con-
servatism—stood for "the idea that Christianity gives the law
to the whole of life; that it must control our business, our
politics, our pleasures; that Jesus Christ is Lord of capital and
counting room, of factory and studio, of school and home."[34]

What was this law of Christ for the whole of life? It was
Beecher's law of love interpreted and applied by one who had
not completely excised the cross from the New Testament
and who believed with Horace Bushnell that Christ had set an
example of self-sacrifice which all mankind might reasonably
be expected to follow. It was the golden rule, the second com-
mandment, the law of brotherhood. "The one thing needful,"
Gladden declared at the fiftieth anniversary of Plymouth
Church, "is the application to all human relations of the Christian law of brotherhood." Discussing the social problems of
the future, he said:

> There is but one social question, and that is the question whether,
> "Man to man, the world o'er,
> Shall brithers be, and a' that."
>
> Just as soon as men are ready to answer that question heartily, in
> the affirmative sense, our social problems will disappear as easily
> as the August sun absorbs the morning mist.

The evils of society are all due to "nothing but the refusal to
accept the simple fact of human brotherhood, and to live in true
brotherly relations." Legislation in certain restricted areas may
help remedy a few specific abuses, but in the end all problems
—whether they be problems of taxation, monopolies, labor
strife, pauperism, crime, or democratic government—will yield
only to the effective application of the spirit of the golden rule.
"We shall never get justice done and peace established until the
law of brotherhood, instead of the law of conflict, is recognized
as the supreme law of the social order." "Take, for example,
the question of taxation," said Gladden. Many of "the evils
under which we are suffering today arise from inequitable
taxation," whereby "the honest man bears far more than his

fair share of the burdens of society." Systems of taxation must
be devised and adopted by which the tax burden shall be more
"equitably distributed and impartially enforced," but even
under the most equitable system the "strong and shrewd" will
still "contrive to evade a large part of their proper contribution." In doing so, however, "these strong and shrewd citizens"
will not be "acting the part of brothers." On the other hand,
if these men, heartily responding "in the spirit of the royal
law," would determine "to put upon his brother no part of his
own load, taxation would cease to be a problem."[35]

It was somewhat disconcerting to Gladden that, "with the
New Testament in our hands for eighteen hundred years, we
have not yet really learned to believe that friendship is better
than strife; and we still go on assuming that the society in
which each one is trying to get all he can away from everybody
else, and to give as little as he can to everybody else, is the only
normal society; that if we should turn right about and give all
we could to everybody, taking from others only that which they
could freely give, we should speedily find ourselves in the highway to ruin." It seemed curious that this could be true, for
Gladden believed that nothing could be more obvious than the
fact that brotherhood pays. It was inconceivable to think that
more "profit" was not to be secured "in helping one another
than in cheating and fighting one another."

To all right reason it is so palpable, so utterly common-sensible,
that it is cheaper and easier and safer and more profitable for
those who are working together to be friends than to be foes, to be
brothers than to be competitors—so perfectly obvious is all this
that one sometimes feels like going out with Wisdom "into the top
of the high places, beside the gates at the entry of the city . . . ,"
and crying with her: "O ye simple, understand prudence, and ye
fools, be ye of understanding heart!"

"What men call 'natural law,' by which they mean the law of
greed and strife," said Gladden, ". . . is not a natural law; it
is unnatural; it is a crime against nature; the law of brother-

hood is the only natural law. The law of nature is the law of sympathy, of fellowship, of mutual help and service."[36]

Gladden was not quite sure as to the source of the failure to recognize and heed the law of brotherhood. At one point he suggested that the "tap-root" of the difficulty was the fact that "most of our theology and our political economy has been built" on the assumption that men are "competitors" rather than "brothers"; whereas a moment or two before he had declared: "We have only to clear our minds of cant and live up to our principles; that is all. We have got the idea; our creed is sound enough; the only trouble with us is that we so imperfectly realize it." But whatever the cause of the failure, Gladden was confident that he was living "in the dawning of a better day," when men would recognize their folly and act their part as brothers.[37]

If the Christian churches were true to the ideals of their Founder, Gladden believed that they could contribute mightily to overcoming strife and conflict by inspiring genuine friendship and good will among men. He was equally convinced that they could not do so while they remained "class" institutions, divided by petty rivalries and corrosive jealousies. It was for this reason that he gave himself without stint to all projects which promised increasing interdenominational co-operation. Gladden did not doubt that an awakening would sweep the churches and that a great tide toward unity would soon set in, yet even if this expectation did not materialize and the churches remained divided and impotent, he was sure that the march of events in the world at large would convince men of the error of their ways and would usher in the day of brotherhood.

All the signs indicate that modern society is being forced by the disastrous failure of the methods of strife to entertain the possibility of cooperation as the fundamental social law. The multiplication of armaments has become not only an enormity, but a howling farce; it is impossible that the nations should go on making fools of themselves after this fashion. The industrial conflict is no less irrational.

And the terrible collapses in big business during the last decade have reduced to absurdity the scheme of the graspers. . . . And the conviction grows that the Golden Rule is, after all, the only workable rule of life; that we must learn how to live by it. This is the sign of promise.

This was 1909. "If it was ever worth while to live, it is worth while to live today. No better day than this has ever dawned on this continent." There is something "that is constantly working to make order out of casualty, beauty out of confusion, justice, kindliness, mercy out of cruelty and inconsiderate pressure," he had affirmed eight years earlier, testifying to his conviction that "what ought to be is going to be." The victory is sure.[38]

In 1893, seven years after Gladden had coined the phrase as the title for his most influential book, George D. Herron was installed in the new chair of applied Christianity at Iowa College. "The world is ruled by ideas," said Herron. "Every few centuries God drops a great idea into the soul of man." The replacement of the spirit of competition and conflict with the "rational self-love" of Gladden's law of brotherhood, did not seem to Herron to be a sufficiently radical principle to effect the transformation of society which Gladden desired. The great idea which God had implanted in Herron's mind and heart was the redemption of society through individual sacrifice, self-denial, and a cheerful bearing of another's burdens. Herron, in turn, dropped this idea into the mind and heart of Charles M. Sheldon, minister of the Central Congregational Church of Topeka, Kansas, who, through a series of parable-novels delivered initially chapter by chapter to his Sunday evening congregations, was to become the greatest popularizer of the social gospel and perhaps its most typical representative.[39]

Sheldon's first three novels—*Robert Bruce, or the Life That Now Is, Robert Hardy's Seven Days,* and *The Crucifixion of Philip Strong*—enjoyed moderate success, but the fourth was destined to win for itself a place beside *Uncle Tom's Cabin* and

Ten Nights in a Bar Room as one of the great American tracts. Within a year after its initial appearance in 1897, *In His Steps, or What Would Jesus Do?* was being printed and sold by sixteen different publishers and its total sales ultimately soared to more than fifteen million copies. In this story of the revolution which occurred in a town when the members of a single congregation resolved to live for a year in accordance with the teachings of Jesus, Sheldon proposed as the solution for all social ills the simple question: "What would Jesus do?" If each church member, whether rich or poor, when faced with a decision, would ask himself that question, said Sheldon, "could it remain true that armies of men would walk the streets for jobs, and hundreds of them curse the church, and thousands of them find in the saloon their best friend?" Nowhere is the romantic sentimentalism and utopianism which characterized the popular understanding of the social gospel more vividly expressed than in the concluding sentence of Sheldon's story. "And with a hope that walks hand in hand with faith and love, Henry Maxwell, disciple of Jesus, laid him down to sleep, and dreamed of the regeneration of Christendom and saw in his dream a church of Jesus 'without spot or wrinkle or any such thing,' following Him all the way, walking obediently in His steps."[40]

VI

Where is the unity to be found in figures as diverse as these princes of the pulpit who dominated the American religious scene during the closing years of the nineteenth century? Surprisingly enough, it is to be found in their beliefs—their common assumptions concerning God, man, and society—rather than in their ethical attitudes and practices. This is surprising because of the unanimity with which they emphasized disposition and conduct as the essence of religion. The purpose of their insistence upon what Beecher called devotional and practical religion as opposed to an intellectual or academic faith, of course, was to ease their departure from the grim tenets of their inherited creeds and to facilitate an adjustment to a new set of convictions which reflected the general satisfaction with things as they were or as they were about to become. It might be the "inspired, sanctified, common sense of enterprising business men" which was operating to make the world more Christlike or it might be Gladden's inexorable march of events which would serve to usher in the day of enlightened self-interest and brotherhood, but the basic confidence was the same. The new creed was authoritative only in a negative sense. It ruled out all notions of human inability and divine wrath, but beyond this the only demand was for sincerity and good intentions.

Happy believers in divine benevolence and human goodness, who invested the realm of nature, including man, with intrinsic tendencies toward redemption (quite independently of grace through Christ, except as he was present "in the spirit of the world" or in "the compulsion to co-operate"), the majority of the preachers of the New Theology found it difficult to conceive of a church which did not embrace humanity indiscriminately. With Daniel Dorchester, they believed that the mission of Christianity was largely accomplished. The world had been "softened and shaded" by Christianity "to her own likeness," and the contrast between the church and the world had almost disappeared because Christianity had so "largely transformed Christendom morally, intellectually, and socially." Thus, "in defiance of all history," observes Commager, "they explained away the Devil and ignored Sin and, in the words of Dean Sperry, 'struck straight for the ultimate optimism in neglect of that preliminary pessimism which the great religions of the world have all presupposed as their premise.' " It was as if God had been "naturalized" and invited, as it were, "to give a weekly editorial commentary" on the vagaries of a society, in the image of which he had been made.[41]

CHAPTER IX

THE CHURCH EMBRACES THE WORLD: *Protestantism Succumbs to Complacency*

By every test but that of influence the church had never been stronger than it was at the opening of the twentieth century, and its strength increased steadily. Everyone was a Christian, and almost everyone joined some church, though few for reasons that would have earned them admission to Jonathan Edwards' Northampton congregation. . . . Never before had the church been materially more powerful or spiritually less effective. HENRY STEELE COMMAGER[1]

"Protestant Christianity entered the nineteenth century on a rising tide," reports Kenneth Scott Latourette, and it came to the end of the century "on a rapidly ascending curve."[2] The momentum of almost two hundred years of vigorous advance had not yet been expended, and the first two decades of the new century found Protestantism at the peak of its strength and influence. These were the halcyon days. Churches were crowded, at least in the cities; costly edifices were being built; programs were proliferating; the moral order of society, in public esteem if not always in practice, was unquestioned; a broad range of humanitarian concerns elicited widespread interest and generous support; and on occasion when an issue was clearly drawn the Christian conscience spoke with an authority which was decisive in party councils. Never before had the churches been able to boast of such a large portion of the population being listed upon their membership rolls, and never before had the members of the churches been so busy—

serving in social settlements, organizing boys' clubs, joining sewing classes, attending "open forums," and conducting campaigns. It was an era of crusades—"movements" they were called—which served to channel the unusual moral idealism and superabundance of zeal generated by the churches into the promotion of a host of good causes. But, within little more than two decades, the churches were on the defensive and were soon to begin a full-scale retreat.

Nothing is more striking than the astonishing reversal in the position occupied by the churches and the role played by religion in American life which took place before the new century was well under way. By the nineteen twenties, the contagious enthusiasm which had been poured into the Student Volunteer Movement, the Sunday School Movement, the Men and Religion Forward Movement, the Laymen's Missionary Movement, the Interchurch World Movement, and other organized activities of the churches had largely evaporated. The two self-denying ordinances of church attendance and Sabbath observance which had long given eloquent testimony to the strength and influence of religious faith in national life were no longer sustained and enforced by the moral conscience of the community. Habits of temperance and sobriety, inculcated by the churches for over a century, disappeared almost overnight. Family devotions survived in most homes only as a childhood memory, grace before meals became increasingly rare, and a rapidly mounting divorce rate gave mute evidence of the disintegration of the Christian family. Religion, which had been one of the principal subjects of serious and intelligent discussion in the literary monthlies and quarterlies, now became consipicuous by its absence, and was usually resurrected only to serve as a target for the satirical shafts of a Mencken. Even as late as 1950, when religion was beginning to receive some wistful attention in "cultural" circles, the *Partisan Review*'s symposium, *Religion and the Intellectuals,* included only one representative out of twenty-nine who could be regarded as standing clearly within the Protestant tradition. Such weighting would have been unthinkable and impossible as late as the second decade of the century, for that generation was only a few years removed from the time when philosophy as the handmaiden of religion was the exclusive preserve of the clergy and political economy—economics, sociology, and political science—was still being taught as a branch of natural theology.

Apart from the fading compulsion to be numbered among the churchgoers and the increasing surrender of church members to the temptations of the automobile, the country club, or a late Sunday morning breakfast, the most vivid illustration of the change which had taken place is to be found in the colleges and universities. Throughout the nineteenth century the president of almost every important college and university was a clergyman, but by the fourth decade of the twentieth century no clergyman occupied the presidential chair of any leading institution of learning. Even among denominational schools the tendency was well established by the twenties to look elsewhere than among the clergy for presidential timber. The predominance of ministers on college faculties disappeared with equal suddenness, and distinctly religious concerns were relegated to the periphery of campus life. As the various disciplines became autonomous, textbooks took on a different character. Sociological texts, which in the early years of the century were primarily concerned with the scientific application of religious principles to society, now exhibited an interest in religion only as a subject of sociological study and analysis. Colleges almost universally up to 1900 and perhaps for a few years thereafter had been accustomed to report the number of "pious" among the students; two decades later most of them would have had difficulty defining the term. Denominational colleges, of course, continued to exist, but the significance of their religious heritage became increasingly difficult to identify and no longer were they able to claim more than a fraction of the 80 per cent of the total student population which had been theirs during the eighties and nineties. The most revealing aspect of this revolution in higher education is the fact that the clergy were such willing participants in the introduction of the new order, extending aid and consent even when the stronger denominational colleges and universities began to cut the tenuous ties which bound them to the churches and to affirm their independence of any specific religious tradition. No new institutions were established to replace those which had been lost and the weaker denominational colleges which remained were left to eke out a meager existence with dwindling support.

So far as most of the outward manifestations were concerned, the years immediately following the signing of the armistice in 1918 were the years which marked the collapse of Protestantism as a dynamic force in American life. It would be plausible to suggest that this was the result of the new social forces which had been released in the post-Versailles era. Certainly there were new problems which made the task of the churches more difficult, but no recognition of the difficulties which the churches faced can obscure how ill-prepared they were to discharge their responsibilities and maintain their position in society. It is scarcely an exaggeration to say that the failure of the churches to resist the tide of secularism was due much more to inner weakness than to any external circumstance. Long before the days of Harding "normalcy" and Coolidge "prosperity," the churches were in process of becoming secular institutions, carried forward by the impetus of past achievements and reflecting all too clearly in their own life the prevailing cultural and social tendencies of the time.

I

While it is true that the period from 1890 through World War I represents the peak of Protestant influence and activity in America, these years also constituted the great testing period which was to determine whether the vigorous advance of the past century was to continue into the new century. At the time there seemed little reason to doubt that the advance would continue, but from the perspective of half a century it is apparent that the continuing forward tide was only the unspent momentum of older impulses which were still exerting their influence through custom, habit, and lingering moral sentiment. Curiously enough, during the very decades when the churches were displaying such remarkable resourcefulness in their attempt to reach and to claim the urban population for the Christian faith, the nerve which impelled them was being cut.

Even before the churches had attained the summit of their prestige and activity, there were indications that a counter tendency had set in. As early as the eighteen eighties a few isolated voices were expressing grave misgivings concerning the continuing strength of the churches. Despite outward signs of prosperity and influence, a small minority detected what seemed to them clear evidence of decline. The crowded churches they regarded as deceptive, for it was not difficult to assemble a large congregation at a time when the population of Brooklyn, for example, had increased during Beecher's ministry alone from sixty thousand to half a million. More significant than the crowded churches was the fact, which Josiah Strong pointed out, that by 1890 the large cities had only half as many Protestant churches in proportion to the population as they had had in 1840. And Bryce, ever sensitive to changing currents, acknowledged that, while churchgoing remained a habit among the large portion of the citizens, it was not keeping pace with the growth of population. Nor was the problem restricted to the cities. A survey of the rural areas of New York State in 1888 revealed many districts where "churches which once were vigorous, thoroughly organized, active, influential, have become, so far as the congregations are concerned, disintegrated and the buildings which once contained them are falling into ruins."[3]

The decline in church attendance which did not become perceptible to the public consciousness until the end of the Wilson administration was accompanied by other disturbing symptoms in the eighties and nineties. As the end of the century approached Bryce noted that the interest of the ordinary person in theological questions was less keen, knowledge of the Bible more limited, and observance of the Sabbath less strict. Most of the leading newspapers were publishing Sunday editions, theaters were beginning to give Sunday performances, and the habit of "resorting to places of public amusement on Sunday" was increasing. Equally significant was what J. M. Buckley described as "the decline and almost total disappearance of discipline in the churches." A leading Methodist editor who was to be counsel for the defense in Borden P. Bowne's trial for heresy, Buckley was deeply disturbed by the laxity which was beginning to prevail.

A half century ago the trial and expulsion of members guilty of immoral conduct was a frequent occurrence, but now it is rare. Only when a member of a church has been guilty of an act intrinsically odious as well as sinful, when public attention has been directed to it and the press has perhaps discussed the character and conduct of the person, only under such circumstances does what is properly called church discipline take place. . . . Not only is this the case, but it is known and it gives "great occasion to the enemies of God to blaspheme," that men of large wealth, however obtained, if they are lavish in its distribution, have no difficulty in finding ministers of the gospel to flatter them and in every possible way to elevate them, so far as their influence can do it, in the communities in which they live.

Not only is this true, said Buckley, but "distinguished" ministers had begun to deliver eloquent discourses designed "to show that there is no place in the Christian church for discipline."[4]

To at least one churchman of the eighties, the barely perceptible outward signs of decline and disintegration were symptoms of an inner decay and weakness in the life of the churches, and he traced this inner decay and weakness to the secularizing tendency—the easing of the tension between the church and the world—of the New Theology. In his book, *Certain Dangerous Tendencies in American Life*, J. B. Harrison observed that, while the nominal faith of the country, in its creeds and symbols, remained unchanged, "the real religion of the people" had become, to a very large extent, "a decorous worldliness." From the vantage point of a Unitarian parsonage, Harrison noted that "the formal observances of religion depended largely upon habit." "Many ministers and multitudes of the more intelligent members of the churches," he continued, "had become skeptical in regard to some of the cardinal doctrines of popular Christianity," and "these doctrines were, in the preaching of the time, habitually so softened and accommodated to the growing doubt that nearly all their original meaning was explained away." Consequently, a "new tide of worldliness rose everywhere and submerged to a great extent a church which it found open and without defense against the flood." In what were to be remarkably prophetic words, Harrison concluded: "There is yet . . . a large amount of moral force and healthful life in the church. Religion is not extinct. But the really significant fact here is that it is constantly losing ground."[5]

In a very real sense the churches had become victims of their own success. They had succeeded in creating a culture that was recognizably Christian, and now—proud of their achievements and pleased that their mission had been so largely accomplished—the churches relaxed and made peace with the world. The progression which followed was clear and remorseless—discipline disappeared, evangelistic fervor faded, faith lost its force, and the churches, living at peace with the world, lost their sense of a distinct and specific vocation in society and devoted their energies to social activities, humanitarian enterprises, and the building of costly edifices.

From satisfaction with the culture, it had been but a small step to the placing of confidence in the power of the culture to nurture and sustain the Christian faith—a step which was formalized during the eighteen eighties by the rise of the New Theology. But even a reasonably Christian culture is, by its very nature, more extensive and complex than the faith it reflects, and it inevitably includes many elements at variance with or hostile to that faith. These elements the churches, no longer possessing an independent perspective of their own, were now to find themselves powerless to resist. Thus, in the words of Francis P. Miller, "a process which began with a culture molded by religious faith" was to end "with a religious faith molded by a national culture."[6] The churches, succumbing to complacency, had embraced the world.

Apart from the decline of church discipline, the most conspicuous result of the surrender to complacency and the easing of the tension between the churches and the world was the loss of evangelistic fervor. The waning of evangelism was due to several factors. For one thing, the optimistic view of human nature which became the principal dogma in the creed of the New Theology served to undercut the evangelistic impulse. William James, in his analysis of the conversion experience, pointed out that the indispensable prerequisite to conversion is "an uneasiness, the sense that there is *something wrong about us*."[7] But it was precisely this "wrongness" that the New Theology was unwilling to admit in any fundamental sense, and this fact was made evident to the community at large when church discipline was allowed to lapse.

The zeal for evangelism also withered because of the role assigned to the church in the New Theology. If man is naturally religious with his deepest desires in harmony with the divine intentions,* if the culture itself serves to nurture the natural Christian graces resident in every human heart, and if the church, indeed Christianity itself, can claim no special revelation apart from the natural order, then the church becomes at best incidental to the work of redemption. The saving grace of God operates quite as effectively outside the churches as within them. In fact, it was widely held by many of the clergy that the churches more often than not hindered rather than helped in the work of redemption, an attitude that was expressed by the quip attributed to the devil in a popular story of the time. When one of the devil's agents, so went the story, complained that he could not make any headway against the Christian faith, the devil was said to have replied: "Then organize it." It was no mere coincidence that the most influential textbook of the New Theology, William Newton Clarke's *Outline of Systematic Theology,* omitted altogether any discussion of the church. If someone had thought to ask him the reason for the omission, he undoubtedly would have replied, for reasons we shall presently examine, that the proper place to discuss the church was in sociology, not theology. If there was no need for an individual to make a sharp break with the past in terms of a conversion experience, there was still less urgency connected with church membership. There might be reasons why a person should join a church but they had little to do with his soul's salvation.

Above all, the churches were diverted from the task of evangelism because they believed the real need to be elsewhere. To revert once more to the familiar premises of the New Theology, if a man is naturally religious and the culture or the so-

* Lyman Abbott put into a syllogism the most widely accepted explanation of the naturalness of religion: "It is natural to love. . . . If religion is love, then religion is natural" (*The New Puritanism,* 62). This was to become, of course, the basic theological assumption of progressive religious education shortly after the turn of the century—the "love-impulse," present in the child at birth, being the "tap-root" out of which the Christian life grows (*Protestant Thought in the Twentieth Century,* ed. A. S. Nash, 234).

ciety operates to develop the natural Christian graces, the absence of those graces in an individual indicates a defect, not
in the individual, but in the culture or the society. Washington
Gladden rejoiced that the "conversion of sinners" was no longer
"supposed to be the preacher's main business," and Edward
Judson, son of the famous missionary to Burma and a distinguished Baptist minister, declared: "The important thing is
not the building up of a church but the Christianization of
society." Graham Taylor was confident that "the world can be
saved if the church does not save it," and he was equally positive that the church could guarantee its continued existence
only by becoming an effective agency of social reform and social service and thus speed the adjustments which were needed
in an evolving but as yet imperfect society.[8]

There was a difference of opinion, to be sure, as to the extent to which the present society needed to be reformed.
Phillips Brooks and Russell Conwell were largely content to
take their stand with things pretty much as they were, while
Washington Gladden and Graham Taylor were convinced that
major reforms were necessary. In between the two extremes
were large numbers interested in particular reforms as universal panaceas for the ills of society—the elimination of un-
employment, poverty, illiteracy, crime, vice, political corruption, and irreligion by the suppression of the liquor traffic, or
the achievement of similar results by giving the vote to women.
The various programs for social reform were supplemented by
the meeting of more immediate human needs—recreational,
educational, medical, and economic—and in this area there
was greater unanimity of opinion concerning what needed to
be done. There might be a question in the minds of some as
to whether the saloons should be regulated or outlawed, but
all could unite in providing "public ice-water fountains" to
slake the thirst of those who otherwise might be tempted to
enter the swinging doors.

The most vivid illustration as to where the real need was

considered to be is to be found in the reaction of the churches to the findings of a survey of the fifteenth assembly district in Manhattan which was conducted in 1897 by the Federation of Churches and Christian Workers of New York City. It was found that in an area containing some forty thousand persons, approximately one-half neither belonged to nor attended any church, and the ten Protestant churches in the area had a total membership of only 1,798, with but seven pastors and two visitors. The churches responded with vigor and enthusiasm to the needs which had been revealed, and two years later the result of "the organized intelligence and love of our churches" having been brought to bear upon the situation was reported. Kindergartens, clubs, and cooking schools had been started, public baths opened, libraries and a new park established, and "one of the most active and successful industrial settlements in the city" organized.[9]

Self-conscious and ill-at-ease, no longer possessing a sense of distinctive vocation of their own, the churches were proceeding to demonstrate their social utility in terms of the contribution they could make to a variety of socially desirable ends. In 1907 these efforts were rewarded by a formal recognition of their new status as a significant social agency, for in that year the American Academy of Political and Social Science devoted an entire issue of its *Annals* to "The Social Work of the Church." By shifting the focus of their concern, the churches had won for themselves a place in society which even the "scientists" were willing to acknowledge. In this very issue of the *Annals,* however, Edward Judson had expressed a disquieting thought concerning the new course which they were following: "Social problems are so difficult and so fascinating that they easily absorb all a minister's time and energy. He neglects his study and the care of his flock. He loses his priestly character and becomes a mere social functionary."[10] Far from presenting the claims of Christianity to the community, the minister in such a situation becomes the spokesman for the community in voicing its needs, and the church, finding its primary orientation in service to the community rather than in service to God, takes its place among other social institutions created by society to serve its needs.

II

The loss of evangelistic fervor in the churches which accompanied their fading sense of a distinctive vocation in the world and the consequent acceptance of the role of a social agency was reflected almost immediately in the marked shift which took place in the character of the instruments which had been devised to win adherents to the Christian faith and members for the churches. Revivalism, to be sure, was in growing disrepute, but revivalism was by no means the sole recruiting technique by which the churches had sought to maintain and perpetuate themselves as voluntary institutions. For almost half a century the churches had been experimenting with real success in the development of alternative methods to the older revivalism, the most notable of which were the Young Men's Christian Association, the Institutional church, the city mission, and the Sunday School. Each of these agencies, which had been functioning vigorously and effectively as the nineteenth century moved toward its close, underwent radical transformation after the turn of the century as all of them adjusted their programs to coincide with the tenets of the New Theology.

The Young Men's Christian Association provides the most striking illustration of the change which took place. An organization of young men dedicated to the winning of other young men to Christ, the Y.M.C.A. had been the most dynamic agency of the churches during the latter half of the century. In their enthusiasm these young men had extended their activities to include an attempt to reach—through prayer meetings, street preaching, tract distribution, and mission Sunday Schools—the total urban population. The local associations did provide recreational facilities, reading rooms, dormitories, and employment services, but these were subordinate to and found their justification only in terms of their relationship to the basic evangelistic purpose of the movement. As early as 1890, however, Graham Taylor was asserting that the primary task of the movement was not evangelistic but "preoccupying and preventive." From an organization *of* young men, the Y.M.C.A. was now transformed into an organization *for* young men with the major emphasis being placed upon the meeting of their recreational needs. After 1900 the "Evangelical Test" as a basis for membership in local associations became increasingly a dead letter and the distinctively religious phases of the program began quietly to disappear. By 1923 a distinguished leader in the movement was able to announce that this creed had changed from "I believe in God" to "I believe," and by 1930, in the absence of any distinctly Christian presuppositions to their program, Y.M.C.A. workers were being urged to study Walter Lippmann's *Preface to Morals* and John Dewey's *Quest for Certainty,* supposedly to provide a philosophical undergirding for their varied activities. Instruction in bond-selling, real-estate promotion, dancing, card-playing, gardening, and interior decoration became the staple fare of the Y's educational program, and members were enlisted on "the fervent plea that summer rates are cheaper and every man should enjoy a swimming pool."[11]

A similar transition was taking place in the program of the Institutional churches. Advocated initially as a recruiting technique which would enable urban churches to survive in areas of deterioration where the population was highly mobile and largely unchurched, the "institutional" program soon became an end in itself. During the early years when the evangelistic concern remained central, the Institutional churches enjoyed amazing success, multiplying their membership with astonishing rapidity, but when they began to fall in line with the new theological temper, discarding the evangelistic features of their program and devoting themselves almost exclusively to social service, their membership dwindled as rapidly as it had increased. Social work alone attracted few recruits. "The minister who engages in social work in order to build up his own church," Edward Judson acknowledged with some dismay, "is doomed to disappointment."[12] Neither Judson nor any of the other leaders of the movement, however, suggested that the Institutional church program should be abandoned; they contended that it should be justified on the basis of meeting human needs rather than in terms of securing converts. This was a laudable purpose but scarcely relevant to the fundamental objective which the program had been designed to serve. Far from being a means of maintaining and securing support for a religious ministry in the central city areas, Institutional churches now became agencies which others had to maintain and support.

In the beginning the Institutional churches had been supported by members of their own congregations, but the new policy upon which these churches embarked resulted in a dwindling membership and the death of two or three of the more substantial contributors always created a serious financial problem. When this occurred, having failed to replace the older members and thus to provide a new source of congregational support, the Institutional churches were forced to become "missions" supported from sources outside their own congregation. The acceptance of the status of a "mission," however, did not imply a resumption of evangelistic activity, for mission work had been undergoing an evolution similar to that of the Y.M.C.A. and the Institutional church. The city missions were no longer necessarily evangelistic centers for they too were being transformed into social agenices. "A decreasing emphasis upon a specific church program and intensification of efforts to help the immigrant worker in the struggle for economic security and social recognition," a study sponsored by the Institute of Social and Religious Research was to conclude, "suggest themselves as the most constructive items on the future program of mission work."[13]

Even in terms of church extension the older vigorous advance was arrested by the withering of evangelistic concern. The earlier spirit is nowhere more vividly expressed than in the response which C. C. McCabe of the Methodist Church Extension Society made to the taunt of Robert G. Ingersoll that "the churches are dying out all over the land." Upon reading Ingersoll's comment in the newspaper, McCabe dispatched a telegram which read:

Dear Robert: "All hail the power of Jesus' name"—we are building more than one Methodist Church for every day in the year, and propose to make it two a day! C. C. McCabe.

The incident caught the imagination of the church people and "Chaplain" McCabe went from ocean to ocean singing:

> The infidels, a motley band,
>   In council met and said:
> "The churches die all through the land,
>   The last will soon be dead."
> When suddenly a message came,
>   It filled them with dismay:
> "All hail the power of Jesus' name!"
>   We're building two a day.

In the twentieth century, however, the church extension societies began a program of retrenchment, in spite of the fact that the population was rapidly mounting and no less mobile. "After the first great era of suburban development," reports Hermann N. Morse, "the old-line denominations began to clam up so far as church extension was concerned. For thirty years after around 1910 they dissolved or merged many more churches than they organized."[14]

It was in the Sunday School, however, that the most crucial surrender was made, for the Sunday School was the agency upon which the churches chiefly relied to replace revivalism as a means by which people could be won to Christ, the churches perpetuated on a voluntary basis, and the influence of the Christian faith exerted in society. Both historically and in practice the Sunday School program was divided into two distinct areas—the children's school which embraced those under fifteen (Beginners, Primary, Junior, and Intermediate departments), and the adult classes which were primarily designed for those age groups subsequently classified as young people and young adults.

Traditionally the Sunday School was almost exclusively a children's school, and adult classes became widespread only after revivalism had begun to decline. The great impetus to adult work came from the "organized class" movement, a highly perfected and carefully devised instrument of evangelism. After 1910, however, it was apparent that the organized classes were losing their evangelistic zeal and were becoming social groups which existed more and more for the sake of the fellowship which they provided and the activities—class parties, baseball teams, entertainments—which they sponsored. Too often the Sunday morning class sessions tended to become either perfunctory or pervaded by the "service club" spirit and were frequently characterized by a ceaseless quest for new topics which would hold the interest of the members. The next decade witnessed a precipitate decline in adult class attendance, and by the nineteen thirties the Sunday Schools had largely reverted to the status of a children's school, with difficulty being experienced in holding the Intermediates.*

By 1903 the children's departments of the Sunday School had become an object of concern to the proponents of the New

---

* The Sunday evening young people's programs—the Christian Endeavor Societies, the Epworth Leagues, the Baptist Young People's Unions, and the Westminster Fellowships—pursued a course and experienced a fate similar to that of the organized classes. There was the same emphasis upon social and recreational activities, the same restless search for lively topics for discussion, and the same dwindling of response.

Theology. In that year William Rainey Harper, president of the University of Chicago, enlisted the interest of a distinguished group of religious leaders in the formation of the Religious Education Association whose purpose was to encourage and assist the Sunday Schools to utilize "progressive" methods of instruction. The familiar indictment that progressive religious education was "strong on technique but weak on content," "more concerned with method than with substance," is scarcely an accurate characterization of the movement. There was content, as H. Shelton Smith has clearly demonstrated,[15] but the content was that of the New Theology which insisted that religion was both natural and normal. Consequently, to permit the educational "experience" to be determined by the immediate interests and capacities of the child rather than to have it defined by any specific body of truth which the churches might be thought to possess, was the sure means by which truly religious personalities would be nurtured and brought to maturity. The emphasis in the Sunday School, therefore, quite rightly should be placed upon one's relationship to society rather than upon one's relationship to God, for it is only out of a growing social experience in which the child makes a happy and satisfying adjustment to his fellows that religious values emerge and the natural religious impulses are developed. Thus George A. Coe, the ablest and most influential figure in the Religious Education Association, noted with dismay in his later years the belated "scramble to get more of God into religious teaching." The educational weakness of this approach, he felt, was that it seeks "to lug God in at the very beginning of the teaching process and will not let God grow out of an experimental pupil-teacher quest for growing values." While an Episcopal bishop might complain that his child was learning to draw airplanes and trucks in Sunday School and had to go to day school in order to learn hymns, many progressive religious educators would not have been unduly disturbed by such a situation, for they would have contended that the day schools

—even without hymns in their music classes—were stimulating and cultivating, frequently more effectively than the Sunday Schools, the growth processes of normal life which are the creative source of true religious experience. Decision Day which had been the focal point of the Sunday School program was quietly discarded. In place of decision, the emphasis was now upon "growth" and "continuous becoming."[16]

There were, to be sure, many values in the new educational approach. It successfully combatted the notion that the Christian life could be achieved by a single transaction, a single decision, or a single experience. It emphasized the importance of what an earlier generation would have called growth in grace, and it implied the need for a perpetual repentance even on the part of those who might justifiably lay claim to the name of Christian. The understanding of the nature and workings of human personality was vastly increased. The methods of instruction were also immeasurably improved and the memorization of such irrelevant facts as the specifications of Solomon's temple began to disappear. The emphasis upon the necessity of relating the Christian faith to the actual issues of life was all clear gain. And, finally, it must be remembered that the practice was often much better than the theory. While any normative authority of the Christian revelation might be denied by some of the theologians of the movement, still the Bible continued to be the staple fare of instruction and a majority of the teachers still drew upon the resources of a less indefinite faith.

On the other hand, the long-term tendency of the progressive religious education movement was to persuade the individual that there was no fundamental contradiction between his own desires and the demands of God, and the net effect was to leave the individual conscience undisturbed and untroubled by any deep-seated conviction of sin. Moreover, with the advent of the new emphasis upon a "student-centered" rather than a "content-centered" curriculum, the day of the "professional" had arrived. The task of teaching in terms of the materials which were now provided was much more difficult and far more complicated. No longer could a teacher have recourse to the clear, definite, and unmistakable statements of a catechism. The goals which now were to be sought were both subtle and intangible, and mastery of the new techniques and methods demanded the skills of the professionally trained. The larger churches hired directors of religious education; state and city directors were employed by denominational and interdenominational agencies; and departments to train them were established in the theological seminaries. But the Sunday Schools could not shed entirely their amateur or lay character. Unlike the public schools, few churches could afford a full staff of professionally trained teachers and almost universally the actual classroom responsibilities were left in the hands of lay volunteers. For a few brief years Sunday School work continued to evoke a measure of enthusiasm, but as the importance assigned to specifically religious instruction declined it was increasingly difficult to find persons of real ability who were willing to devote time and energy to Sunday School teaching. More often than not, they were secured, but it was not an easy task. The theory demanded an activity program and in too many instances the Sunday School program degenerated into an effort to keep the more obstreperous busy and occupied. Actually, of course, the practice had antedated the theory. J. M. Buckley, viewing the impact of the New Theology, had complained as early as 1889 that the test of a successful Sunday School superintendent was rapidly becoming a question of his ability "to give the children and the young people a good time."[17]

Buckley's observation can be defended as illustrating the general drift that had set in, but it must not be allowed to obscure the corresponding truth that the Sunday Schools did not completely abdicate their former responsibilities. Indeed, they provided in large part the sole remaining evangelistic outreach of the churches. The theory may have been faulty and the content meager, but the surprising fact is that the Sunday Schools continued, as well as they did, to impart knowledge of the Christian past, to awaken devotion, and to nurture Christian character—ample evidence of the essential healthy-mindedness and Christian spirit of many of those who engaged in Sunday School work. Nevertheless, the Sunday Schools were suffering from a deep-seated malady which could not be ignored and which ultimately was to force a complete re-examination of the educational theory and practice of the churches.

III

The fading of the older evangelistic impulse did not mean that the churches were not concerned with preserving their own institutional life. No institution willingly accepts its own demise. Furthermore, if the churches were to serve as effective instruments of social reform and social service, their membership had to be maintained. And, while classification as a social agency was gladly accepted by many of the churches, there was a strong conviction that in one respect at least they were something more than that. The one distinctive vocation of the church in society was to bear witness to the essential oneness of humanity. The church could and should be a center of fellowship which would give visible expression to the fundamental unity of mankind. The problem was to get the people into the church so that the oneness of humanity—the brotherhood of man—might be made evident to the community at large. Discipline, of course, could be relaxed. An indiscriminate welcome into the fellowship of the church could be extended to all members of the community. The errant and the wayward need not be excluded from the fold. But the relaxation of discipline in itself would scarcely draw people into the church's fellowship. A positive program to enlist interest and participation was necessary. The basic presuppositions of the older evangelism having been rejected and the familiar instruments of recruiting church members largely diverted to other ends, new techniques had to be devised.

Of particular concern to many churchmen at the turn of the century was the widening gulf which existed between the church and the workingman. The laboring classes were being lost and there was widespread discussion as to how this tide might be reversed. No better illustration of the confused mind of the church exists than the suggestions which were made as to the means by which the gap between the worker and the church might be bridged and the laboring men won back to the church. One might expect the proposal of a mission to workers somewhat analogous to the Seamen's Friend Societies of the nineteenth century or to the subsequent lay apostolate to workers among Roman Catholics, but the proposals that were made were much less direct. Graham Taylor suggested that "open forums" on Sunday evenings to discuss social issues would be of real help. C. B. Thompson acknowledged that ministers owed a spiritual responsibility to both rich and poor and ought generally remain impartial in disputes between capital and labor so that the church might maintain its status as an inclusive institution, yet, in view of the present alienation of the laboring man and because his lot was the more difficult one, ministers might do well to champion occasionally the workingman's cause. William M. Balch proposed that representatives of labor be invited to speak before the men's brotherhoods of the churches, that study groups be formed to discuss the industrial problem, and that churches should endeavor to be "uncompromisingly democratic." Charles Stelzle, minister of New York's Labor Temple urged that Labor Day Sunday be observed, that ministers should deliver distinctly social messages in a prophetic spirit, and that "institutional" programs should be developed to meet the specific needs of the working class.[18]

Apart from the specific expedients advocated as a means of winning the laboring man to the church, the more typical approach to the problem of recruiting members was the utilization of the principle of the "added attraction." Entertainments, sociables, broom drills, debating and literary societies were among the early devices that were employed, and they were followed by the organization of sewing circles, women's auxiliaries, men's brotherhoods, athletic teams, and amateur theatricals. More and more congregations began to compete with one another in terms of the size and elegance of their church buildings and furnishings. The more prosperous churches began to specify that gymnasiums, bowling alleys, and social halls be included in the plans for their new edifices, even when the Y.M.C.A. and the public school, to say nothing of neighboring congregations, had already provided these facilities for the community. Constant efforts were made to "dress up" the services in order to make them more appealing. Sermons were shortened, pulpit gowns appeared, and the ancient prayer books and liturgies were raided to give the congregation something to do, although "in reciting the ancient formulations" the worshipper was not necessarily supposed to accept "the ideas he utters." In the more fashionable churches well-trained professional soloists, quartettes, and choirs had early been employed, and in these churches, Bryce tells us, "the congregation would not think of spoiling the performance by joining in the singing."[19]

A more systematic and forthright attempt to sell religion and fill the pews was initiated by a group of businessmen who had organized the Men and Religion Forward Movement in 1911 for the purpose of conducting a nationwide campaign to "find 3,000,000 men missing in participation in church life" and to double the enrollment of all men's Bible classes. "Going after Souls on a Business Basis" was the title of an article in *Collier's Weekly* which applauded as well as described the campaign. Religion, the organizers of the movement were convinced, could be sold, for it produces tangible benefits—honesty in government, obedience to law, sobriety, social tranquillity, and world peace. And they proceeded to sell it, with all the brisk efficiency, detailed organization, and sales technique which they had mastered in the marts of trade. "Enlistment of men in the program of Jesus as the world program of daily affairs" was their slogan. Basing the campaign on the premise that "the army of the Lord moves on its stomach," dinner meetings were scheduled from coast to coast. Each local effort was preceded by a flood of publicity and a Period of Preparation. Then speakers and specialists arrived for an intensive eight-day campaign. The Follow-up Period ended with a Conservation Day. The Men and Religion Movement did get results, according to Gaius Glenn Atkins. "It increased church attendance and membership, 'decreased vulgarity and profanity,' reclaimed backsliders and widened the social vision of the churches." But by 1914 its energy was spent. In contrast to the earlier evangelistic efforts of the churches, its continuing impact was not great.[20]

IV

The decline of discipline and the waning of evangelistic zeal were not the only symptoms which testified to the steady secularization of the churches. Equally significant was the relinquishment by the churches of any sense of responsibility for the intellectual life. The most clear-cut evidence of the intellectual retreat of the churches was their growing conviction that they had no real stake in the field of higher education. Denominational colleges and universities which the churches had maintained through long years of struggle, sacrifice, and careful stewardship were now surrendered without protest into the custody and service of the general community. This abdication was a third major consequence of the acceptance of the New Theology.

Someone has remarked that after Jonathan Edwards the American churches did not produce a single first-rate Christian thinker, but the force of this observation must be qualified by the recognition that the American people were not much addicted to philosophy and that with the exception of Edwards they had not produced a first-rate thinker of any kind, in the exact sense of the term. During the greater portion of their history, Americans had been too busy subduing a continent and building a nation to be able to devote much time to reflection, but what thinking had been done was Christian thinking carried on within the general framework of the inherited faith and drawing upon the resources of past systematic intellectual formulations. Over the years, to be sure, a loosening had taken place at many points within the predominant intellectual system, but few denied the fundamental importance of religious presuppositions or challenged the validity of a Christian orientation in scholarly pursuits. In the twentieth century this point of view was completely altered, and the ideal of the Christian scholar was replaced by the concept of independent "scientists"—social, physical, biological—pursuing their investigations in autonomous fields of inquiry unhampered by any religious commitment. This new scholarly ideal was both welcomed and sanctified by the New Theology.

It is something of a paradox that a movement which professedly sought to gain intellectual respectability for the churches should have constituted an anti-intellectual force, yet this was precisely the role of the New Theology. How this totally unintended and unexpected outcome developed can readily be understood. Under the impact of the serious intellectual problems raised by the newer scientific thought and Biblical studies, a segment of religious leadership had begun to retreat into "a defensive, armor-clad system" which sought to imprison the mind of the church in a rigid orthodoxy and make impossible any attempt to rethink theological questions in the light of modern knowledge. But what began as a greatly needed and honest effort to counter the retreat into a rigid orthodoxy and to stake out a domain for man's mind, free from the shackles of obscurantism, led many to adopt the disastrous expedient of defining religion largely in terms of sincerity and sentiment, and of stressing openness of mind as the Christian's most prized possession. While the struggle to remove the dead-weight of outmoded intellectual formulations was critically important and while the ultimate consequence of the struggle was to be both salutary and beneficial, the immediate consequence for the first few decades of the twentieth century was to strip the faith of any normative content, and the New Theology was forced to depend more and more, for its most characteristic affirmations, upon what was described as the unfolding revelation of God to be found in the scientific study of man, society, and the natural world. As a result, theologians had little to contribute to intellectual discussions for their place had been usurped, and the real theologians, who served as arbiters of Christian truth and made plain the mind of God, were the autonomous scholars who stood outside the faith in terms of their intellectual inquiries. Churchmen, it was popularly supposed, had neither an intellectual vocation nor an intellectual responsibility. They simply appropriated the conclusions of supposedly objective scholarship, and could therefore safely encourage their institutions of higher learning to cut the ties which bound them to the churches and to seek support from the community at large.

It was this intellectual retreat more than anything else which made it so difficult for the churches to deal systematically and effectively with the new and critical problems of society which were beginning to arouse their deep concern. Doing little more than reflect the tendencies of the time, the churches were placed at the mercy of social forces over which they could exercise no control. Far from constituting a creative and formative force in society, the churches were being successfully reduced to mere creatures of society, with the influences dominant in the world largely dominant in the churches also. In no substantial respect did they differ from other associations of men, and lacking the inner integrity of an independent and consistent understanding of the basic dilemmas of man in relationship to his fellows, the churches were no longer equipped, as they had been in an earlier day, to play an independent role in recasting the structure of society or, indeed, to assume any real and distinctive responsibility for the more immediate needs of the community.

The most ironical feature of the course adopted by the proponents of the New Theology was that it was not conspicuously successful in gaining adherents for the churches from among "the cultured despisers of religion" which had been its ostensible object. Unquestionably the identification of the faith with contemporary cultural tendencies did make it possible for some thoughtful persons, imbued with the new scientific outlook in one of its several forms, to maintain their connection with the church, but the chief consequence was to further persuade the intellectually emancipated that religion in general and Christianity in particular made no real difference. By attempting to demonstrate the affinity of the Christian faith to what members of the intelligentsia had already accepted on other grounds, the churches succeeded only in demonstrating that they had little of consequence to contribute and that the person outside the church could justifiably remain indifferent. Thus, even in terms of the limited objective of recommending the church and its gospel to the unbelievers in academic circles, the New Theology largely failed to achieve its end, and the steady drift of the intellectuals from the churches was, if anything, accelerated.*

* It must be acknowledged that the alienation of the intellectuals did not occur without an assist from the Fundamentalists. Whatever its original mo-

Among the great mass of the people, the intellectual retreat of the churches was not accompanied by the explicit alienation from the church which had occurred among the intellectuals, but among them the lack of any normative standard caused the faith largely to lose its force. While church membership continued to mount, it did so because the demands which were made were not great and because church membership carried with it a mark of respectability. The relationship thus established, however, was increasingly casual, and the laity became progressively illiterate religiously. Before the end of the nineteenth century, an Andover professor had complained that the laity "no longer hold the independent convictions which their fathers had, the fruit of their own theological reading and reflection. Said one of them at a juncture of affairs at which his official position called for an opinion of a doctrine of theology: 'The clergy must take care of that; I go with the majority.' "[21] Unfortunately, the responsibility could not be evaded quite so easily, for in most American denominations the laity had the decisive voice in the selection of the minister. In many of the churches, in the absence of any specific theological orientation, it was pulpit manner and ability to get along with the young people that counted most when it came to calling

---

tivation, Fundamentalism soon became identified with obscurantism and, after its initial phase at least, was as rigid an expression of a cultural loyalty as was the New Theology. "Not all though many of these antiliberals," writes H. Richard Niebuhr (*Christ and Culture*, 102), "show a greater concern for conserving the cosmological and biological notions of older cultures than for the Lordship of Jesus Christ. The test of loyalty to him is found in the acceptance of old cultural ideas about the manner of creation and the earth's destruction. More significant is the fact that the mores they associate with Christ have at least as little relation to the New Testament and as much connection with social custom as have those of their opponents." As a phase of the rural-urban conflict, the Fundamentalist controversy was much more cultural than religious. The Fundamentalist counterattack, however, did serve two ends. The violence of its campaign and the "smear" tactics it employed drove many moderates to the defense of the most extreme positions of the New Theology. The Fundamentalist position also served to justify the contention of the religiously emancipated that the churches, despite their pretensions to the contrary, did represent a culturally out-of-date way of thinking which modern man could not accept.

a pastor. More and more membership in a particular church was determined by accident rather than by conviction, and, while the average church member was sure that the church was something to be supported along with other good causes, neither the intellectual nor the ethical implications of the faith he professed extended much beyond the patterns of thought and behavior which were already current in society.

V

The most surprising outcome of the new temper which had invaded the churches was a decline in co-operative activities. The sectarian spirit was absent but institutional interests had become paramount. The Sunday School Movement, with its interdenominational training institutes and mass city, county, state, and national conventions of lay workers, its interdenominationally organized classes, and its uniform lessons throughout all the churches, was diverted into denominational channels and only the top echelon of officials continued to meet periodically to draft co-operatively, as an economy measure, the graded lessons which were now published in denominational disguise. In similar fashion, the Society of Christian Endeavor was replaced by denominational "leagues" and "unions," and the Student Christian Movement was to a very large extent replaced by denominational student foundations. The Student Volunteer Movement continued to exist but only on the periphery of the denominations' efforts to recruit missionary personnel, and the Y.M. and Y.W.C.A.'s shifted from an interdenominational to a nondenominational basis and ultimately came to regard themselves as completely independent of the churches. The great interdenominational revival campaigns were a thing of the past, and the churches were largely content to scramble competitively to enlist the interest of new arrivals in the community. Occasionally a limited co-operative visitation program would be proposed with detailed safeguards to prevent poaching upon one another's preserves, but not infrequently it was discovered that similar denominational programs were in conflict with the proposed effort and since they took precedence little could be done. The interdenominational rescue missions tended to languish for lack of support. The Women's Christian Temperance Union which had brought the women from the various churches together and enlisted their interest in a wide variety of civic concerns was replaced by no organization which was able to secure an equally widespread participation and the League of Women Voters filled the vacuum left by its decline.

Of the great tide of co-operative activity which characterized the late nineteenth century, a stated and officially recognized procedure for holding conferences among denominational officials to adjust specific conflicts in institutional interests was practically all that remained by the nineteen twenties and thirties. Resolutions were adopted, a few commissions with limited objectives were formed, union Thanksgiving and Good Friday services made a brave show of Christian solidarity, and extensive discussion of the tragedy and sinfulness of the existing divisions served to quiet many an uneasy conscience. In contrast to public confessions of guilt coupled with inactivity, nineteenth-century Christians tended to put first things first. They regarded denominationalism as not necessarily either sinful or tragic, but on the whole natural, inevitable, and, in spite of obvious liabilities, of real positive value in serving as a check to human aberration, undue pretensions, institutional lethargy, and theological irrelevance; and, without a burden of guilt to be eased by protracted discussion, they had proceeded to work together gladly, co-operatively, and for the most part harmoniously in the common cause. A nineteenth-century churchman might well have suggested that the problems which plagued the churches in the twentieth century were less the result of denominational divisions than of feebleness of faith and a consequent unwillingness to assume the responsibilities imposed upon the churches by their voluntary status. The churches were being subjected to that "moral coercion which makes man work," but as yet the pressure was not sufficient to cause them to do much more than offer excuses for the lack of vigor and vitality in their institutional life.

The persisting complacency and lack of real concern on the part of the churches can be seen most clearly in the field of the rural church. As soon as the churches began to give their attention to the needs of the new metropolitan centers following the Civil War, it was recognized that the rural churches were the chief source of Protestant strength even in the cities, and by the eighties and nineties it was becoming evident that the rural churches were in serious difficulty and beginning a disastrous decline. In 1908 a White House commission voiced its alarm at the plight of the rural churches, and little more than a decade later statistical studies revealed that the rural areas now had the smallest percentage of church members of any section of the population, even without taking into account the unduly large proportion of nonresident and inactive members on the rolls of the rural churches. Having had a meager and inadequate ministry over a long period of years, many rural churches had little conception of and little desire for any type of ministry different from that to which they had become accustomed. With the rural churches largely powerless to help themselves and with the rural people in danger of becoming the most secular element in the population, a few tentative gestures of concern were made by the various denominations. A few secretaries were appointed, a modest literature was produced, scattered institutes were held, fellowships of rural ministers were organized, and an increasing number of theological seminaries added professors of rural church work to their faculties. But the most impressive feature of this response to a critical and urgent need which affected the future prospects of every church was its pitiful lack of vision and support. At best only an oblique attack upon the problem was permitted, and the very real achievements of the limited personnel assigned to the task were accomplished on budgets that in most denominations did not exceed the expenditures of three or four good-sized city churches. By 1950, more than half a century after the acute nature of the problem had first been recognized, a large-scale generously supported frontal attack upon the problem, such as characterized the nineteenth-century reaction to similar situations, had yet to be made.

The neglect of the rural churches can be explained only in terms of a basic indifference on the part of the more prosperous churches and the denominations as a whole to the ultimate fate of the Christian cause, an indifference which permitted time, energy, and financial resources to be diverted to purposes of more immediate institutional and denominational aggrandizement. While the proportionate giving to missions, even though supported by the assiduously cultivated humanitarian impulse, steadily declined as the new century advanced, the amount being spent on church buildings and current expense rapidly mounted. Willard L. Sperry has told the story of "a paddle-wheel steamer on one of our western rivers which could make only so much steam in her boilers; when she blew her whistle the paddles stopped going around." He then remarked that many of our American churches were in something of "the same desperate state." The most that many of them could do was "to call attention to themselves."[22]

While the details varied, it was largely the story of the Halfway Covenant all over again. And it had all begun so early with a spirit of complacency and an easing of the tension between the church and the world. Long before the advent of the automobile, the motion picture, the radio, and Sunday golf, disintegration had set in. Discipline declined, evangelistic fervor faded, faith lost its force, and the churches living at peace with the world, lost their sense of a distinct and specific vocation in society.

CHAPTER X

A LONELY PROPHET: The Continuity of the Great Tradition

In Rauschenbusch . . . the reign of Christ required conversion and the coming kingdom was crisis, judgment as well as promise. Though his theory of the relation of God and man often seemed liberal he continued to speak the language of the prophets and St. Paul. H. RICHARD NIEBUHR[1]

Among the more conspicuous figures of the American religious scene during the first two decades of the twentieth century, Walter Rauschenbusch was one of the few who ran counter to the prevailing tendencies of the time. He is important in that he provides a connecting link between the older tradition of the American churches and the new evangelicalism which was beginning to arise out of a chastened liberalism during the nineteen thirties and forties. Rauschenbusch's thought was at once both reminiscent of the evangelicalism of Lyman Beecher and Charles G. Finney and prophetic of the theological insights which were being reasserted as the mid-century point was approached. In a very real sense, Rauschenbusch bears witness to the fact that the continuity of the great tradition of American religious life was never completely severed by the surrender of the churches to complacency.

By the twentieth century, as we have seen, the older evangelicalism had moved in two directions. On the one hand, revivalism had been rendered largely devoid of content, with theological tags being substituted for serious theological inquiry, and had degenerated into institutionalized procedures for obtaining a highly individualistic salvation. On the other hand, the surviving humanitarian concern of nineteenth-century evangelicalism had been largely divorced from the theological understanding which had provided its structural support.* With remarkable success, Rauschenbusch avoided the dangers represented by both these tendencies. The superficialities of the late revivalism he emphatically rejected; and, while profiting by the positive contributions of the new scientific and Biblical studies, he skillfully escaped the snares into which so many of his contemporaries were stumbling with their New Theology.

Rauschenbusch achieved distinction as a major prophet of social Christianity; and when attention is focused upon those aspects of the social gospel which were able to survive the outbreak of a world war, a world depression, and the rise of totalitarian regimes, he may justly be described as "the real founder of social Christianity in this country" and as "its most brilliant and generally satisfying exponent."[2] Yet, in his own time, these aspects of his thought were not generally appreciated. His greatest significance is that he establishes the relationship of present theological tendencies to the tradition which shaped our most characteristic institutions and informed our culture.

I

Graduating from seminary in 1886 and being denied an appointment as a missionary to India, Rauschenbusch accepted the pastorate of a small German Baptist Church in the tough Hell's Kitchen neighborhood of New York City. Here for eleven years he ministered to a congregation of German immigrant working people. In 1897 came the call to join his father as an instructor in the "German Department" of the Rochester

*The two tendencies can clearly be seen among the men whom Dwight L. Moody enlisted in his revivals. His Chicago colleagues moved in the first direction, whereas the bright young men he recruited in the colleges tended to follow the path being blazed by Henry Ward Beecher.

Theological Seminary, and five years later he was asked to take the chair of church history in the English faculty, a post which he held until his death in 1918. Although well known in his own denomination, it was the publication of *Christianity and the Social Crisis* in 1907 that established him as a national figure. Almost overnight attention was centered upon him as a major voice of the Christian church.

While Rauschenbusch could not wholly escape the sanguine temper of his time, there are relatively few traces of sentimental optimism to be found in his writings. In contrast to Shailer Mathews who was to suggest that, even if the confident expectation should turn out to have been only a pious hope, it was much "better to plan for Utopia than for Hell,"[3] Rauschenbusch was firm in his rejection of such dubious counsel and spoke strong words of caution to those who had imbibed the heady wine of inevitable progress.

The continents are strewn with the ruins of dead nations and civilizations. History laughs at the optimistic illusion that "nothing can stand in the way of human progress." It would be safer to assert that progress is always for a time only, and then succumbs to the inevitable decay. One by one the ancient peoples rose to wealth and civilization, extended their sway . . . , and then began to decay within and to crumble without, until the mausoleums of their kings were the haunt of jackals, and the descendants of their conquering warriors were abject peasants slaving for some alien lord. What guarantee have we, then, that our modern civilization with its pomp will not be "one with Nineveh and Tyre"?

This was 1907, almost three decades before such sober words began to creep into the pulpits. The cry of "crisis," Rauschenbusch acknowledged, is wearisome. "Every age and every year are critical and fraught with destiny." Yet, he continued, all the evidence of "the widest survey of history" clearly indicates that Western civilization has reached "a decisive point in its development." The possibility that "some Gibbon of Mongol race" will "sit by the shore of the Pacific" and "write on the 'Decline and Fall of the Christian Empire'" cannot be dismissed. If this does occur, he will probably describe the present era "as the golden age when outwardly life flourished as never before, but when that decay, which resulted in the gradual collapse . . . , was already far advanced."[4]

Can the Western world, asked Rauschenbusch, escape the fate which has overtaken preceding civilizations? For a nation or a group of nations, he observed, death would seem to be no inevitable necessity as it is for an individual. The strength of a society could be "indefinitely prolonged if the people were wise and just enough to avert the causes of decay. There is no inherent cause why a great group of nations, such as that which is now united in Western civilization, should not live on in perpetual youth, overcoming by a series of rejuvenations every social evil as it arises, and using every attainment as a stepping-stone to a still higher culture of individual and social life." "It has not yet been done," he acknowledged, and the question remains, Can it be done?[5]

One thing is clear from his writings. Rauschenbusch early rejected the notion that the ills of society could be corrected by a mere tinkering with external social arrangements. Before leaving New York for Rochester, he had asserted that the twin supports for any enduring hope for society are "a combination of personal regeneration and social reform."

Most of the social reformers claim that if only poverty and the fear of poverty could be abolished, men would cease to be grasping, selfish, overbearing and sensual. We do not see it so. We acknowledge that evil surroundings tempt to evil actions and strengthen evil character and we go as far as any in the earnestness of our protest against any social institution which makes null the prayer: "Lead us not into temptation." But we can conceive of a state of society in which plenty would reign, but where universal opulence would only breed universal pride and wantonness.

"The Kingdom of God," he wrote in 1912, "includes the economic life," but "no outward economic revolution will answer our needs. It is not this thing or that thing our nation needs, but a new mind and heart. . . . We want a revolution both inside and outside." "The social order," he affirmed in his Nathaniel W. Taylor Lectures, "cannot be saved without regenerate men." Only "converted men," he had earlier declared, are the sure ground of hope. "Create a ganglion chain of redeemed personalities in a commonwealth, and all things become possible."[6]

II

"The pioneers of the social gospel," Rauschenbusch recognized, had "had a hard time." Some "lost their faith"; others came "out of the struggle with crippled formulations of truth" —"a kind of dumbbell system of thought with the social gospel at one end and individual salvation at the other." The traditional theology, he believed, was at least partially responsible for "this spiritual wastage," since "it left these men without spiritual support and allowed them to become the vicarious victims of our theological inefficiency."

If our theology is silent on social salvation, we compel college men and women, workingmen, and theological students, to choose between an unsocial system of theology and an irreligious system of social salvation. It is not hard to predict the outcome. If we seek to keep Christian doctrine unchanged, we shall ensure its abandonment.

It was for this reason, as well as for its obvious academic and intellectual credentials, that Rauschenbusch welcomed the new movement of Biblical and historical criticism.[7]

The new historical and Biblical studies served several purposes. By emancipating the minds of men from what Rauschenbusch called "ancestor worship"—an unyielding reverence which would permit no questioning even of those dogmas and

beliefs from which all vital life had vanished—a door was
opened to the needed theological reconstruction. The concept
of Biblical inerrancy, he pointed out, had served to discourage
prophecy—the ministry of the Spirit—within the churches;
the rejection of Biblical inerrancy cleared a path for its restoration. "Present inspiration" and "living prophetic spirits," he
asserted, are "essential equipment" in the work of redemption.
The recognition that all institutions—religious no less than
secular—were historically conditioned conferred freedom from
bondage to ecclesiasticism. In the same manner, a historical
view permitted one to see how reconciliation with God had
again and again become identified with an acceptance of the
established customs of society, thus throttling any creative
response to the changing needs of men in their corporate life.
Finally, the new methods of historical understanding made it
possible for the Christian past to speak to "men of modernized
intelligence." No longer was it necessary for men "to believe
with all their hearts what they could not possibly understand
with all their heads."[8]

The new spirit released by the changing intellectual climate,
at its best, represented a recovery of that dynamic element in
religious life which revolted "against the biblicism which made
the Scriptures a book of laws for science and for morals, against
the revivalism which had reduced regeneration to a method
for drumming up church members, and against the otherworld-
liness which had made heaven and hell a reward and a punishment." On the other hand, as Rauschenbusch well knew, the
critical spirit did not represent all clear gain. It had its own
peculiar temptations. "The attacks on our inherited theology
have usually come," he wrote, "from the intellectuals who are
galled by the yoke of uncritical and unhistorical beliefs brought
down from pre-scientific centuries. They are entirely within
their right in insisting that what is scientifically impossible
shall not be laid as an obligatory belief on the neck of modern

men in the name of religion." Yet, we must also remember that "the rational subtractions of liberalism do not necessarily make religion more religious." "Critical clarifying is decidedly necessary, but power in religion comes only through the consciousness of a great elementary need which compels men to lay hold of God anew." The critical spirit, it was all too evident, could be embraced not for the sake of releasing the rigorous demands of prophetic religion, but simply because the conventional demands of orthodoxy were irksome and resented. Thus the New Theology, which was the primary religious expression of the new Biblical and historical views of Rauschenbusch's day, won its principal following among the cultured and the comfortable rather than among the humble and the distressed. For many of them it was a release from bondage and little more, and there is a degree of justice in the comment that many of them were not so much "liberal" as they were "loose" in their religious faith.[9]

Looking back, one is impressed by Rauschenbusch's remarkable success in escaping the chief pitfalls of the New Theology. His writings, to be sure, reflected the thought of his contemporaries, at many incidental points their influence was predominant, but he rejected with amazing consistency almost all the major tenets of the New Theology. His technique was irenic. Where agreement existed, he affirmed that agreement; where disagreement existed, he continued to affirm but usually neglected to point out the denials that were involved. Consequently, the points at which he diverged in his thinking from the other advocates of the social gospel are apt to pass unnoticed and give the impression of being unpremeditated and almost unconscious.*

* Apart from his rejection of the doctrine of inevitable progress and his recognition of the perennial element of crisis in human history, it should be pointed out that much of Rauschenbusch's social analysis lacks the sturdy quality and real insight which, on the whole, characterizes his religious thought. His critique of specific existing social institutions, as well as his proposals for social reconstruction, tend to be utopian and to reflect the mild "progressive" radicalism of his time. They thus give evidence of the fact that he had

Rauschenbusch, as we have seen, indulged in no superficial optimism, and he harbored no illusions concerning the inevitability of progress. Far from religion being natural, he held that true faith could arise only out of a sense of crisis—both personal and social. "There is nothing else in sight today," he insisted, "which has the power to rejuvenate theology except the consciousness of vast sins and sufferings, and the longing for righteousness and a new life." In terms of a theology which came to grips with the basic issue of life, as Rauschenbusch saw it, the stylized conversion of late revivalism, with its institutionalized procedures for staking out a claim in the life to come, had no place. "To one whose memories run back twenty or thirty years, to Moody's time," he wrote, "the methods now used by some evangelists seem calculated to produce skin-deep changes. Things have simmered down to signing a card, shaking hands, or being introduced to the evangelist." But no less irrelevant to the central issue were the assurances which were being given of a natural harmony which existed between God and man. Neither alternative would do. The crisis was real, and the judgment which provoked it was real. And so Rauschenbusch returned to an older tradition which insisted that the tension could be resolved only by pressing forward into a new life free from its former bondage. Sin, repentance, grace, salvation, the kingdom, the church—all these were interpreted in terms strikingly reminiscent of Charles G. Finney and the earlier revivalists. Both the consciousness of sin and the message of salvation must be enlarged and intensified, but they must not be rejected.[10]

III

The test of any theology, said Rauschenbusch, is "the question whether it does justice to the religious consciousness of

---

not entirely eliminated "the dumbbell system of thought." His conception of the Kingdom, on the other hand, gives evidence of extended and mature reflection which is directly related to his religious presuppositions.

sin." "By our very nature we are involved in tragedy." We are driven by "imperious instincts and desires," and "the weakness or the stubbornness of our will and the tempting situations of life combine to weave the tragic web of sin and failure" from which none of us can escape. "We have the impulse to live our life, to exercise our freedom, to express and satisfy the limitless cravings in us, and we are impatient of restraint." As a result, "we set our desires against the rights of others and disregard the claims of mercy, of gratitude, of parental love." We attempt to establish our own "private kingdom of self-interest," and this leads from "selfishness" to "godlessness," from defiance of the "common good" to rebellion against the "universal good." Thus "we frustrate our possibilities; we injure others; we disturb the divine harmonies. We are unfree, unhappy, conscious of a burden which we are unable to lift or escape."[11]

Although "many modern theologians are ready to abandon" the doctrine of original sin, said Rauschenbusch, "I take pleasure . . . in defending it." The notion of total depravity, to be sure, must be rejected, but there is no blinking the fact that "depravity of will and corruption of nature are transmitted wherever life itself is transmitted." Yet the doctrine of original sin does not tell the whole story. The inner drives of self-interest and self-love are strengthened and reinforced by "the kingdom of evil," the demonic structures in society. Sin is transmitted not only by the constitution of our being, but also by social tradition, customs, and institutions, so that "one generation corrupts the next."[12]

"One cause of distrust of the social gospel," Rauschenbusch acknowledged, "is that its exponents often fail to show an adequate appreciation of the power and guilt of sin." Blame for wrongdoing seems to be placed on the environment, and "instead of stiffening and awakening the sense of responsibility in the individual, it teaches him to unload it on society." There is truth in such an accusation. "The emphasis on environment and on the contributory guilt of the community, does offer a chance to unload responsibility, and human nature is quick to seize the chance." Seldom do we overtly rebel against God. "We dodge and evade. We kneel in lowly submission and kick our duty under the bed while God is not looking." Even Adam "began soon after the fall to shift the blame. This shiftiness seems to be one of the clearest and most universal effects of original sin."[13]

The actual effect of the social gospel, when properly understood, Rauschenbusch insisted, was not the easing of the burden of guilt. Quite the reverse was true. Far from diminishing the consciousness of sin, the social gospel enlarged and intensified it, accentuated the sense of crisis, and plunged the individual soul into a new baptism of repentance. Not only the individual but the social group indulges in rationalization to avoid a conviction of sin—to explain, to excuse, to justify the surrender to evil and the rebellion against God. A person can quite easily throw the cloak of respectability over his individual sins, but the social gospel has a more searching eye. It ferrets out hidden motives, brings to light the disturbing fact of the common involvement of men in the kingdom of evil, and reveals the emptiness of all pretensions to self-righteousness. "The sin of all is in each of us, and every one of us has scattered seeds of evil, the final multiplied harvest of which no man knows." No man can escape the demand for repentance.[14]

Redemption, for Rauschenbusch, sprang from repentance and was fulfilled in faith. Faith involved both trust and commitment—an "expectancy and confidence in the coming salvation" both personal and social, and "an energetic act of the will." Christ's death was "an essential part of the redemptive process," for it is Christ who convicts us of sin and awakens faith. By his death, Christ had demonstrated "the power of sin" in human life; revealed the love of God for men (a "monumental fact telling of grace and inviting repentance and humility"); and displayed the power of "prophetic suffering" to redeem men and to inspire them to carry on the work which had been begun, comforting and sustaining them in their sufferings by the consciousness that they were "bearing the marks of the Lord Jesus." Like Finney, Rauschenbusch insisted that conversion involved a radical shift from self-interest to what the earlier revivalists called "disinterested benevolence," and its consequence was to put men to work for the kingdom. Redemption, said Rauschenbusch, turned men from a life centered upon themselves to "a life going out toward God and men,"* and this new obedience must find expression in seeking "to overcome the evil in the present world, not by withdrawing from the world, but by revolutionizing it." Thus redemption must lead to "the progressive transformation of all human affairs by the thought and spirit of Christ."[15]

At the center of Rauschenbusch's thought, illuminating and giving meaning to his faith, was his conception of the Kingdom of God—the Reign of God in a redeemed society of men. Almost from the beginning of his ministry to the end of his life, he was struggling to understand and to express the full meaning of the doctrine of the Kingdom. He found no easy answers. A simple identification of the good society with the teachings of Jesus would not do. He sought to come to terms with the eschatological problem, but never succeeded in a way that was wholly satisfactory to himself. The ethical concern, he was convinced, must remain central. The notion of development he could not surrender, although he had some difficulty in relating the concept to the New Testament record. His ultimate

---

* "Of course in actual life," Rauschenbusch admitted, "there is no case of complete Christian transformation" (*A Theology for the Social Gospel*, 98). One cannot escape the need for a continuing repentance and a continuing redemption. "Paul's description of the struggle of the flesh and spirit in his life is a classical expression of the tragedies enacted in the intimate life of every one who has tried to make his recalcitrant Ego climb the steep path of perfection: 'The good which I would, I do not; but the evil which I would not, that I practice'" (*ibid.*, 58).

conclusion was that the Kingdom of God could be understood only in terms of miracle.

The Kingdom of God is divine in its origin, progress, and consummation. It was initiated by Jesus Christ . . . , it is sustained by the Holy Spirit, and it will be brought to its fulfillment by the power of God in his own time. . . . The Kingdom of God, therefore, is miraculous all the way, and is the continuous revelation of the power, the righteousness, and the love of God.[16]

The Kingdom of God, he was also convinced, was both a judgment and a promise, both a present reality and a future hope whose final consummation could only be beyond history. The promise must not be allowed to obscure the judgment and the necessity for repentance, nor should the judgment with its sense of crisis be allowed to obscure the promise. Similarly, the present reality of the Kingdom must not obscure its incompleteness, nor should the beyondness of the Kingdom lead men to discount its present reality.

The promise of the Kingdom was in itself a judgment. "Sin is always revealed by contrast to righteousness," said Rauschenbusch. "We get an adequate intellectual measure of it and feel the proper hate and repugnance for it only when we see it as the terrible defeat and frustration of a great good which we love and desire." Thus "a clear realization of the nature of sin" and our own involvement in it "depends on a clear vision of the Kingdom of God." Conversely, from the judgment and the repentance and new life it evokes springs added confirmation of the promise, for "a mind set free by God and energized by a great purpose is an incomputable force." On the other hand, there is no final historical consummation of the Kingdom. "At best there is always but an approximation to a perfect social order. The Kingdom of God is always but coming."

In Christ's thought the Kingdom of God was to come from heaven to earth, so that God's will would be done on earth as it is in heaven. So then it exists in heaven; it is to be created on earth. All true joys on earth come from partial realizations of the Kingdom of God; the joy that awaits us will consist in living within the full realization of the Kingdom. Our labor for the Kingdom here will be our preparation for our participation hereafter.

Yet, even if the future of the Kingdom does lie beyond time "among the mysteries of God," to ask for faith in the possibility of a new social order is to ask for no utopian delusion. "We know well that there is no perfection for man in this life; there is only growth toward perfection." In terms of personal religion, we rightly "look with seasoned suspicion at any one who claims to be holy and perfect, yet we always tell men to become holy and to seek perfection. We make it a duty to seek what is unattainable. We have the same paradox in the perfectability of society. We shall never have a perfect social life, yet we must seek it with faith."[17]

If the Kingdom is a promise and a hope, it is also a present reality. It is both present and future. "Like God it is in all tenses, eternal in the midst of time." It is "always coming, always pressing in on the present, always big with possibility, and always inviting immediate action." To those who thrust it wholly into the future and postpone their response, it is but "a theory and not a reality." It is a reality only to those who press forward and appropriate it now.

Every human life is so placed that it can share with God in the creation of the Kingdom, or can resist and retard its progress. The Kingdom is for each of us the supreme task and the supreme gift of God. By accepting it as a task, we experience it as a gift. By laboring for it we enter into the joy and peace of the Kingdom as our divine fatherland and habitation.

And the real hope for society lies only with those who have appropriated it now, with those for whom the Kingdom has become their "fatherland and habitation."

Important as was social reconstruction in breaking the power of the kingdom of evil, the Kingdom of God could be entered

only by a path which led through the death of self to a rebirth
into a new life in which God's will is done. Even the judgment
implicit in catastrophe, without the redeeming judgment of
Christ's kingdom, was not likely to touch the issue of the future.
As Finney, who was one of the chief inspirers of the abolition
crusade, could write his memoirs without mentioning the Civil
War; so Rauschenbusch could view World War I only with
the detached eye of a saddened heart. In the midst of the eager
expectations of a nation caught up in a great crusade to make
the world safe for democracy and fighting a war to end war,
Rauschenbusch wrote: "I am not as sure as others that a victory for the allies would, of itself, free the world from imperial-
ism." There is, to be sure, "a great historic opportunity for our
nation. . . . We can lift the whole contest above a fight for
territory and trade privileges and make it a battle for the
freedom of the nations and the achievement of international
order and peace." But Rauschenbusch was far from sanguine.
"President Wilson will have a tremendous task to translate his
idealistic utterances into realities against the pressure of selfish
interests at home and abroad. Again and again in the past, the
peoples have been led to slaughter by noble hopes only to be
cheated at the peace table." Rauschenbusch, like Finney and
Edwards and the other men of the older tradition, had "little
faith in progress toward true peace by any means save those
of the Christian revolution." With Lyman Beecher, who had
come to recognize the folly of seeking to sustain a Christian
order by legislation alone, Rauschenbusch knew that what the
spirit of the people requires is a much sounder foundation than
what the laws demand. Important as it was to have principles
written in the statute books, it was much more important to
have them written in the hearts and minds of men. The only
sure control was that control which governed the fountainhead
of action—the inner life—"where the desires and motives of
the soul are born."[18]

One of the most important aspects of Rauschenbusch's thought was expressed in his conviction that the church was of "indispensable importance" in the work of salvation. "The individual is saved, if at all," he asserted, "by membership in a community which has salvation." Nothing is more apparent than the inadequacies of the existing churches, but that does not diminish their importance. "What chance would a disembodied spirit of Christianity have, whispering occasionally at the key-hole of the human heart?" On the other hand, the church too often does not even whisper, because it fails to "embody Christ" in its life.

If the church is to have saving power, it must embody Christ. He is the revolutionary force within it. The saving qualities of the church depend on the question whether it has translated the personal life of Jesus Christ into the social life of its group and thus brings it to bear on the individual. If Christ is not in the church, how does it differ from "the world"? It will still assimilate its members, but it will not make them persons bearing the family likeness of the first-born son of God.

The task of the church, then, is to create "a Christian duplicate of the social order for its members" and, to the extent that it is necessary, to exist "in sharp opposition not only to the state but to the whole social life surrounding it." For it is only by embodying Christ in its life and carrying his spirit "into human thought and the conduct of public affairs" by the control which it exerts over the lives of its members, that the church can influence the world. Thus everything depends upon "the spiritual virtues of the church group."[19]

Churches may become "social agencies to keep their people stupid, stationary, superstitious, bigoted, and ready to choke their first-born ideals." They may identify the church with the Kingdom of God, and instead of pointing men to God point them only to themselves. They may became subservient to and dependent upon the state.* In all such instances, the church has ceased to be "the power of redemption" and has become its "object." Even as important as "social activities" are, they must not be substituted for religion. "If the church comes to lean on social preachings and doings as a crutch because its religion has become paralytic, may the Lord have mercy upon us." The function of the Christian church is, first of all, to "enlist the will and love of men and women for God, to mark them with the cross of Christ," and then "send them out to finish up the work which Christ began." From its basic religious task, the church dare not depart.[20]

IV

Walter Rauschenbusch was a lonely prophet. The influence which he exerted in terms of his fundamental convictions was negligible. Few, except among his own students, grasped the fundamental structure of his thought. They had found a less demanding gospel, and what influence Rauschenbusch did exert during his own generation was limited primarily to the contagion of his own devotional life and the impetus he provided for participation in a variety of movements for social reform. If he had been as good a historian as he was a theologian or at least as familiar with the more recent past as he was with the ancient past, Rauschenbusch would have recognized the tradition in which he stood. His conception of the Kingdom of God was—except for his awareness of the importance of social conditioning—essentially identical with the Kingdom of Christ as it had been preached by the earlier revivalists. Had he understood this, he would have spent less time attempting to draw distinctions between his theology and the old theology, and those who were captivated by his spirit would have been less

* "The separation of church and state," said Rauschenbusch, "has the double advantage of removing the clerical influence from political life, and the political influence from church life. It leaves the church unmuzzled to speak out, if it has anything to say" (*Christianity and the Social Crisis*, 188).

confused as to his basic convictions. To the end of his life, he was an evangelical in an era when evangelicalism as a dynamic movement had quite disappeared. "It has been my deepest satisfaction," he said in a letter written shortly before his death, "to get evidence now and then that I have been able to help men to a new spiritual birth. I have always regarded my public work as a form of evangelism, which called for a deeper repentance and a new experience of God's salvation."[21]

What won Rauschenbusch national recognition were those points in his books and addresses where he reflected the influence of what many other people were saying—incidental facets of the New Theology and aspects of contemporary political and economic radicalism. The distinctive and basic elements of his message went unnoticed. The churches honored him as a prophet, with both applause and denunciation, but they went their way quite oblivious to his sober words of warning and rebuke. The churches, victims of their own complacency, had first to embrace the world and demonstrate the folly of their waywardness, before they could be recalled to an awareness of their distinctive vocation in society.

CHAPTER XI

THE RENEWAL OF THE CHURCHES: The Recovery of the Great Tradition

This is our situation. As Christian people we believe that the social life of the country must be quickened and sanctified by the power of the Christian religion; that the children of the country must receive a Christian nurture; that the people of the country must be established in Christian character; and that the spirit of Christian righteousness must permeate all our affairs; and yet to do this great and needed work, the state in this country will not and cannot give us any assistance. . . .

Here the Christian faith must commend itself to the people, as it did in apostolic days, by what it can show itself to be worth and by the fruits which it can bring forth, and by nothing else. When this is fully realized by the Christian church, that the . . . Christian character of our American society depends on it and what it shall do, then, I believe, will the Christian church in this country throw itself on God, [and] . . . will do an apostolic work. DAVID H. GREER, rector of St. Bartholomew's Episcopal Church, New York City, in an address before the Evangelical Alliance, 1889.[1]

The basic problem of American Protestantism in the twentieth century is spelled out by the "disturbing discrepancy" which now exists between the size of the churches and the influence which they exert in American life. In dealing with this situation, it is surprising that it is so seldom recognized that the American churches must look primarily to their own historical experience for guidance. As Daniel Jenkins, the British theologian, has pointed out, the whole question of

Christian duty and the role of the church in a democratic society has never received much attention from the theologians of the past. For the first three centuries of Christian history the state was the Roman Empire, and "the recognition of the church by Constantine was the recognition of the church by that empire, which was far from a modern democracy." While it is true that the Reformation in several respects was directly related to the growth of the modern democratic state, none of the Reformers functioned within a true democracy and most of their thinking presupposed the authority of a Christian prince. Even Britain during "the period of its supremacy in world affairs . . . was only in process of becoming democratic." Although English divines did struggle with the problem for a few brief years during the seventeenth century, it has been in the United States alone that the churches over an extended period of time have had to face squarely the problem of their relationship to and responsibility within a democratic state.[2]

It should be obvious that in a democracy everything yields to the supremacy of public opinion and that public opinion to be dependable must be grounded on personal conviction. Thus the influence of the Christian faith upon the political order will always be determined by the success of the churches in creating an informed and committed electorate. It should be equally evident that to the extent that the churches succeed in creating a Christian climate of opinion an effective defense is established against secular tendencies in the larger social order and the culture itself. Recent experience of the American churches should have made the point clear that the total community cannot be trusted to instruct itself in terms of Christian duty or to generate, nurture, and sustain the Christian faith. It is a responsibility which inevitably and unavoidably rests upon the churches. One great merit of a frank acceptance of the full implications of the voluntary principle in religion— the complete separation of church and state— is that it represents an explicit recognition of the plain facts of life as they exist in a democracy, and it makes definite and unequivocal the responsibility, inherent in the very nature of a democratic society, which the churches must assume. Not only is the responsibility of the churches made clear by the separation of church and state, the churches are subjected to an added coercion which makes it necessary for them to discharge this responsibility if their own institutional life is to remain strong and vigorous. Depending solely upon voluntary support, they are forced to seek and to secure conviction if only to preserve their own existence. American experience, to be sure, offers no guarantee that the churches will not forget the tension which exists between the demands of God and the desires of men and enshrine social gods upon their altars, nor does it guarantee that churches which have forsaken the distinctive note and the earnestness of a Christian discipline of life will not be content to become the dwindling societies of the elderly, sustained only by loyalties dating from an earlier and more vigorous time. The American churches have demonstrated, however, that by voluntary effort a reasonably Christian democratic society can be achieved.

It is curious how unwilling the American churches have been to heed the lessons of their own historical experience. Perhaps it is because such a thoroughgoing reconstruction of their own institutional life is demanded, and institutions are always hesitant to resort to drastic measures. Even after European churches have been confronted by the problems implicit in a democratic society, have witnessed the bankruptcy of their old assumptions as their governments began to reflect a growing secularism or to transform themselves into totalitarian regimes, and increasingly have been forced to decide whether they are to be Christ's church or the church of a national religion, many American churchmen are still fascinated by the idea that a democratic state can somehow assume the role of a Christian prince and thus relieve the churches of their responsibility to maintain the hold of the Christian faith among the people. By this means the fundamental issue is evaded, the dereliction of the churches remains unacknowledged, and the door is opened to a progressive secularization which in the end will force the churches openly to betray the Gospel or to become mere islands of resistance in a pagan society.

I

The present situation of the American churches is strikingly similar to the plight of New England Congregationalism after the full effects of the Half-way Covenant in terms of the indiscriminate admission of church members had begun to be felt. Alec Vidler, editor of an English theological journal, has confessed that the "babel of church-sects" in the United States strikes him as "a very horrid thing." A true church of Christ, he observed, should claim "all the people dwelling in a particular urban or rural area as citizens of the kingdom of Christ" and thus stand forth and bear witness that "the work of Christ in every land is to bind men together in one universal family or kingdom without regard to their different racial origins, trades and professions, income brackets, class interests, political parties, etc." But, said Vidler, the American churches "seem complacently to regard it as their task to cater for the religious needs of such individuals or such sections of the population as will patronize them."[3]

By his comments Vidler revealed himself to be an inaccurate reporter and in this instance, a poor theologian. The American churches almost wholly shared his sentiments, and this was precisely their major problem. Vidler's prescription, far from curing the malady from which the churches were suffering, would only serve to aggravate it. The work of Christ is not primarily to bind men together into one universal family but to relate men through faith to God. It was because so many of the American churches were putting the cart before the horse and seeking to make the church, first of all, a friendly fellowship which bore witness to the unity of mankind that its class character was accentuated. The common relationship to God in Christ which would have transcended and overcome the natural barriers which separate man from man was subordinated and the churches inevitably assumed the complexion of the customary social groupings.

The extent to which the majority of the American churches shared Vidler's point of view and adopted a policy which in application was even more indiscriminate than the principle of birthright membership can be illustrated by a pamphlet issued by the Commission on Evangelism and Devotional Life of the Congregational Christian Churches. Utilizing bold face type to give the proper emphasis, this bit of evangelistic literature asserts that the Congregationalists "have seen the need for churches which shall meet the religious requirements of **all** the people in a given community. . . . A Congregational community church is a place of friendly cooperative Christian enterprise that fits the mood and standards of a community. Its membership is open to all. . . . Members of such a church control their own church affairs."[4] The key phrases, of course, are obvious—a church designed to fit "the mood and standards" of a community, "open to all" who may wish to join for one reason or another, and subject in the determination of all matters of faith and practice to a majority vote of what in the sixteenth and seventeenth centuries would have been called a mixed multitude—a company of people bound together by few ties deeper than personal friendship and by few convictions stronger than the mere fact that their names appeared on a common membership roll. So casual were the demands of the churches, even in terms of such minimal responsibilities as attendance and the payment of "dues," that the pull of an emotional loyalty to a college fraternity, service club, lodge, trade union, professional association, or veterans' organization frequently far exceeded that exerted by the church.

The consequences of the adoption of this "open membership" or "community church" policy, which in practice if not always in name was the common assumption upon which many of the churches of the major Protestant denominations proceeded, cannot be described as anything less than disastrous. A careful survey conducted by the Institute of Social and Religious Research of the fourteen thousand inhabitants of a single community could find no basis for a clear-cut line of division, beyond the simple fact of church affiliation, which would serve to distinguish the unchurched from the churched portions of the population.[5] There was nothing that could remotely be described as a godly public opinion, and the relationship between Christian faith and political decision was impossible to identify. The constraint exercised by every kind of professional organization and special interest group, except the church, determined the political attitudes of church members. Even the Society of Friends, which once was so skilled in the exercise of group discipline, was represented in public life by the divided counsels of such diverse personalities as Joe Grundy, Republican boss of Pennsylvania, Herbert Hoover, Alger Hiss, Whittaker Chambers, Richard Nixon, and Paul Douglas. In England, where a similar collapse of the Free Churches had robbed the nation of its "nonconformist conscience," the feeble complaint of a few High Church clerics concerning the remarriage of the once-divorced Foreign Secretary produced only taunts in the daily press and served to reveal the emptiness of the pretensions of the churches to speak with authority even on questions of private morals. Far from being able to shape the life of the total community, the inner life of the churches had become so largely determined by external social influences as to deny in practice "the right of the Christian gospel to shape the Christian community" itself.[6]

If the indiscriminate admission of members made it impossible for a Presbyterian session, a Baptist covenant meeting, or a Methodist class to function effectively as an instrument for maintaining "a lively sense of the judgment of God upon the corporate life and public activities" of church members, and thus rendered the churches impotent in terms of their influence upon society as a whole; the lowering of the bars to church membership also left the churches with no means of preserving the integrity of the faith they professed. It is apparent that in churches with a democratic or representative system of government, the ultimate authority in matters of faith as well as of practice resides in the congregation or in the commissioners, elders, and ministers whom they elect. But even in churches with a closed system of clerical control, the laity in a democratic society can exercise a determinative influence, for when any church depends upon popular support a strong element of coercion is introduced.* Thus the Roman church with its tightly knit system of clerical authority recognizes that an implicit faith on the part of the people is not adequate in a democracy and expends prodigious effort to make sure that its membership has a firm grasp of the essentials of the faith. While the freedom of a church to say what it has to say may be preserved, if it imposes no tests for membership and makes no provision for discipline, it will not only display no distinctive quality of life but in due time will have nothing to say except that which everyone will be saying.

A third consequence of the attempt of the churches to be inclusive institutions embracing, largely upon their own terms,

* Perhaps it should be said that the only alternative to dependence upon voluntary support is dependence upon the support of the state—an alternative presenting its own peculiar perils which, even in terms of the authority exercised by a Christian prince, are evident enough in the record of history. Voluntary support has the obvious advantage of permitting a church to define the terms upon which it shall receive members and thus to determine by whom it shall be coerced and to a large degree the nature of the pressures to which it shall be subjected. It has freedom, in other words, through the control which it can exercise over its membership, to strive to be Christ's church.

as many of the community as can be persuaded to join is that the possibility of any effective evangelism is thereby destroyed. Lyman Beecher discovered that a revival of religion always depended upon a "purified" church, and it was only after the covenant had been renewed and two or three excommunications had demonstrated the determination of his church at Litchfield to restore discipline and order that a revival had begun. If the members of a church do not believe in their own Gospel sufficiently to take it seriously, they can scarcely expect the world outside to do so. Thus the churches become obstacles to the persuasiveness of their own message. The churches can never make good their claim to possess the good news of redemption in the eyes of either the simple or the sophisticated unless they appear visibly as a society distinct from the larger society about them. The basic need, then, for an effective evangelism is not the devising of new techniques. It is a deepening of the quality of life exhibited by particular local congregations, until the very quality of that life bears witness in some small measure to the transforming power of the Christian Gospel.

Even the worship of the churches has been affected by the laxity of discipline and the consequent heterogeneous character of the congregations. Corporate worship presupposes a prepared people. "An ignorant or careless congregation will sterilize the most magnificent liturgy into dead formalism, and will freeze up the most gifted leader of extempore worship"; whereas "a genuinely consecrated company will make any form eloquent and make up for all sorts of deficiencies on the part of the pastor." The leaders of the liturgical movement in modern Roman Catholicism have recognized this fact and have been emphasizing the necessity of Bible study, an explicit faith, and a personal witness to the social and ethical consequences of the gift of grace. While Roman Catholics have been pulling their altars from the walls and encouraging congregational participation, Protestant worship has become increasingly casual in its demands for preparation on the part of the worshiper. Many Protestant churchmen are at a loss either to explain or to understand the scruples which caused their fathers to bar the ignorant and the scandalous from the Lord's Supper and "fencing" the table has long fallen into disuse.[7]

No mere restoration of the disciplinary habits of churches in the nineteenth century, of course, will be adequate. The moralistic pettiness, legalism, and at times overweening pretensions to absolute truth, which characterized many of the old church trials and contributed so greatly to bringing the exercise of church discipline into disrepute, must be avoided. Indeed, such trials probably should never have been held. But certainly the churches, no less than the Rotary Clubs, ought to insist upon the fulfillment of the institutional obligation of attendance and support. They should insist that a definite program of instruction should precede reception into the full membership of the church. They should make clear certain other generally accepted obligations of the Christian in terms of marriage, family life, and community responsibilities. An insistence, as a prerequisite to membership, that within the Christian fellowship there is no place for distinctions of race, class, or nationality would not be inappropriate. Beyond this, definite procedures for the enlistment of full congregational participation in group discussions to determine the meaning of the Christian faith and its implications with reference to the specific decisions Christians must make in personal, social, and political life should be established. Long ago John Woolman within the Society of Friends demonstrated the efficacy of discussion and persuasion as an effective instrument of group discipline in the forming of a corporate conscience on a specific issue, and such organizations as the National Education Association, the Daughters of the American Revolution, and the National Manufacturers Association have demonstrated in recent years that excommunication is not a necessary adjunct to the development of a common point of view within a particular group. A more radical proposal would be to return to the practice of "fencing" the Lord's Table. By insisting upon the renewal of the covenant prior to Communion and by providing an opportunity for confession and the reconciliation of members at variance with one another, the Lord's Supper might be made more meaningful as a visible expression of their unity as members of the body of Christ, and at the same time constitute an effective disciplinary procedure which would have the real virtue of necessitating a revival of the Presbyterian "session," the Methodist "class," and the Baptist "covenant meeting" as important elements in church life.

Thus far we have sought to make clear that an indispensable prerequisite to the renewal of the churches as a dynamic force in American life is the recovery of discipline. The recovery of discipline, in turn, is dependent upon the recovery of the distinctive note of the Christian faith. In the past, the prosperity and prestige of the churches, as well as the relatively untroubled state of the world, encouraged a spirit of complacency which served to keep God at a respectable distance and softened the stringency of his demands. But now the complacency has departed and, both in Europe and more recently in America, the voice of God which in "the old days of security" was "pleasantly muffled" is beginning to be heard again. The end of the older era in America was marked by Henry Nelson Wieman's announcement in 1932 of his intention "to promote a theocentric religion as over against the prevalent anthropocentric one,"[8] although it was left to others to grasp the full meaning of the impasse which had been reached. By 1940 theological discontent was showing itself in many places and a decade later, with the theological revival making its influence felt in most of the theological seminaries, the intellectual fiber of the Christian faith was beginning to be reasserted and once more theology was beginning to contribute fundamental insights to intellectual discussions.

The theology which had shaped American institutions and informed American culture during the nineteenth century was Calvinism as modified by revivalism and expressed systematically in the New England Theology. It was this understanding of the Christian faith which so largely disappeared during the last two decades of the century. Walter Horton has recalled the comment of Frank Hugh Foster that "in 1880 the chairs of theology at all the Congregational and some of the Presbyterian seminaries were occupied by adherents of the New England school, and fifteen years later every one had been filled by some one of an entirely different temper. 'As it were, in a night,' he says, the New England Theology 'perished from off the face of the earth'—a most serious break in our one strong link with the Protestant Reformation." During the succeeding decades the churches were living largely off the dwindling reserves of moral force and religious habit accumulated in the earlier era. This ebb of religious life and vitality is now beginning to be arrested and evidence is multiplying that recovery has set in. The centrality of Biblical faith is again being asserted in Protestant churches and numerous signs suggest that the current theological revival will lead to a chastened and more comprehensively interpreted form of evangelicalism in which the lessons learned in the struggle to free the faith from the fetters of a culturally impoverished orthodoxy will not have been forgotten. In the end the people in the churches will make the decision, and, through "honest inquiry and discussion," they constitute "a surer organ of perception" into the nature of God's will "than any ecclesiastical functionary."[9]

It is not yet clear whether or not the theologians who have played such an important role in the renewal of theological interest in the seminaries are fully aware of the obligations imposed upon them by the voluntary status of the churches in society. A British churchman has complained that in Europe theology "rarely gets out of the classroom and the theologian's study," and remarked that the theologians spend too much time and energy merely talking to one another.[10] While the intellectual world cannot be neglected without dire consequences, the restriction of theological concerns to academic circles is a luxury that can be ill afforded in a world where churches almost everywhere are on their own. Theology must always be able to adopt the language of the man in the street, speaking to his need simply and persuasively, awakening faith, and winning conviction. It must be preachable. The most fatal expedient, of course, is to let preachableness determine the content of the Christian message, but this danger must not be allowed to obscure the need to be understood, the need to speak directly and intelligibly to the condition of men. It may be a disturbing symptom that as yet, unlike the theologians of the Reformation period and the seventeenth century who almost immediately turned their attention to the composition of catechisms for the instruction of the common people, no major theologian of the twentieth century has produced a comprehensive manual for the instruction of the laity. It is also not clear as yet whether or not there is a full realization of the necessity for corporate discipline if, through the everyday decisions of Christian people, the Christian faith is to be made relevant to and influential within the political, economic, and social order. The implications of this necessity for the doctrine of the visible church would seem to be very great. In the absence of a Christian prince, a gathered, disciplined community would appear to be an indispensable requirement.

II

The greatest single obstacle to the thoroughgoing reconstruction of church life that is demanded is a continued unwillingness on the part of many Christians to admit its necessity. This is due partly to the resistance which any institution will offer to measures of radical reform, and partly to the illusion that the state can somehow come to the aid of the churches and thus the necessity for drastic measures can be avoided. But the greatest obstacle is to be found in the popular cry for Christian unity as a means of restoring power, prestige, and influence to the Christian cause, and in a similar cry for unity on the part of others who have come to regard the divisions which exist between the churches as a scandalous and tragic denial of the unity to be found in Christ and who therefore insist that the primary duty of Christians in our time is to bring about a reunion of the churches.

The popular demand for unity is largely based on the assumption that the indifference with which the pronouncements of the churches are treated springs from the fact that the churches are divided, that bigness has virtue and power of its own, and that there is no hope for successful resistance to the forces of secularism unless the churches can speak with one voice. The churches must present a united front. Either they unite or they will perish. The demand for unity, which springs from a sense of embarrassment that the Church of the Christ through whom men are knit together in love by faith should exhibit disunity in its visible institutional structure, also betrays a pragmatic concern for the effectiveness of the Christian witness in our time. How may the churches speak to a divided world when their own unity is lacking? The heavenly vision of the perfect harmony of the redeemed, therefore, must have its institutionalized counterpart on earth, supposedly to demonstrate the practicality of Christ's kingdom as a present historical possibility. There can be no question as to the validity of the concern which both these demands for unity express, but there is a question as to whether the immediate objective they seek will accomplish the end they desire, and also whether a concentration upon the overriding importance of Christian unity may not serve to divert attention from the more basic necessity for a fundamental reordering of life within the existing churches.

An emphasis upon the primary importance of Christian unity can lead to several unhappy results. Since the prospect of the reunion of Christendom as a whole is sufficiently remote, the quest for unity can become an essentially utopian enterprise. It can also by an insistence upon the necessity for a total consensus prevent co-operation and a united witness by those among whom real agreement does exist. It can also foster the illusion that a church which will "hold in creative tension members of various classes and races" can be achieved merely by lumping together denominational units which have not previously broken the power of caste and color in their separate institutional existence. Finally, a preoccupation with the unity of the visible church as the supreme end to be pursued can result in a practical displacement of God as the object of faith and devotion. While the basic compulsion on the political level in the twentieth century is to seek the adjustments, compromises, and resolution of tensions which will permit some semblance of unity to be achieved among the peoples of the earth, no such primary compulsion rests upon the churches. Whereas the primary compulsion of the political order may be described as horizontal that of the churches is vertical. The churches have the prior obligation of a distinctive message and a distinctive life to maintain, and unity among the churches can be achieved only when they find themselves, through study, discussion, and prayer, in substantial agreement as to what constitutes that message and that life.

It is this last danger of making unity an end in itself rather than the consequence of shared convictions that constitutes the greatest danger. A desire for unity can very easily encourage a willingness to adopt the principle of comprehension as a basis upon which particular churches might unite and thus produce a new church with little or nothing to say, plagued by disparate views, and with no possibility of developing an effective corporate discipline. It is precisely the absence of procedures for self-discipline which has rendered the major denominations in America so largely impotent, and has frequently made it possible for small disciplined religious bodies to speak with more power and influence than those which possess memberships many times as large. The pronouncements and resolutions which the American clergy have been able to agree upon from time to time in their denominational assemblies and the National Council of Churches frequently exert little influence because they do not represent the corporate conscience of the churches, lay opinion being sharply divergent from that of the clergy. The adoption of an explicit policy of comprehension as a basis for church union, far from increasing the influence of the churches, would only serve to aggravate the problem which already exists.

One of the chief handicaps under which the Church of England has labored over the course of its history has been the policy of comprehension which it was forced to pursue as a result of its connection with the state. With no corporate conscience of its own, the impact of the Church of England upon society has been largely limited to that made by parties within the church which were able to develop a cohesiveness and discipline quite apart from the total life of the church. If this situation has begun to change in the twentieth century, it is because, with the growing recognition that the church could no longer safely rely on the state even for institutional advantages, Anglicans have become increasingly self-conscious as a distinct and separate people within the nation and have begun to develop a definite position and point of view of their own. Parties continue to exist within the church but the strong tendency is toward the center with an emphasis upon the distinctively Anglican heritage and with a growing awareness, particularly evident in discussions of baptism and confirmation, of the importance of discipline.

While it would be wrong to be complacent about the denominationalism of American religious life, denominationalism ought not to be regarded as pure tragedy or unmitigated evil. Denominationalism has its scandalous aspects and it does testify to the pervasiveness of human perversity, sin, and fallibility—even in ecclesiastical construction. On the other hand, the scandalous aspects of the denominational system ought not to blind us to the distinct values which it possesses. It has the merit of frankly recognizing that "sectarian" or "denominational" differences are to be expected and that the true Church of Christ composed of all those in whom Christ lives and works and reigns can never be fully represented by a single ecclesiastical structure. Thus it stands athwart the tendency of any religious institution to absolutize itself and to claim God as its own exclusive possession, and provides a basis for co-operation between denominations in areas of common agreement by acknowledging that all denominations or bodies of Christians, however imperfect, may be regarded as true churches to the extent that they are striving by the grace of God to become a more perfect representation of the universal Christian community. It also has the advantage of making possible an alternative spiritual home for those who become alienated by the pretensions or polices of a particular church and thus avoids the vigorous anticlerical sentiment which tends to arise where such an option does not exist. Above all, it avoids the necessity for undue comprehension and thus makes possible within the various denominations the development of that corporate discipline which is indispensable to an effective Christian witness in a democratic society—a requirement which becomes increasingly imperative when the society at large is becoming progressively more secular. "Whatever the weaknesses of the 'sectarian' church, which has set the pattern for American church life," Reinhold Niebuhr has written, "one should think that the prevailing secularism of modern culture might give the idea of an exclusive church new validity.[11]

To suggest that denominationalism has value is not to justify the continued separate identity of all existing denominations. For many practical reasons it is obvious that there are too many denominations in the United States, and in the absence of any significant theological differences between many of them there is no reason why all the existing denominational divisions should be perpetuated. There would seem to be sufficient theological unity for the various Presbyterian, Congregational, and Reformed groups to coalesce without impairing their common witness, and this may be true of the Methodists as well. Nor need the lack of full agreement with the remaining denominations be a bar to a united witness and action in areas where agreement does exist. The recognition of this fact was an important aspect of Lyman Beecher's "great discovery." By means of voluntary societies the American churches have demonstrated, again and again, their ability to meet specific needs through co-operative effort. One possible weakness of the National Council of Churches may be that in its very effort to be comprehensive and to represent all the interests of the churches, it may retard and restrict co-operation. Fortunately, this danger has been minimized by providing for a large degree of autonomy within the various divisions of the Council, by facilitating the participation of a denomination in a single area of concern, and by making it possible for denominations to dissociate themselves from actions desired by the majority which they would find embarrassing. Thus, the possibility exists of securing the widest possible participation while avoiding the necessity for delay until full agreement can be reached.

Finally, if discipline is to be recovered and the integrity of the Christian witness and life is to be made more secure, there must be a new awareness of the importance of a wider "order" than the emphasis on "congregational" autonomy, as practiced by almost one-third of the American denominations, makes possible. On the one hand, an individual congregation is "not powerful enough and its resources are not great enough to maintain the uniqueness of the Christian witness against the world." A local congregation occupies a particularly vulnerable position in terms of its obligation to bear witness to the Christian faith against the sinful forces of the community when it has become more fearful of the authority of a bishop than of "the influence of the village big-wig upon the faith and morals of the church." On the other hand, the problems and concerns which trouble the Christian conscience are no longer restricted to the common life of "the isolated settlements and small towns of agrarian America." The effective social community has become vastly larger than the old congregational neighborhood. Thus "a structure designed to discipline only the immediate neighborhood to Christian living" can serve only "to disqualify Christians from their responsibility to the larger communities of industry, commerce, state, and culture."[12]

Actually, as we have seen in an earlier chapter, the reason for an insistence upon congregational autonomy within these denominations has largely long since disappeared, and most of them are functioning on a semipresbyterian basis.* The insistence upon congregational autonomy had presupposed the existence of a national church, in that it was assumed that congregationally organized churches would replace the established church and constitute collectively its equivalent. The genuine expectation was that what, in the midst of controversy, was regarded as false worship would wither and die, leaving a free field to a thoroughly "reformed" worship. The thing to be feared in this situation, particularly after the Presbyterian

---

* In 1934 Shailer Mathews had warned the Northern Baptists that they were moving unwittingly step by step toward a presbyterian polity (R. G. Torbet, *A History of the Baptists* [Phila.: Judson Press, 1950], 457), and the tendency was even more pronounced among Southern Baptists. The Congregationalists themselves had never practiced the full theory of congregational autonomy for any extended period of time or with any great consistency.

party had consolidated its position in the English House of Commons, was a new usurpation of divine sovereignty by ecclesiastical authority and the emergence of just such a system of religious absolutism as the Puritans in general had been rebelling against. Consequently, in their ecclesiastical construction they sought to guard against the possibility of "new presbyter" becoming merely "old priest writ large," in the same way that in political construction they sought to guard against the threat of tyranny by the reservation of powers to local government and a carefully devised system of checks and balances. The confident expectation that the wisdom, virtue, and Biblical authority of the reforms which these congregationally-minded Puritans proposed would carry the day without dissent, of course, failed to be fulfilled, and the resulting denominational system provided its own check against undue ecclesiastical pretensions and tyranny in the total life of a nation. If in the future there should be a coalescence of religious groups to the extent that the resulting institution would tend to dominate the life of the country, we might again be compelled to begin thinking in terms of the rights of local congregations, but that danger would seem to be sufficiently remote. For even that most unlikely of all possibilities, a union of all Protestant bodies, would scarcely accomplish such a predominance of influence in America today, and if such a union were attempted it would unquestionably produce new dissent. In the meantime, the problem is to provide procedures whereby a denomination can actualize Christian discipline in those areas of life which transcend the local community, and deal with the waywardness which local congregations can display when left with no outside resource to help them withstand the social pressures of their own community. In the present situation, then, the theory and practice of congregational autonomy would seem to serve no useful purpose and actually involve distinct liabilities in dealing with the most pressing contemporary needs of the churches.

III

The argument of this book may be briefly summarized. In a democracy there is no substitute for an informed public opinion, and consequently there can be no substitute for a church which seeks to stand apart from the culture with something to say that is distinctly its own, with procedures for group discipline to form a corporate conscience on specific issues, and with an aggressive missionary spirit which will serve to extend its influence. Only thus can an informed Christian public opinion be created. When religion, by this means, is restored to a central place in life, religious presuppositions will find expression even in the work of the public schools, in the same way that secularization came first in life and was then reflected in the schools.[13] But it cannot be legislated or coerced. It must be a free expression of the mind of the community which will take substance, not in formal courses of religious instruction, but in the basic assumptions of the teachers and the writers of textbooks.

The constitutional provision for the separation of church and state has the great merit of making this responsibility of the churches explicit and of fostering those qualities of initiative, responsibility, relevance, resourcefulness, liberality, missionary zeal, and lay participation, which Philip Schaff, against the background of his knowledge of religious conditions in his native land, described as the characteristic consequences of the acceptance of the voluntary principle in religion.[14] The separation of church and state has the additional virtue of guaranteeing the freedom of a church to be a church, to determine its own life, and to appeal to a "higher law" than the statutory enactments of the state. For this reason alone, if for no other reason, the separation of church and state ought resolutely to be guarded—the more so when the prevailing culture is so largely secular.

Disestablishment was "the best thing that ever happened in Connecticut," and the separation of church and state will be the best thing for both the churches and the nation in the twentieth century, if the responsibilities it defines are freely acknowledged and the necessary reconstruction in the life of the churches takes place. When we begin to recognize that the Christian faith can commend itself to the people only "by what it can show itself to be worth and by the fruits which it can bring forth," and to realize that "the Christian character of our American society" depends on the churches and what they shall do, then, in the words of David H. Greer, "the Christian church in this country" will again "throw itself on God" and "will do an apostolic work." The truth of Daniel Dorchester's confident declaration once more will become self-evident. "From a careful study of the history of American Protestantism, we have risen up to declare the conviction that the purely voluntary are the best, the purest, and the most favorable conditions for the religious life of any people."[15]

SUGGESTIONS
FOR FURTHER READING

There may be readers who will have come to the end of this book in full agreement as to the validity of its major contentions concerning "the voluntary nature and responsibility of the church, the sin of surrender to contemporary culture, the distinctive quality of the Christian faith and life, and the need for disciplined churches which stand for the Eternal Gospel amid all temporary changes," and yet who find the brief theological tags which have been introduced into the discussion unsatisfying. For these readers, H. Richard Niebuhr's account of the shifting theological currents of these same years, in *The Kingdom of God in America*, will serve as a welcome supplement and corrective. Present theological tendencies are admirably surveyed by Daniel D. Williams in *What Present-day Theologians Are Thinking*. For a brief yet exceedingly perceptive discussion of the American religious scene, Henry Steele Commager's chapter on "Religious Thought and Practice" in *The American Mind* is unsurpassed. Willard L. Sperry's *Religion in America*, written for British consumption, provides several illuminating and incisive insights. *Protestant Thought in the Twentieth Century*, edited by Arnold S. Nash, is explicitly designed to acquaint the nontechnical reader with the changing emphases in the major fields of theological study. The political and social issues which have confronted the churches during the past century and a half are spelled out by James Hastings Nichols in *Democracy and the Churches*. A perceptive diagnosis of the malady from which the churches are suffering is to be found in the three essays by Wilhelm Pauck, Francis P. Miller, and H. Richard Niebuhr, published under the title *The Church Against the World*. The parallel situation among the English churches is depicted in *P. T. Forsyth: Prophet for Today* by Robert McAfee Brown. W. E. Garrison's *A Protestant Manifesto* is an informed statement of the basic convictions of Protestantism. Wise words of caution with regard to the danger which lurks in an uninhibited and undisciplined ecumenical enthusiasm are to be found in *Positive Protestantism* by Hugh Thompson Kerr, Jr. The serious reader, of course, will not neglect the essays by Paul Tillich in *The Protestant Era*.

NOTES

Chapter I. THE PROBLEM THE CHURCH IS FACING

1. Willard L. Sperry, *Religion in America* (N. Y.: Macmillan Co., 1946), 69, 257.
2. Review by L. Wendell Fifield in *Advance*, July 9, 1951, 24.
3. Henry P. VanDusen, *God in Education* (N. Y.: Charles Scribner's Sons, 1951), 103.
4. James Hastings Nichols, "Separation of Church and State," *Christian Century*, LXV (1948), 266.
5. Washington Gladden, ed., *Parish Problems* (N. Y.: Century Co., 1887), 366.
6. For an illuminating discussion of this point, consult Paul V. Harper, "Let the Church Educate," *Christian Century*, LXIV (1947), 1552-54.
7. Henry S. Commager, *The American Mind* (New Haven: Yale University Press, 1950), 167-68.
8. Harry Emerson Fosdick, "A Religion with Its Feet on the Ground," *Church Monthly*, XII (1938), 105.

Chapter II. AN AXIOM OF ALL AMERICANS

1. James Bryce, *The American Commonwealth*, 2 vols. (N. Y.: Macmillan Co., 1910), II, 766.
2. *Ibid.*, 781-82.
3. *Ibid.*, 763, 766, 770.
4. *Ibid.*, 765-66.
5. J. H. Nichols, "Separation of Church and State," *Christian Century*, LXV (1948), 266.
6. C. H. Moehlman, *The American Constitutions and Religion* (Berne, Ind., 1938), 63.
7. Philip Schaff, *Church and State in the United States* (N. Y.: Charles Scribner's Sons, 1888), 34.
8. *Ibid.*, 15, 35, 40, 78. Daniel Dorchester, *Christianity in the United States* (N. Y.: Hunt and Eaton, 1890), 771. H. A. Rommen, *The State in Catholic Thought* (St. Louis: B. Herder Book Co., 1945), 599-604. Charles A. Beard, *The Republic* (N. Y.: Viking Press, 1943), 165.
9. Bryce, *op. cit.*, II, 767.
10. *Ibid.*, 768-70.
11. *Ibid.*, 777.
12. *Ibid.*, 779, 874.
13. *Ibid.*, 763, 779, 874.
14. Alexis de Tocqueville, *Democracy in America*, ed. Phillips Bradley, 2 vols. (N. Y.: A. A. Knopf, 1945), I, 308.

15. Bryce, *op. cit.*, II, 775, 776, 778, 779, 780, 790.
16. *Ibid.*, 789-90.
17. *Ibid.*, 773, 789.
18. *Ibid.*, 774, 779.
19. Tocqueville, *op. cit.*, I, 308. Cf. 314.
20. Bryce, *op. cit.*, II, 778, 780, 786, 874.
21. *Ibid.*, 290, 790.
22. Tocqueville, *op. cit*, I, 303-5
23. *America in Perspective: The United States Through Foreign Eyes*, ed. H. S. Commager (N. Y.: Random House, 1947), 85, 87.
24. Tocqueville, *op. cit.*, I, 307-9, 312.

Chapter III. FAITH AND FREEDOM

1. Quoted in H. Richard Niebuhr, *The Kingdom of God in America* (New York: Harper & Brothers, 1937), 68.
2. J. H. Nichols, "Separation of Church and State," *Christian Century*, LXV (1948), 265.
3. A. S. P. Woodhouse, *Puritanism and Liberty* (London: J. M. Dent and Sons, 1938), Introduction, 37.
4. *Ancient Bounds*, as reprinted in Woodhouse, *ibid.*, 250.
5. William Haller, *The Rise of Puritanism* (N. Y.: Columbia University Press, 1938), 23.
6. Ernst Troeltsch, *Protestantism and Progress* (N. Y.: G. P. Putnam's Sons, 1912), 124-25.
7. J. H. Nichols, *Democracy and the Churches* (Phila.: Westminster Press, 1951), 29. Bryce, *op. cit.*, I, 306. André Siegfried, *America Comes of Age* (N. Y.: Harcourt, Brace and Co., 1927), 33.
8. Charles O. Paullin, *Atlas of the Historical Geography of the United States*, ed. J. K. Wright (Wash., D. C.: Carnegie Institution, 1932), 50.
9. Quoted in H. Richard Niebuhr, *op. cit.*, 68.
10. *Ibid.*, 69.
11. *The Bloudy Tenent of Persecution*, as reprinted in Woodhouse, *op. cit.*, 284.
12. Niebuhr, *op. cit.*, 70.
13. Woodhouse, *op. cit.*, Introduction, 73-74.
14. *An Apology for Church Covenant, ibid.*, 300; *The Saints' Apology, ibid.*, 301
15. L. J. Trinterud, *The Forming of an American Tradition* (Phila.: Westminster Press, 1949), 17, 18, 180.
16. Robert Barclay, *An Apology for the True Christian Divinity* (London, 1765), 94.
17. Isaac Pennington, *Works*, 4th ed. (Phila., 1863), II, 371.
18. John Cotton, *An Exposition of the Thirteenth Chapter of Revelation* (London, 1656), 72.
19. Niebuhr, *op. cit.*, 80.

20. Cotton, *op. cit.*, 17.

21. Niebuhr, *op. cit.*, 81-2.

22. Thomas Hooker, *Survey of the Summe of Church Discipline* (London, 1648), preface. Philip Schaff, ed., *The Creeds of Christendom*, 3 vols. (N. Y.: Harper & Brothers, 1919), III, 438. W. T. Whitley, *History of British Baptists* (London: C. Griffin and Co., 1923), 94.

23. Woodhouse, *op. cit.*, Introduction, 45. *The Last Book of John Smyth, Works*, 2 vols. (Cambridge: University Press, 1915), II, 752.

24. *Ancient Bounds*, Woodhouse, *op. cit.*, 259.

25. Nichols, "Separation of Church and State," *Christian Century*, LXV (1948), 266. *The Bloudy Tenent*, in Woodhouse, *op. cit.*, 287. Schaff, *Church and State*, 11-12.

26. *The Bloudy Tenent*, in *op. cit.*, 287.

27. Woodhouse, *op. cit.*, Introduction, 85.

28. *Ibid.*, 44, 60.

29. Nichols, *Democracy and the Churches*, 40.

30. Niebuhr, *op. cit.*, 124.

31. Nichols, *Democracy and the Churches*, 40.

CHAPTER IV. LYMAN BEECHER'S GREAT DISCOVERY

1. Henry K. Rowe, *History of Religion in the United States* (N. Y.: Macmillan Co., 1924), 54.

2. C. M. Rourke, *Trumpets of Jubilee* (N. Y.: Harcourt, Brace and Co., 1927), viii.

3. *Autobiography, Correspondence, etc., of Lyman Beecher, D.D.*, ed. Charles Beecher, 2 vols. (N. Y.: Harper & Brothers, 1871), I, 344.

4. S. E. Mead, *Nathaniel W. Taylor, 1786-1858: A Connecticut Liberal* (Chicago: University of Chicago Press, 1942), 41, 43. Much of the material in this chapter is based upon this penetrating study.

5. *Autobiography*, I, 344, 452-53.

6. This was Beecher's conviction as early as 1812. The account of the conditions into which New England had fallen is quite obviously overdrawn, but it does accurately reflect Beecher's own analysis of the situation. Actually, even in terms of Beecher's own criteria, the churches were not utterly decadent. Revivals had never completely died out and discipline had never totally disappeared. During the preceding ten or twelve years, under the leadership of Dwight, there had been a marked resurgence in both respects.

7. *Autobiography*, I, 271.

8. Dorchester, *op. cit.*, 151, 201.

9. Mead, *op. cit.*, 47.

10. *Ibid.*, 49.

11. *Ibid.*, 101.

12. *Autobiography*, I, 329-30.

13. Mead, *op. cit.*, 76-77.

14. *Autobiography*, I, 241, 244, 415-16.

15. Mead, *op. cit.*, 83-94, discusses Beecher's publishing activities in detail.
16. *Autobiography*, I, 150-56.
17. *Ibid.*, II, 218.
18. *Ibid.*, I, 241.
19. *Ibid.*, 273, 275.
20. Mead, *op. cit.*, 80-82.
21. *Autobiography*, I, 345.
22. A. G. Koch, *Republican Religion: The American Revolution and the Cult of Reason* (N. Y.: Henry Holt and Co., 1933), 281.
23. Niebuhr, *op. cit.*, 119.
24. Tocqueville, *op. cit.*, I, 312.
25. *Autobiography*, II, 343, 453. K. S. Latourette, *A History of the Expansion of Christianity*, Vol. IV (N. Y.: Harper & Brothers, 1941), 374.
26. *Autobiography*, I, 452.
27. H. K. Rowe, *op. cit.*, 54.
28. Mead, *op. cit.*, 51.

CHAPTER V. THE GREAT CENTURY

1. K. S. Latourette, *op. cit.*, VI, 442.
2. C. A. and M. R. Beard, *The Rise of American Civilization*, 2 vols. (N. Y.: Macmillan Co., 1927), I, 90, 661.
3. Charles R. Keller, *The Second Great Awakening in Connecticut* (New Haven: Yale University Press, 1942), 100.
4. W. W. Sweet, *Religion on the American Frontier*; Vol. III, *The Congregationalists* (Chicago: University of Chicago Press, 1939), 13. Keller, *op. cit.*, 71. J. T. Adams, *The March of Democracy* (N. Y.: Charles Scribner's Sons, 1932), 258.
5. Horace Bushnell, *Barbarism, the First Danger* (N. Y.: American Home Missionary Society, 1847), 28-29.
6. Merle E. Curti, *The Growth of American Thought* (N. Y.: Harper & Brothers, 1943), 261.
7. Whitney R. Cross, *The Burned-over District* (Ithaca, N. Y.: Cornell University Press, 1950), vii, 19.
8. *Ibid.*, 14.
9. Henry Scougal, *The Life of God in the Soul of Man*, ed. Winthrop S. Hudson (Phila.: Westminster Press, 1948), 15.
10. Keller, *op. cit.*, 211, 220.
11. Cross, *op. cit.*, 42.
12. Bushnell, *op. cit.*, 31.
13. Cross, *op. cit.*, 151-2; Mead., *op. cit.*, 202; Gilbert Seldes, *The Stammering Century* (N.Y.: John Day, 1928), 104.
14. Cross, *op. cit.*, 153.
15. *Ibid.*, 152, 155, 254.

16. Gilbert H. Barnes, *The Anti-Slavery Impulse, 1830-1844* (N. Y.: Appleton-Century Crofts, 1933), 11. Lyman Beecher, *Autobiography*, I, 268.
17. Seldes, *op. cit.*, 203.
18. S. E. Mead, "Revivalism and the Emergence and Growth of the Denominations in America," mimeographed lecture, May, 1949.
19. T. R. Roosevelt, *The Winning of the West*, 6 vols. (N. Y.: G. P. Putnam's Sons, 1900), IV, 21.
20. Peter Cartwright, *Autobiography*, ed. William P. Strickland (N. Y.: 1856), 243.
21. Bushnell, *op. cit.*, 31.
22. Vernon L. Parrington, *Main Currents in American Thought*, 3 vols. (N. Y.: Harcourt, Brace and Co., 1927), II, 167.
23. Ralph Gabriel, *The Course of American Democratic Thought* (N. Y.: Ronald Press, 1940), 33.
24. H. Paul Douglass in Harold Stearns, ed., *America Now* (N. Y.: Literary Guild, 1938), 513.
25. Gabriel, *op. cit.*, 98-99.
26. Latourette, *op. cit.*, IV, 1, 4; V, 469; VI, 442, 443, 450; VII, 450.
27. J. H. Nichols, *Primer for Protestants* (N.Y.: Association Press, 1947), 75.
28. Elie Halévy, *A History of the English People in the Nineteenth Century*, 4 vols. (N. Y.: Peter Smith, 1949), I, 399-400.
29. Latourette, *op. cit.*, VI, 443.
30. *Ibid.*, 444.
31. Halévy, *op. cit.*, I, 387, 590-91.
32. H. B. Smith, *Tables of Church History*, quoted in Lyman Beecher, *Autobiography*, I, 345.
33. Carl Sandburg, *Abraham Lincoln: The War Years*, 4 vols. (N. Y.: Harcourt, Brace and Co., 1939), III, 370.
34. *Ibid.*, I, 39, 47, 49, 54.
35. Nichols, *Democracy and the Churches*, 79.
36. Sandburg, *op. cit.*, I, 133-35.
37. *Ibid.*, III, 370, 378, 380-81.
38. *Ibid.*, IV, 92.
39. *Ibid.*, IV, 92-94.
40. Gabriel, *op. cit.*, 121-22.

CHAPTER VI. THE CITY AND THE CHURCHES

1. Helen Campbell and others, *Darkness and Light* (Hartford, Conn. 1891), 40. Howard B. Grose, *Aliens or Americans?* (N. Y., 1906), 194. H. K. Rowe, *op. cit.*, 88.
2. Beard, *Rise of American Civilization*, I, 637.
3. *Ibid*, 635.
4. A. M. Schlesinger, *Political and Social Growth of the American People, 1865-1940* (N. Y.: Macmillan Co., 1941), 40-41.

5. Samuel L. Loomis, *Modern Cities and Their Religious Problems* (N. Y.: Baker and Taylor Co., 1887), 10, 27-28.
6. Charles L. Brace, *The Dangerous Classes of New York* (New York, 1872), 34-35.
7. W. C. Hollenbeck, *Urban Organization and Protestantism* (N. Y.: Harper & Brothers, 1934), 13, 15, 16.
8. C. H. Hopkins, *History of the Y.M.C.A. in North America* (N. Y.: Association Press, 1951), 4-5.
9. *Ibid.*, 16-19, 23.
10. *Ibid.*, 26-30, 45-47, 81-83, 362.
11. *Ibid.*, 88-92.
12. A. I. Abell, *The Urban Impact upon American Protestantism* (Cambridge: Harvard University Press, 1943), 11, 13.
13. *Ibid.*, 14-15.
14. *Ibid.*, 30, 36, 45-46, 50-55; See also *National Needs and Remedies: Discussions of the General Conference of the Evangelical Alliance* (N. Y.: Baker and Taylor Co., 1890), 265. For Moody's concern for the training of lay workers equipped to do home visitation as a primary objective of the Chicago Bible Institute, see William R. Moody, *The Life of Dwight L. Moody* (N. Y.: Fleming H. Revell Co., 1900), 338-39, and William R. Moody, *D. L. Moody* (N. Y.: Macmillan Co., 1930), 373.
15. Abell, *op. cit.*, 15.
16. *Ibid.*, 31-32.
17. *National Needs and Remedies*, 17, 20, 64-65, 101.
18. *America: The National Catholic Weekly*, December 14, 1930.
19. Beard, *Rise of American Civilization*, II, 247.
20. W. W. Sweet, *Story of Religion in America*, 2nd rev. ed. (N. Y.: Harper & Brothers, 1950), 334.
21. Beard, *Rise of American Civilization*, II, 396.
22. Halévy, *op. cit.*, I, 475.
23. W. E. Garrison, "Characteristics of American Organized Religion," *The Annals of the American Academy of Political and Social Science*, March, 1948, 21. H. S. Commager, *The American Mind* (New Haven: Yale University Press, 1950), 191. Leo XIII, Encyclical Letter, "The Christian Constitution of States" (1885).
24. Abell, *op. cit.*, 182, 183.
25. Latourette, *op. cit.*, IV, 283. Latourette's conclusion apparently is based upon the study of Theodore Abel, *Protestant Home Missions to Catholic Immigrants* (N. Y.: Institute of Social and Religious Research, 1933).
26. Latourette, *op. cit.*, IV, 283.
27. Abell, *op. cit.*, 6, 140.
28. Edward Judson, "The Church in Its Social Aspect," *The Annals of the American Academy of Political and Social Science*, November, 1908, 436. Josiah Strong, *The Challenge of the City* (N. Y.: Young People's Missionary Movement, 1907), 198, 210.

29 *Ibid*, 211-15. Abell, *op. cit.*, 150-51.

30. Strong, *op. cit.*, 218-22. Abell, *op. cit.*, 150, 157.

31. *Ibid.*, 161-63.

32. *Ibid.*, 122, 137. Nichols, *Democracy and the Churches*, 114.

33. Rowe, *op. cit.*, 88. Grose, *op. cit.*, 194.

CHAPTER VII. THE END OF AN ERA

1. W. L. Sperry, *Religion in America* (N. Y.: Macmillan Co., 1946), 161.

2. Gilbert Seldes, *The Stammering Century*, 141.

3. William R. Moody, *D. L. Moody* (N. Y.: Macmillan Co., 1930), 339, 459. C. H. Hopkins, *History of the Y.M.C.A.*, 158, 187-89, 303, 305.

4. *Ibid.*, 187.

5. Moody, *D. L. Moody* (1930), 194-95, 221-22, 356-57.

6. *Ibid.*, 244-45.

7. *Ibid.*, 249.

8. *Ibid.*, 265-67, 277, 489, 520.

9. *Ibid.*, 287-98, 338, 385.

10. *Ibid.*, 310-11, 319, 334, 373-75. William R. Moody, *The Life of Dwight L. Moody* (N. Y.: Fleming H. Revell Co., 1900), 293-94. Hopkins, *op. cit.*, 188. *The International Messenger*, VII, September, 1900. E. T. Thompson, *Changing Emphases in American Preaching* (Phila., Westminster Press, 1943), 128.

11. Seldes, *op. cit.*, 140-41.

12. The discussion of the disintegration of revivalism is largely based upon the discriminating and incisive analysis by Sidney E. Mead, "Revivalism and the Growth of the Denominations in America," mimeographed lecture, May, 1949.

13. D. D. Williams, *The Andover Liberals; a Study in American Theology* (N. Y.: King's Crown Press, 1941), 7.

14. Niebuhr, *Kingdom of God in America*, 179-80.

15. Moody, *D. L. Moody* (1930), 339. Hopkins, *op. cit.*, 379.

16. Moody, *D. L. Moody* (1930), 311, 517. *International Messenger*, VII, September, 1900.

17. Moody, *Dwight L. Moody* (1900), 97, 99, 103. E. M. Fergusson, *Historic Chapters in Christian Education in America* (N. Y.: Fleming H. Revell Co., 1935), 30, 49.

18. *Ibid.*, 39-41, 122-23. M. C. Brown, *Sunday School Movements in America* (N. Y.: Fleming H. Revell Co., 1901), 94-112.

19. Fergusson, *op. cit.*, 143. *The Encyclopedia of Sunday Schools and Religious Education*, ed. J. T. McFarland and B. S. Winchester (N. Y.: Thomas Nelson and Sons, 1915), I, 81-82. *Organized Sunday School Work in America, 1908-1911; Official Report of the Thirteenth International Sunday School Convention* (Chicago: International Sunday School Association, 1911), 277, 280.

20. *Ibid.*, 281, 284-85.

21. Dorchester, *Christianity in the United States*, 687.

CHAPTER VIII. PRINCES OF THE PULPIT

1. Commager, *The American Mind*, 163.
2. *Ibid.*, 41-54.
3. Bryce, *The American Commonwealth*, II, 775.
4. *Ibid.*, 286-87, 827, 932.
5. Gabriel, *The Course of American Democratic Thought*, 148-49.
6. J. H. Randall, Jr., "The Churches and the Liberal Tradition," *Annals of the American Academy of Political and Social Science*, March, 1948, 150.
7. Phillips Brooks, *The Candle of the Lord and Other Sermons* (N. Y.: E. P. Dutton and Co., 1899), 7-8.
8. *National Needs and Remedies*, 301-3, 306, 311. C. E. Macartney, *Six Kings of the American Pulpit* (Phila.: Westminster Press, 1942), 148-49.
9. *National Needs and Remedies*, 301, 309-10.
10. Brooks, *New Starts in Life and Other Sermons* (N. Y.: E. P. Dutton and Co., 1897), 88. *Essays and Addresses* (N. Y.: E. P. Dutton and Co., 1894), 371. Henry F. May, *Protestant Churches and Industrial America* (N. Y.: Harper & Brothers, 1949), 64-65.
11. George A. Gordon, "The Theological Problem for Today," in *The New Puritanism*, ed. R. W. Raymond (N. Y.: Fords, Howard, and Hulbert, 1897), 143, 146, 151. W. E. Garrison, *The March of Faith* (N. Y.: Harper & Brothers, 1933), 96.
12. *The New Puritanism*, 160-61, 169-70.
13. *Ibid.*, 151. *The Dictionary of American Biography* (N. Y.: Charles Scribner's Sons, 1929), III, 87.
14. Brooks, *Essays and Addresses*, 178. Henry F. May, *op. cit.*, 67.
15. E. T. Thompson, *Changing Emphases in American Preaching*, 69.
16. *Ibid.*, 65-66.
17. *Ibid.*, 67-68, 88. *The New Puritanism*, 55, 58-60. Henry Ward Beecher, "Progress of Thought in the Church," *North American Review*, CXXXV (August, 1882), 116. May, *op. cit.*, 86.
18. *Ibid.*, 40. Thompson, *op. cit.*, 75, 84.
19. *Ibid.*, 65, 86-87, 94. Garrison, *March of Faith*, 92.
20. *North American Review* (August, 1882), 99-117.
21. *Ibid.* Thompson, *op. cit.*, 89.
22. *The New Puritanism*, 63, 67-68.
23. A. M. Schlesinger, *The Rise of the City, 1878-1898* (N. Y.: Macmillan Co., 1933), 198. May, *op. cit.*, 55 n.
24. Paxton Hibben, *Henry Ward Beecher* (N. Y.: George H. Doran Co., 1927), viii. Newell Dwight Hillis, *All the Year Round* (N. Y.: Fleming H. Revell Co., 1912), 162-63. William R. Moody, *D. L. Moody* (1930), 533.
25. A. R. Burr, *Russell H. Conwell and His Work* (Phila.: John C. Winston Co., 1917), 314.
26. May, *op. cit.*, 69, 70, 94.

27. *Ibid.*, 69-70. Garrison, *March of Faith*, 57.
28. R. R. Conwell, *Acres of Diamonds* (N. Y.: Harper & Brothers, 1890), 19; quoted by Gabriel, *op. cit.*, 149. Conwell, *Acres of Diamonds*, 11; as printed in Burr, *Russell H. Conwell and His Work* (Phila.: John C. Winston Co., 1908). There are variations in the text of Conwell's lecture in the various editions.
29. R. H. Conwell, *What You Can Do With Your Will Power* (N. Y.: Harpers & Brothers, 1917), 1-2, 7, 21. Burr, *op. cit.*, 1908 ed., 270. R. H. Conwell, "The Lodge and Church," printed in *Temple Review*, Pamphlet No. 1. *The Congregationalist*, June 21, 1876, 196; quoted by May, *op. cit.*, 51.
30. Gabriel, *op. cit.*, 149. Conwell, *Will Power*, 4, 7-8. Conwell, *Acres of Diamonds* (N. Y.: Harper & Brothers, 1915), 18, 19, 21; as quoted by May, *op. cit.*, 200. *Acres of Diamonds*, as printed in Burr (1908), 11.
31. Albert H. Smith, *Russell H. Conwell* (N. Y.: Silver, Burdett and Co., 1899), 334. Gabriel, *op. cit.*, 149-50.
32. *Ibid.*, 153.
33. *Ibid.*, 311. Thompson, *op. cit.*, 140-41.
34. C. E. Macartney, *op. cit.*, 109. Washington Gladden, "Social Problems of the Future," in *The New Puritanism*, 176.
35. *Ibid.*, 182-87, 191.
36. *Ibid.*, 194-95. Washington Gladden, *Social Facts and Forces* (N. Y.: G. P. Putnam's Sons, 1899), 220.
37. *The New Puritanism*, 202, 207, 211.
38. Thompson, *op. cit.*, 175. Washington Gladden, *Recollections* (Boston: Houghton Mifflin Co., 1909), 306, 419-20, 430-31.
39. *Ibid.*, 298. Gabriel, *op. cit.*, 321.
40. *Ibid.*, 321-22. May, *op. cit.*, 209-10. Schlesinger, *The Rise of the City*, 342.
41. Dorchester, *op. cit.*, 698. Commager, *op. cit.*, 164-65.

CHAPTER IX. THE CHURCH EMBRACES THE WORLD

1. Commager, *The American Mind*, 166-67.
2. Latourette, *History of the Expansion of Christianity*, IV, 20, 458; VI, 5.
3. Strong, *Challenge of the City*, 54. *National Needs and Remedies*, 23. Bryce, *American Commonwealth*, II, 782, 785.
4. *Ibid.*, 782-83. *National Needs and Remedies*, 93-94.
5. J. B. Harrison, *Certain Dangerous Tendencies in American Life* (Boston: Houghton, Osgood and Co., 1880), 7-9, 28.
6. *The Church Against the World*, ed. H. Richard Niebuhr (N. Y.: Harper & Brothers, 1935), 102.
7. Seldes, *Stammering Century*, 142, 148.

8. Edward Judson, "The Church in Its Social Aspect," *Annals of the American Academy of Political and Social Science*, Nov., 1907, 440. Gladden, *Recollections*, 58. Strong, *op. cit.*, 198.
9. C. H. Hopkins, *The Rise of the Social Gospel in American Protestantism* (New Haven: Yale University Press, 1940), 276-77.
10. Judson, *op. cit.*, 437.
11. Hopkins, *History of the Y.M.C.A.*, 377, 518, 519, 522.
12. Judson, *op. cit.*, 438.
13. Theodore Abel, *Protestant Home Missions to Catholic Immigrants*, 107.
14. W. W. Sweet, *Story of Religion in America*, 2nd rev. ed., 337. H. N. Morse, "Evangelizing A Procession," *Christian Century*, LXVIII (1951), 1337.
15. H. Shelton Smith, "Christian Education", *Protestant Thought in the Twentieth Century*, ed. A. S. Nash, 225-46.
16. *Ibid.*, 241. W. L. Sperry, *Religion in America*, 173.
17. *National Needs and Remedies*, 93.
18. Hopkins, *Rise of the Social Gospel*, 247-51.
19. Sweet, *Story of Religion in America*, 414. Bryce, *op. cit.*, II, 787.
20. Gaius Glenn Atkins, *Religion in Our Times* (N. Y.: Round Table Press, 1932), 160-64.
21. Dorchester, *Christianity in the United States*, 673.
22. Sperry, *op. cit.*, 129.

Chapter X. A LONELY PROPHET

1. H. R. Niebuhr, *Kingdom of God in America*, 194.
2. Reinhold Niebuhr, *An Interpretation of Christian Ethics* (N. Y.: Harper & Brothers, 1935), preface.
3. Shailer Mathews, *The Spiritual Interpretation of History* (Cambridge: Harvard University Press, 1916), 106.
4. Walter Rauschenbusch, *Christianity and the Social Crisis* (N. Y.; Macmillan Co., 1907), 279-80, 285.
5. *Ibid.*, 280.
6. D. R. Sharpe, *Walter Rauschenbusch* (N. Y.: Harper & Brothers, 1942), 92-93. Walter Rauschenbusch, *Christianizing the Social Order* (N. Y.: Macmillan Co., 1912), 458-62, and *A Theology for the Social Gospel* (N. Y.: Macmillan Co., 1917), 194.
7. *Ibid.*, 7, 9.
8. *Ibid.*, 6, 13, 16, 118-19, 192-94.
9. Niebuhr, *Kingdom of God in America*, 185-86. Rauschenbusch, *A Theology for the Social Gospel*, 11.
10. *Ibid.*, 5, 14, 96-97.
11. *Ibid.*, 32, 46-47, 52.
12. *Ibid.*, 57-58, 60.
13. *Ibid.*, 32-33, 47-48.
14. *Ibid.*, 33-37, 56, 91.

15. *Ibid.*, 52, 98, 101-2, 267, 270-73, 279. *Christianity and the Social Crisis*, 412. *Christianizing the Social Order*, 458.
16. *Theology for the Social Gospel*, 139.
17. *Ibid.*, 50-52, 141, 227, 238-39. *Christianizing the Social Order*, 460. *Christianity and the Social Crisis*, 420-21.
18. *Theology for the Social Gospel*, 141. *Christianizing the Social Order*, 459-60, 465. Niebuhr, *Kingdom of God in America*, 149-50, 158. Sharpe, *op. cit.*, 387-88.
19. *Theology for the Social Gospel*, 118-29.
20. *Ibid.*, 128, 144. *Christianity and the Social Crisis*, 181, 185, 187-88, 198. *Christianizing the Social Order*, 462-64.
21. Sharpe, *op. cit.*, 435.

CHAPTER XI. THE RENEWAL OF THE CHURCHES

1. *National Needs and Remedies*, 203-4.
2. Daniel Jenkins, *Europe and America: Their Contributions to the World Church* (Phila.: Westminster Press, 1951), 48-49.
3. Alec Vidler, "The Appalling Religiousness of America," *Christianity and Crisis*, Dec. 22, 1947, 5.
4. *The Congregational Churches: For What Do They Stand?* (N. Y.: Commission on Evangelism and the Devotional Life of the Congregational Christian Churches, 1942).
5. H. P. Douglass and E. deS. Brunner, *The Protestant Church as a Social Institution* (N. Y.: Harper & Brothers, 1935), 46.
6. J. H. Nichols, *Democracy and the Churches*, 238.
7. J. H. Nichols, "The Recovery of Puritan Worship," *Christian Century*, LXVIII (1951), 531. Ernst B. Koenker, "Objectives and Achievements of the Liturgical Movement in the Roman Catholic Church Since World War II," *Church History*, XX (1951), 17-24.
8. Nash, *op. cit.*, 117.
9. *Ibid.*, 107. Nichols, *Democracy and the Churches*, 79.
10. Jenkins, *op. cit.*, 70.
11. Reinhold Niebuhr, *Christianity and Crisis*, Dec. 22, 1947, 6.
12. Reinhold Niebuhr, "The Ecumenical Issue in the United States," *Theology Today*, II (1945-46), 533. Nichols, *Democracy and the Churches*, 240.
13. W. E. Garrison, *Christian Century*, LXVIII (1951), 844.
14. Philip Schaff, *Church and State in the United States*, 78-83.
15. *National Needs and Remedies*, 204. Daniel Dorchester, *op. cit.*, 777.

INDEX

Set in Linotype Old Style No. 7
Format by Edwin H. Kaplin
Manufactured by The Haddon Craftsmen, Inc.
Published by HARPER & BROTHERS, *New York*